# the TRAVELLER'S GUIDE to
# planet earth

BBC
EARTH

the **TRAVELLER'S GUIDE** to
# planet earth

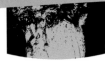
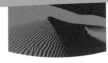

# Tony Wheeler's planet earth

## Co-Founder, Lonely Planet

## 01.
### GREAT PLAINS

**Life on the Highest Plateau** (Tibetan Plateau) **p194**

One lap of Mt Kailash and all the sins of my lifetime are washed away. Well, this lifetime; it would take another 107 circuits to clean up all my lifetimes.

Those sin-cleansing capabilities are just a sample of the magic of western Tibet. It's a place of endless vistas, forgotten cities and people whose beliefs seem to merge with the landscape. The final magic is revealed when my travels end and I turn east for the drive to Lhasa. How many places in the world can you end up a solid week's drive from the nearest airport?

## 02.
### ICE WORLDS

**The Ice Continent** (Antarctica) **p162**

It's the sheer simplicity of Antarctica that is so amazing. There is no rainbow spectrum of colours; everything is either blue (the sky and sea), white (the snow, the ice and half of every penguin) or black (the rocks, the whales and the other half of those penguins). The wildlife is equally simple, equally dramatic – you don't get hundreds of different animals or birds, but the lack of variety is made up for by sheer numbers. One penguin is a delight; 10,000 are mind blowing. It's hardly surprising that far from being a one-off experience of a lifetime, a visit to Antarctica seems to inspire return trips.

## 03.
### DESERTS

**The Outback** (Australia) **p124**

The cities are beautiful, the Great Barrier Reef is a wonder, but it's the outback – the desert – that really brings Australia home. I've never done an Australian outback trip that wasn't a great experience – whether it's roller-coasting in a 4WD up and down the thousand sand dunes across the Simpson Desert, or trekking along the rocky spine of the Larapinta Trail. Yet, that Australian love affair always carries a hint of danger: the outback can also be that edgily dangerous lover who has a knife hidden under the bed.

# Mark Brownlow's planet earth

## Episode Producer, Planet Earth

## 01.
### FRESH WATER
**Angel Falls
(Venezuela) p30**

If you suffer from vertigo this is not the place for you. With no safety rail to steady you, peering over the near-1000m drop of the world's tallest waterfall is a heart-in-the-mouth experience. Such is the height of these falls, that long before the water can reach Devil's Canyon below, it is blown away as a fine mist. Away in the distance lies the inspiration for Arthur Conan Doyle's *The Lost World*: a prehistoric land of impenetrable jungle and isolated mountain plateaus. Is that a pterodactyl I can see in the distance?

## 02.
### FRESH WATER
**Lake Baikal
(Russia) p60**

The booms of fracturing ice echo all around you as the planet's largest freshwater lake begins to melt. The harsh Siberian winter is finally retreating under the radiant spring sunshine and the lake's metre-thick icy crust is breaking up. This is not exactly what you want to hear when crossing the world's deepest lake by camper van. But it's only during this three-week window in March, when conditions are just right, that you can squeeze through an ice hole into the freshwater wonderland below. Dramatic ice sculptures and green forests of living sponge provide the backdrop for the lake's unique population of bizarre creatures – from giant amphipods to the comical Baikal seal.

## 03.
### SHALLOW SEAS
**Great White in Flight
(off the coast of South Africa) p258**

Few things prepare you for such a display of raw brutality, a sobering reminder that for many animals life is a battle for survival. The war zone is Seal Island, 19km off Simon's Town, a sleepy coastal resort in the Eastern Cape. The victim, a doe-eyed Cape fur seal pup, is on its daily trek out to its fishing grounds. The enemy is every swimmer's worst nightmare: a one tonne great white shark At dawn it is possible to take a ring-side view on board a charter boat and witness jaw-dropping attacks as these terrifyingly huge sharks torpedo out of the water. It's voyeuristic and bloody, but mesmerising. On returning to shore you may think twice about jumping on that surf board. Ignorance is bliss.

# MOUNTAINS
## *Planet Earth,* Episode Two

To gaze up to the summit of one of Earth's great mountains is to feel the insignificance of man. No other natural environment is quite so humbling. Humans may be changing the face of the globe, but our achievements pale in significance when compared to nature's steal-your-breath, stop-you-in-your-tracks towering hunks of good old-fashioned rock. Perhaps this is the reason travellers are frequently drawn to them. Wildlife is less enticed – mountains generally offer a harsh home, with thin air and capricious conditions. But this just makes the flora and fauna that do flourish at our planet's lofty extremes all the more extraordinary.

# SIMIEN MOUNTAINS
## Ethiopia

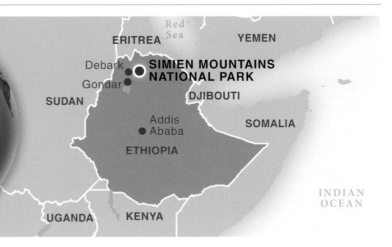

The Simien Mountains may not be Africa's highest peaks, but they are arguably the most dramatic, offering a massive 4000m-high table of rock riven with gullies. The trekking is fairly easy, but immensely rewarding, taking you along the edge of a plateau that falls sheer to the plains far, far below. Come not only for the views, but also for the excitement of sitting among a group of 100 gelada baboons, or watching magnificent walia ibexes joust on the rock ledges.

## On Screen

*Planet Earth* travels from Ethiopia's lowest point – the Danakil Depression – where continuous lava flows build new mountains, to its highest tips, where large troops of gelada baboons scale impossible rock faces and graze grassy plateaus beside walia ibexes.

## When

December to March is the driest time, but in October – after the rainy season – the scenery is greenest and the wildflowers are out. During the main rainy season, between June and September, mist often obscures the views and trails can be slippery underfoot; however, you're still assured of several hours of clear, dry weather as the rain tends to come in short, sharp downpours.

**(top) Dallol, Danakil Depression, Ethiopia**
Volcanic explosion craters mark Earth's lowest known subaerial volcanic vents. The most recent, Dallol, with its colourful hot brine springs, sits at 48m below sea level.

**(bottom) Gelada Baboons**
A species of Old World monkey found only in the Ethiopian Highlands, the gelada is largely terrestrial, and spends much of its time foraging in grasslands.

# EXPERIENCE

The view through the flap of your tent is nothing short of extraordinary: escarpments stepping down in rock staircases from the plateau to the brown smudge of the plains far below. It's as though you've camped at the edge of the world, and yet you've walked for just two days since leaving the trailhead town of Debark. There is abundant grass here at Chenek for your tent, and also for the gelada baboons, the efficient little brown lawnmowers that are grazing near camp. In their customary way they are sitting on their bums to eat, the blazes on their chests flashing pink in the light. You know that their eating habits make them unique in the monkey world, but still, it is odd to watch a primate nibbling on grass.

You begin to walk – this morning you are heading for the nearby summit of Mt Bwahit, a peak about 150m short of being the highest along the range. You are setting out early because of the tantalising prospect of spying walia ibexes, the southernmost ibex species in the world. Around 20 minutes out from camp you are rewarded: your guide stops and points to a couple of brown specks on an escarpment a few hundred metres away. Through the binoculars they grow into life forms – the ibexes you have come to see. Their horns, curled back from their heads as if slicked down with gel, look almost as sharp as the leaves of the giant lobelias growing across the mountain slopes, some of which tower above your head, resembling pineapples on poles.

You continue to the summit of Mt Bwahit, the scarcity of air at this altitude slowing you down and sending your lungs into overdrive. The views are worth it, though, stretching across the range and its deep, shadowed ravines and valleys. You are truly atop the so-called 'roof of Africa'.

As you head back down to camp, far below, the pressure on your lungs eases; you can see that the gelada baboons are still grazing, and in such numbers that it almost looks as though the ground is moving. Grazing among them are a few ibexes, their horns looking regal now that you see them a little closer, like a tribal headdress or a crown – befitting for an animal living atop this most imperial of African mountain ranges.

**Erta Ale, Danakil Depression, Ethiopia**
Erta Ale, a basaltic shield volcano, is the most active volcano in Ethiopia. The summit caldera is renowned for its long-term lava lakes.

# TAKING ACTION

## As You Saw It

To enjoy this experience you'll need to first get fit and acclimatise. To really get in among the sharp pinnacles and the troops of gelada baboons you will be trekking for days, and with the highlands of Ethiopia averaging 3500m above sea level (and rising to 4543m), you should not underestimate the effects of the altitude.

## Adding to the Experience

From the mountains, head to the depths of the Danakil Depression, which dips to more than 100m below sea level (and is among the hottest places on earth). Here you can view continuous lava flows building and moulding new mountains in much the same way the Simiens were formed around 40 million years ago.

## Alternative African Peak–Bagging Experiences

If standing on the summit of the Simiens' highest peak, Ras Dashen, brought you a sense of accomplishment, you may fancy a bit more peak bagging across Africa; here's a selection of the continent's loftiest.

✿ **Mt Kilimanjaro** (Tanzania) 5896m

✿ **Mt Kenya** (Kenya) At 5199m the summit is attainable only to climbers; hikers head for the trekkers' summit of Point Lenana.

✿ **Mt Stanley** (Uganda) A 5109m technical ascent.

✿ **Mt Speke** (Uganda) A 4890m technical ascent.

✿ **Mt Meru** (Tanzania) 4566m

✿ **Jebel Toubkal** (Morocco) 4167m

# WHILE YOU'RE THERE

## Lalibela

The rock-hewn churches, dimly lit passageways and hidden crypts and grottoes of the 'new Jerusalem' make Lalibela an African wonder. There are 11 rock-hewn churches around the town.

## Tigray

Rock-hewn churches with an adventurous twist: here, around 120 churches have been cut into the top of rock spires in seemingly impossible-to-reach positions. Visiting them involves steep climbs or scrambling up almost-sheer rock faces using toeholds.

## THE BLEEDING HEART BABOON

The gelada baboon is one of Ethiopia's most fascinating endemic mammals. In fact, not a baboon at all, it makes up its own genus of monkey. Of all the nonhuman primates, it's by far the most dexterous. It also lives in the largest social groups (up to 800 individuals in a group have been recorded), is the only primate that feeds on grass, and has its 'mating skin' on its chest and not on its bottom – a convenient adaptation, given that it spends most of its time sitting.

The gelada also has the most complex system of communication of any nonhuman primate and the most sophisticated social system: the females decide who's boss, the young males form bachelor groups, and the older males perform a kind of grandfather role looking after the young.

Although the males sport magnificent leonine manes, their most striking physical feature is the bare patch of skin on their chest. This has given rise to their other popular name: the 'bleeding heart baboon'. The colour of the patch indicates the sexual condition of not just the male (his virility), but also his female harem (their fertility).

Although shrinking, the gelada population is the healthiest of Ethiopia's endemic mammals. Its current population is thought to number between 40,000 and 50,000.

## Lake Tana

Ethiopia's largest lake is also the source of the Blue Nile, which converges with the White Nile near Khartoum (Sudan) before flowing to the Mediterranean Sea. Boat trips to visit the lake's monasteries are the main activity here. You can also head downstream to the quiet village of Tis Isat to see the gentle Nile suddenly pour over the side of a sheer chasm and explode into a melange of mists and rainbows at the Blue Nile Falls.

## Gondar

Often called the Camelot of Africa, this town's masterpiece is its Royal Enclosure, a 70,000-sq-metre, World Heritage–listed compound containing numerous castles and palaces.

# GETTING YOU THERE

Treks in the Simien Mountains begin in the town of Debark, which has two morning buses to Gondar (3½ hours). Ethiopian Airlines flies once or twice daily to Gondar from the capital, Addis Ababa (or you can ruin yourself on the two-day bus trip). There are regular flights to Addis Ababa from around Europe, the Middle East and Africa.

# EXPLORING THE SIMIEN MOUNTAINS

Cooks, scouts (park rangers, armed in case of encounters with wild animals), mules and guides can all be organised at the park headquarters in Debark. The scouts are compulsory; official guides are recommended and will help translate while in villages.

There are also numerous tour operators or travel agencies in Addis Ababa, and several more in Gondar, that can organise transport, guides, equipment rental and food. However, they charge you a lot more to hire exactly the same services from the park headquarters that you can easily arrange yourself.

## FAST FACTS

The Simien Mountains contain around 20 peaks above 4000m.

The range was formed by countless volcanic eruptions around 40 million years ago. Layer upon layer of molten lava poured until it reached a thickness of 4000m.

The mountains are home to three of Ethiopia's larger endemic mammals: the walia ibex, the gelada baboon and the Ethiopian wolf.

Of Africa's 10 endemic mainland bird families, eight are represented in Ethiopia, with only rockfowls and sugarbirds absent.

The Ethiopian wolf is the world's rarest *canid* (dog family member) – in 2005 only 71 wolves were counted around the Simien Mountains.

# ROCKY MOUNTAINS
## North America

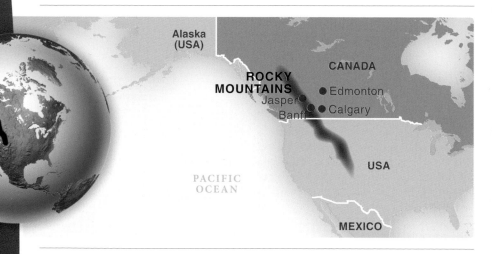

North America's mightiest mountain chain – part of the great line of mountains that extends from Alaska to Patagonia – is littered with wonderful national parks, protecting a host of wildlife and peaks beaten into shape by millennia of wild weather. Wander away from the crowded trailheads and you can spend time among more animals than people, from the cute (marmots) to the colossal (grizzly bears).

## On Screen

On *Planet Earth* you watch winter avalanches give way to spring, and grizzly bears emerge from hibernation. And as the seasons turn, the grizzlies head for the barren and bouldery heights of the range in search of an unusual treat: moths, rich in fat to help the bears through the next winter's hibernation.

## When

To really explore the upper reaches of the Rocky Mountains, the summer season (June to September) is best. In many places, the high passes aren't clear of snow until well into July.

**Mt Edith Cavell, Jasper National Park, Canada**
A short, self-guiding trail at the foot of Edith Cavell's north wall leads to a small melt-water lake and Angel Glacier.

"Summer reveals the true nature of the Rockies. Stripped of snow, the peaks bare their sculpted forms."

# EXPERIENCE

The marmot stands atop the cairn like a rodent mountaineer surveying the miles of mountain country, disappearing only as you rise to the broad top of Big Shovel Pass. A pair of bighorn sheep is less fazed by your presence and continues to graze, moving among the mass of wildflowers sprinkled like confetti about the meadow sloping down from the pass. The shrill warning whistles of the marmots, alerting others to your presence, screech through the air.

Wherever you look – left, right, ahead, behind – there are mountains, and it is as though the Rockies envelop you. The views seem endless, as they should since you are making the longest alpine crossing of any hiking trail in the Canadian Rockies. Walking the Skyline Trail, you will hover above the tree line on the Maligne Range for more than a day. It's like a scenic flight on legs, and the most exposed section of the crossing is just ahead.

Through a rock fall of orange boulders you approach Curator Lake and begin climbing to the Notch, the highest and steepest of the Skyline's passes. The earth is beginning to freeze and crunch beneath your feet as you climb to the cold heights. Ahead, the path crosses a barren ridge top. Such a contrast...just a few hours ago you'd been knee high in a sea of flowers; this ridge is as bleak as a desert.

Beside its views, the thing the Skyline Trail is most famous for is the number of bears along the range. Though it feels as though you can see forever, you still wonder if they are about, somewhere, somehow out of sight. This morning you watched a pair of hikers set out carrying a virtual bear arsenal – bear bells (otherwise known around here as 'dinner bells' because of their supposed ineffectiveness), bangers and mace – making you feel rather underdressed, as you've chosen to rely on just the noise you'll make walking to alert and discourage bears.

For an hour you amble along the lifeless ridge, sometimes blinded by cloud and sometimes blinded by beauty. Mt Edith Cavell rises tall across the valley, striped with snow; near to it is Whistlers Mountain, topped by the gondola station from Jasper. In a few minutes it will be buried in cloud, filling you with a certain cruel satisfaction; you feel as though you've earned your view, while those on the gondola have not.

A long, winding descent from the ridge takes you past a tarn coloured as brilliantly as a volcanic lake. A short distance on you see something strange, something you haven't seen for what seems like an eternity: green things on brown stands. Trees.

(top) Bighorn Sheep
A male bighorn's horns can reach over 1m in length and are the main weapon used in clashes over females. Their size also dictates the sheep's position in the herd.

(bottom) Mt Rundle, Banff National Park, Canada
Mt Rundle towers over the town of Banff in Banff National Park, one of four connected national parks that make up the heart of the Canadian Rockies.

# TAKING ACTION

## As You Saw It

The sort of ridge tops shown on the *Planet Earth* series can be reached on a number of hiking paths, most notably Canada's Skyline Trail. Spending 25km of its 45km in alpine terrain, this is the longest alpine traverse in the Canadian Rockies. The hike, best broken into three days, begins on the shores of Maligne Lake and ends near Jasper.

## A Less-Intense Experience

If your objective is to see a bear, but you don't fancy the exposure of hiking into the mountains, consider a morning drive along the Bow Valley Parkway between Banff and Lake Louise. Regarded as one of the most reliable roads in North America for wildlife viewing, it runs beside the Bow River and offers the chance to see elk, bighorn sheep and bald eagles, as well as black and grizzly bears.

## Alternative Rockies-Hiking Experiences

Montana's Glacier National Park is one of the best places in North America for sighting wildlife as you walk through the Rockies. Consider the following trails and destinations.

✿ **Dawson-Pitamakin Loop** This circuit walk passes through areas that rangers have used as bear-study areas.

✿ **Hidden Lake Overlook** This straightforward 5km-return hike leads to a lookout point over Hidden Lake, where you are likely to see bighorn sheep.

✿ **Fishercap Lake** A short walk from the Many Glacier trailhead towards Swiftcurrent Pass, you can turn down to this small lake, where there are regular moose sightings.

# WHILE YOU'RE THERE

## Icefields Parkway

Billed by tourism authorities as the 'most beautiful road in the world', the journey from Lake Louise to Jasper passes through deep valleys, beneath sharp peaks and past duck-egg-blue lakes. The scenery is amazing and the wildlife plentiful, and the eponymous icefield sits like icing on the Rockies. Other highlights include the Athabasca Glacier – where the Columbia Icefield breaks through the mountains and reaches down towards the road – and the surging Athabasca Falls. It's a great drive, and an even better cycling tour.

# BURGESS SHALE

High in the Rocky Mountains, inside Canada's Yoho National Park, is a place that's something of an evolutionist's heaven. The Burgess Shale – described by Stephen Jay Gould as containing 'the world's most important animal fossils' – is located high on the slopes of Mt Stephen and Mt Field. It preserves the 515-million-year-old Cambrian fossils of marine creatures that were some of the oldest life forms on earth. In this small space there are hundreds of thousands – if not millions – of fossils that, when discovered in 1909, were the world's first-recorded soft-tissued fossils, and the oldest fossils to shed light on the evolution of life.

It is illegal to enter the Burgess Shale except on guided hikes led by the Burgess Shale Geoscience Foundation (www.burgess-shale.bc.ca). It's a 20km-round walk from the Takakkaw Falls car park. Walks go to Walcott's Quarry, where Charles Walcott (one of America's preeminent scientists) discovered the Burgess Shale. Visitors get to poke about the rocks looking for fossils – such ancient treasures as *marrella*, trilobites, *vauxias*, brachiopods and the parochially labelled *Canadaspis* and *Yohoia*.

## Cave & Basin

This national historic site, with its hot sulphur springs in a cave, is the site where the evergreen town of Banff was founded, and the raison d'être for Canada's first national park. There's no bathing allowed anymore, but you can head down the road to the Upper Hot Springs for a soak.

## Yellowstone National Park

Even older than Banff National Park, Yellowstone was the world's first national park, created in 1872, and it remains among the most famous reserves in the world. Come for copious wildlife, gushing geysers (the park is home to half the world's geysers), waterfalls and alpine lakes. See p188 for more.

# GETTING YOU THERE

Edmonton and Calgary are the nearest airports to Jasper and Banff, respectively. The Banff Airport Shuttle runs between Calgary airport and both Banff and Jasper. The Maligne Lake Shuttle (www .malignelakeshuttle.com) operates a bus service between Jasper and the trailheads for the Skyline Trail.

# EXPLORING THE ROCKY MOUNTAINS

Campsite bookings along the Skyline Trail can be made through the Parks Canada office (pnj.jnp@pc.gc.ca) in Jasper. And if hiking just doesn't get you high enough, you can enter the realms of mountaineering in the Canadian Rockies. The following operators offer mountaineering expeditions and instruction out of Banff.

✿ **Yamnuska** (www.yamnuska.com) Beginner courses through to private guided expeditions, plus rock and winter ice climbing.

✿ **Chute High Adventures** (www.alpineadventureguide.com) Personalised mountaineering trips.

# IN THE SHADOW OF THE BLUE TOWERS

## Torres del Paine, Chile

BOLIVIA

BRAZIL

PARAGUAY

PACIFIC
OCEAN

URUGUAY

ARGENTINA

ATLANTIC
OCEAN

CHILE

**PARQUE NACIONAL
TORRES DEL PAINE**

Puerto
Natales

Everything about this place is truly wild – the weather, the cruelly jagged granite peaks, the habitats and, especially, the animals. In addition to herds of guanacos and stealthy pumas, you'll probably spot flocks of flightless rheas and flamingos, as well as soaring condors. And with some 250km of marked hiking trails, it's a trekker's paradise.

## On Screen

The environment of Parque Nacional Torres del Paine is as dangerous and ever-changing as it is beautiful – especially for guanacos, who must contend with vicious climatic variations as well as the attentions of the park's number one predator: the puma. *Planet Earth* tracks a group of pumas through the peaks and valleys of the southern Andes as the mother struggles to provide food for four young – showing us a unique family portrait of the region's prime land hunter.

## When

The austral summer (December to March) offers the best chance of warmer, drier weather – though storms can blow up at any time. The park gets busy in high summer, so shoulder seasons (early December and March) offer a good compromise for trekkers.

**Torres del Paine, Chile**
Spectacular granite pillars jutting up some 2800m, the Torres del Paine dominate the landscape of Parque Nacional Torres del Paine.

"The Andes have the most unstable mountain weather on the planet – truly, all seasons in one day."

# EXPERIENCE

This climate is crazy – your zip's whizzing up and down like a yo-yo. Forget four seasons in one day – you're experiencing all of them in the space of five minutes. One moment you gaze up to admire a swath of unbroken ultramarine sky, the sun caressing your back; in the blink of an eye, the blustering wind teases the clouds from around the higher peaks and drags them down to surround you in a chill mist. While seconds earlier you'd been stripping down to your smalls; now you're buttoning up your collar as snow is driven almost horizontally into your face.

On the slopes above you, the herd of guanacos you'd been watching lies down in the undergrowth. You can almost hear the resigned sigh as they huddle together, stoically awaiting the passing of the storm.

And pass it does. As quickly as it blew up, the cloud breaks and a rainbow streams down to the hillside, close enough to touch. Then, as if at a signal, the guanacos leap to their feet, instantly alert, staring down at the valley beneath them. You glance across, at first spotting nothing untoward among the dun-coloured rocks and scrub. Then a cluster of shapes emerge, flowing like liquid across a patch of open ground: a puma family – a mother and four cubs, though in truth the youngsters don't give away much size to mum.

The wary guanacos mutter amongst themselves in timid grunts, scuttling away up the hillside as the pumas slink towards the lakeshore to drink, stealthily padding down the shale slopes. Stealth won't help them in this open landscape, though, you think – not in daylight, at least.

You camp in a remote spot, thankful that the wind has finally died down and the flapping of your tent has subsided enough for you to sleep. You wake with a start during the night, sure you heard screaming; poking your head out of the tent, the moonlight glistens off the snow patches on the peaks above, but there's nothing else to be seen. Exhausted after your day's hike, you quickly nod off again.

In the morning the peaks are still visible, free from their cloaks of mist – for the time being. Quickly you strike camp and set out, watching the cloud shadows scud across the variegated brown-green valley floor. In the distance a dash of vivid red, twitching slightly, catches your attention. As you approach, you realise what was screaming last night: one of your guanacos – or what's left of it – is being tugged around by the hungry puma cubs and their hunter mum. She left her attack till cover of dark, when the guanaco herd lost the visual advantage they held in the open ground. As always, mother knows best.

**(top) Parque Nacional Torres del Paine, Chile**
Located between the Andes and the Patagonian steppe, Parque Nacional Torres del Paine was nominated a Unesco biosphere reserve in 1978.

**(bottom) Guanacos**
Guanacos can hold more oxygen in their blood than many other mammals, enabling them to live in the thin air of the high Andes, at altitudes of up to 4500m.

# TAKING ACTION

## As You Saw It

Those soaring granite peaks are unmistakable – the Torres del Paine (Towers of Paine), which lend their name to southern Chile's most popular national park. The area is blessed with lakes, mountains, glaciers and forests. This southern tip of the Andes is accessible on day trips from nearby Puerto Natales, but to really appreciate the variety of its scenery – and for a better chance of spotting its guanaco herds and elusive pumas – lace up those boots and get hiking on one of the fine trails criss-crossing the park.

## Adding to the Experience

The two main hiking routes offer jaw-dropping views of both the Towers and the park's jagged Cuernos (Horns). The most popular trail is the 'W', a one-way, three- to five-day east–west trek along the northern sides of lakes Nordenskjöld, Pehoe and Grey. The Circuit is a more challenging affair, extending the 'W' to a loop around the northern side of the peaks, giving access to the full range of habitats. Allow at least five days, ideally more to account for unpredictable (though not unexpected) changes in weather. Note that the park gets very busy during January and February – you'll need to book accommodation in advance.

## Alternative Puma-Spotting Experiences

The puma – known in North America as the cougar – is shy and tricky to spot, though present pretty much the length of the Americas. Try:

✿ **Parque Nacional Alerce Andino** (central Chile) Hike among lush alerce forest.

✿ **Banff National Park** (Alberta, Canada) Keep your eyes peeled for wolf, bear, elk, moose and, if you're really fortunate, cougars.

✿ **Parque Nacional Huascarán** (Peru) Hike the trails of the Cordillera Blanca, staying alert for signs of pumas.

✿ **Cascade Mountains** (Oregon, USA) Almost 6000 cougars roam the state's mountains.

# WHILE YOU'RE THERE

## Cueva del Milodón

This large cave was the resting place of the remains of a 4m-high giant sloth, discovered in the late-19th century. The species was reputedly the inspiration for Bruce Chatwin's book *In Patagonia*.

## Kayak the Río Serrano

Get a different perspective on the mountains and glaciers – a three-day kayaking trip along the river visits Glaciar Balmaceda.

# IN PATAGONIA – IN MY IMAGINATION...

Englishman Bruce Chatwin wrote Patagonia's seminal travel narrative, a book blending visual description with social commentary, history and local legends. Chatwin claimed his six-month odyssey through Patagonia in 1975 was inspired by seeing a scrap of skin from a prehistoric giant sloth, like the one found in the Cueva del Milodón some 25km northwest of Puerto Natales. The resulting book, In Patagonia, was published in 1977 and became recognised as a classic of travel literature.

But perhaps the book is more fiction than fact. After its publication numerous local characters publicly denied the truth of many of the events and conversations described in its pages. As it transpired, Chatwin had a tendency to exaggerate or subvert the facts; he died of AIDS in 1989, but during his final illness claimed it was the result of a bite from a Chinese bat.

Regardless of whether or not every word is absolutely truthful, *In Patagonia* remains arguably the most evocative and inspiring description of the region.

### Parque Nacional Los Glaciares

Hop over the border into Argentina to gawp at the mighty Glaciar Perito Moreno, a vast, creaking river of ice that calves massive bergs into the channel below.

### Sail Through the Fjords

Board a cruise ship or a more down-to-earth Navimag ferry to sail through fjords and past glaciers from Patagonia to Puerto Montt.

## GETTING YOU THERE

Parquo Nacional Torres del Paine is 112km north of Puerto Natales, the main transport hub for the area. Buses operated by several companies shuttle to the park a couple of times daily in summer, departing Puerto Natales early morning and early afternoon. The journey takes about 2½ hours to Laguna Amarga, the starting point for the 'W' trek. Buses pick up from the Administración (park headquarters; for the end of the 'W') in the afternoon.

## EXPLORING PARQUE NACIONAL TORRES DEL PAINE

Though you'll probably want to undertake one of the treks to get a real feel for the area, it's also possible to join one-day minibus tours from Puerto Natales, which provide views of the peaks from the road looping through the southeastern part of the park. There are plenty of other options for tours and activities in the park, including kayaking, climbing, glacier trekking and horse riding. Numerous travel agents in Puerto Natales organise tours.

# FRESH WATER
## *Planet Earth, Episode Three*

Find fresh water and you'll find wildlife in abundance. Even the smallest trickle can harbour surprising diversity; visit one of the world's great freshwater repositories – a vast lake, a spewing delta, the sprawling web of a continent-wide river system – and the species count skyrockets. You'll see life in all directions: flying over, swimming under, floating on and drinking from the source – an encyclopedia of creatures congregates in these lush and luxuriant habitats. Whether you choose to paddle a stream, sail across a lake or stand in the spray of a tumbling waterfall, you can bet you will not be alone.

# ANGEL FALLS

## Parque Nacional Canaima, Venezuela

Caracas

TRINIDAD & TOBAGO

ATLANTIC OCEAN

VENEZUELA

ANGEL FALLS ○

GUYANA

COLOMBIA

SURINAME

BRAZIL

The inspiration for the 'Paradise Falls' featured in Pixar's *Up,* Angel Falls is a spectacular and perhaps surprisingly familiar sight. And for anyone trying to collect all of the planet's superlatives in their travel list, adding the tallest waterfall is certainly a worthy endeavour.

## On Screen

The mysterious tepuis (flat-topped mountains) of Venezuela appear as isolated plateaus towering over the jungle. Here is Angel Falls (Salto Ángel), where waters plunge unbroken for nearly a kilometre. Any pilot who ventures here risks treacherous winds and sudden white-outs, but after four attempts by the *Planet Earth* crew to film, the clouds briefly and miraculously part.

Angel Falls, Parque Nacional Canaima, Venezuela
Angel Falls was known locally as Kerepakupai-merú ('waterfall of the highest place' in Pemón), long before its 'discovery' by Jimmie Angel.

## When

The amount of water going over Angel Falls depends on the season, and the contrast can be dramatic. In the dry months (January to May), it can be pretty faint – just a thin ribbon of water fading into mist before it reaches the bottom; boat access is impossible at the peak of the dry season. In the rainy season, however, particularly in the wettest months (August and September), the waterfall is a spectacular cascade of plummeting water – but you run the risk of the view being obscured by clouds.

"Angel Falls is the world's highest waterfall: more than 3000ft high."

# EXPERIENCE

Prior to landing in Canaima, a remote indigenous village in the southeastern region of Guayana province, you skim through the pages of Sir Arthur Conan Doyle's *The Lost World* for the umpteenth time. Long before there was *Up* (and *Jurassic Park,* for that matter), Doyle inspired you with tales of prehistoric animals thriving on a remote plateau in the middle of the Amazon basin.

Glancing out the aeroplane window, you admire this impossibly lush corner of Venezuela, home to the majority of the country's indigenous groups; the Pemón, Warao and Yanomami constitute about 10% of the region's total population. And then there are the anvil-like tepuis punctuating the seemingly endless rolling savannahs. Logic aside, you wonder for a moment if there are in fact still dinosaurs roaming about somewhere below.

You touch down in Canaima, which despite functioning as little more than a base camp for Venezuela's number-one natural attraction, is absolutely gorgeous in its own right. Sitting at the heart of everything is the Laguna de Canaima: a broad blue expanse framed by a palm-tree beach with a dramatic series of seven picture-postcard cascades and a backdrop of tepuis.

Tourism infrastructure here is better than you've seen elsewhere in Venezuela, but it's still not easy going. Routine currency exchanges are complicated by an active, dollar-hungry black market, but you take these financial challenges on the chin, like everything else. Besides, Venezuela remains a fairly inexpensive place to travel, and the people are warm and well mannered.

A short boat trip later and, at long last, you're standing in front of Angel Falls. Pouring off the towering Auyantepui, one of the largest of the tepuis, this cascade is no less than 16 times the height of Niagara Falls. As your guide is quick to point out, the waterfall is not named, as one might expect, for a divine creature, but rather the American bush pilot Jimmie Angel, who landed his four-seater aeroplane atop Auyantepui in 1937 while searching for gold.

As an encore to the main event, you leave the relative safety of the boat and hike up behind the falls, where you enjoy the backstage experience of the hammering curtains of water. Their colour is a rather curious shade of pink, caused by the high level of tannins from decomposed plants and trees. You rather foolhardily search for a triceratops, but sadly come up empty-handed.

**(top) Roraima Tepui**
Lying on the Guiana Shield in the southeastern corner of Canaima National Park, Mt Roraima forms the highest peak of Guayana's Highland Range.

**(bottom) View from Roraima**
Although it's one of the easier tepuis to climb and no technical skills are required, the trek up Roraima is long and demanding – a five-day round trip with time to explore the plateau.

# TAKING ACTION

## As You Saw It

Angel Falls is in a distant wilderness with no road access. The village of Canaima is the major gateway to the falls, but it doesn't have an overland link to the rest of the country either, and must be accessed by small plane from Ciudad Bolívar. From Canaima you take either a light plane or a boat to the falls.

## Adding to the Experience

Most visitors who go to the falls by boat opt to stay overnight in hammocks at one of the camps (set up by tour companies, some in conjunction with local communities) near the base of the falls. The trip upriver and the experience of staying at the camp are almost as memorable as the waterfall itself.

## Alternative Waterfall Experiences

Our planet is full of dramatic waterfalls, and each one is utterly unique in size and scope.

✿ **Victoria Falls** (Zambia–Zimbabwe border) 108m tall, 1708m wide at its maximum.

✿ **Iguaçu Falls** (Argentina–Brazil border) 82m tall, 275 cataracts set in a horsehoe shape 2.7km in total width.

✿ **Niagara Falls** (US–Canada border) 53m tall, 790m wide at its maximum.

# WHILE YOU'RE THERE

## Gran Sabana

Wide-open grassland that seems to be suspended from endless sky, the Gran Sabana (Great Savannah) invites poetic description. Scores of waterfalls appear at every turn, and tepuis sweep across the horizon, their mesas both haunting and majestic. More than 100 of these plateaus dot the vast region from the Colombian border in the west to Guyana and Brazil in the east, but most are here in the Gran Sabana. One of the tepuis, Roraima, can be climbed; this trip is an extraordinary adventure.

The largest town on the savannah is Santa Elena de Uairén, close to the Brazilian border. The rest of the sparsely populated region is inhabited mostly by the 15,000 indigenous Pemón people, who live in nearly 300 scattered villages.

## Los Roques

Island-hopping is the primary activity on Los Roques, a group of nearly 300 shimmering, sandy islands and islets that lie in aquamarine waters some 160km due north of Caracas. It's pricier than the mainland because everything is imported, but for those who love undeveloped beaches, snorkelling and diving, the trip is worth every bolívar. There are no high-rise hotels and you can walk barefoot on Gran Roque's sand streets. The whole archipelago, complete with the surrounding waters,

## LIFE IN THE MOUNTAIN STREAMS

Along the coast of South America moisture rises from the surface of the sea as water vapour and travels inland on the wind. Coastal ranges force the moist air upward, and as it cools and condenses into clouds, rain falls in dramatic sheets, providing vitally important fresh water. Here, a tropical downpour happens almost every day of the year. In the upper reaches of the mountains the high-energy flows of water are cold and low in nutrients, but high levels of ambient oxygen are conducive to life. Invertebrates dominate, including the hellgrammite, which has a flattened body to reduce drag and bushy gills to extract oxygen from the current. Blackfly larvae also thrive, relying on a ring of hooks to anchor themselves to the rock, with a backup silken safety line in case they lose hold. And bamboo shrimp spend most of their time just sitting and sifting passing particles with their fan-like forearms, proving that there is such a thing as a free meal.

was made a national park in 1972. The great majority of the islands are uninhabited except by pelicans and can be visited by boat from Gran Roque. The surrounding waters are known for their sea life, particularly lobsters – 90% of all lobsters consumed nationally come from here.

## GETTING YOU THERE

Rutaca airlines (www.rutaca.com.ve) connects Ciudad Bolívar to Caracas. From here, most tour operators fly to Canaima.

## EXPLORING ANGEL FALLS

In Ciudad Bolívar and Canaima everyone and their mother can arrange onward travel to Angel Falls – shop around, ask fellow travellers and bargain for the best price.

### TEPUIS

Tepuis, which means 'House of the Gods' in the local Pemón language, are the remains of one enormous block of sandstone that was eroded, over 200 million years, by a succession of lakes and seas. The sandstone itself, referred to by geologists as the Guiana Shield, was formed two billion years ago and is both the oldest rock in South America and some of the oldest rock in the world.

## FAST FACTS

Venezuela is the 5th-largest oil-exporting country in the world – at almost 2.5 billion barrels per day.

The country's official name is the Bolivarian Republic of Venezuela in honour of the great Latin American political leader, Simón Bolívar.

Boasting a huge diversity of wildlife in a variety of protected habitats, Venezuela is one of the top 20 biodiverse countries in the world.

Venezuelan women have won five Miss Worlds, five Miss Universes and countless other beauty contests.

Venezuela is one of the five founding members of the Organization of the Petroleum Exporting Countries (OPEC), which was established in response to low oil prices.

# RIVERS STALKED BY NOCTURNAL GIANTS
## Honshū, Shikoku & Kyūshū, Japan

RUSSIA

CHINA

NORTH
KOREA

Sea
of
Japan

JAPAN

SOUTH
KOREA

Tokyo

PACIFIC
OCEAN

**SALAMANDER
RIVERS**

Honshū

Shikoku

Kyūshū

East
China
Sea

*"With the spring melt in Japan, monsters stir in their dens."*

**(left) Japanese Giant Salamander**
Until protection was conferred in the 1950s, Japanese salamanders were hunted for their meat. Its Chinese sister species, lacking such protection, is now listed by IUCN as Critically Endangered; the Japanese salamander is listed as Near Threatened.

**(right) Shiratani River, Yakushima**
Miyazaki Hayao's animated *Princess Mononoke* was inspired by the thick, lush forest of Yakushima Island, a Unesco World Heritage Site.

Giant salamanders are the world's largest amphibians. They can live for up to 80 years, allowing them to grow to up to 2m long – now that's something worth seeing. And even if you don't catch a glimpse, it's no hardship hanging out by the crystal-clear mountain streams they inhabit – a good excuse to leave behind the bustle of Japanese cities to experience the country's wilder side.

## On Screen
Taking the cameras below the surface of the icy streams of Japan, *Planet Earth* captures the nocturnal hunt of *Andrias japonicus* – the giant salamander. The 2m-long creature lurks on the riverbed, dark and grotesque, waiting for its fishy supper.

## When
The best seasons to visit Japan are spring (March to May) and autumn (September to November), when the temperatures are fine and the flora is at its best – cherry blossoms in the former season; russet-orange leaves in the latter.

Giant salamanders are nocturnal, so you'll only see them in action after dark. They mate in late August, when hundreds of the beasts congregate at nest sites.

PETER SCOONES/BBC

TAKASHI YAGIHASHI/SEBUN PHOTO/GETTY IMAGES

# EXPERIENCE

You hope it's got a good personality; the Japanese giant salamander isn't the most comely of specimens – in fact, if you're honest, it's downright ugly. A fat, flat lizardy beast, its patchy black skin is covered in a pox of warty nodules. As you lower your gaze from the icy splendour of a mountain stream, a mini-waterfall gushing over a carapace of sparkling ice, it's not surprising the creature hides itself from all this beauty by living a nocturnal, submarine existence.

Of course, that's nonsense; the salamander cares not a jot what you think of its aesthetics. It is the master of this watery domain – there are no other predators to compete with, no bigger beasts to fear. When it lurks, coiled and immobile in the subaquatic gloom, its form is practically indistinguishable from the speckled rocks around it. When it sets off on a prowl, its full extent is revealed: swim-walking along the riverbed, propelled by stubby digits and a sinuous tail, you can see it's a frankly horrifying 1.5m long. A real-life dragon in modern-day Japan – and one, much like dragons proper, few people will ever see.

So, back to those warts. Far from being an embarrassing outbreak, this aquatic acne has a specific purpose. The giant salamander has very poor eyesight in a very dark world; being myopic and nocturnal means it needs another trick up its sleeve. Or, in this case, on its back. The nodules on giant salamanders' bodies are highly sensitive to the slightest changes in water pressure, picking up vibrations much like the hairs in a human's ear. You watch as an unsuspecting fish floats by; the creature senses the movement and – bam! – with lightning speed lunges forward and catches its dinner.

This doesn't mean our monster has it easy, though. You may have seen him catch a feed, but it's pretty slim pickings in the icy meanders of Japan – a few fish, the odd frog or unfortunate passing crustacean – as the cold deters much life. Luckily, the salamander is a light eater, surviving on infrequent meals thanks to an exceptionally slow metabolism; in fact, it can go without food for weeks, lurking hungrily under rocks by day to conserve its meagre energy reserves. Or maybe this unfortunate-looking creature is body conscious after all, and is just watching its figure.

**Swimming Hole at Kirishima-Yaku National Park, Kyūshū**
Kirishima-Yaku National Park boasts chains of volcanic mountains with beautiful crater lakes, extensive beaches and hot springs.

# TAKING ACTION

## As You Saw It

You'll need a toasty dry suit if you want to take a dip in Japan's chilly rivers. In winter air is whisked over from Siberia, so there's plenty of snow on the ground and ice in the streams. You'll also have to stay up late for salamander action – they are strictly nocturnal – and keep your fingers crossed, as their numbers are in decline (the International Union for the Conservation of Nature classifies them as a Near Threatened species). Oh, and be careful – captive salamanders have been known to give their handlers a nasty bite.

## Adding to the Experience

Giant salamanders live in the rivers of western Honshū, Shikoku and Kyūshū; this is fascinating country to explore. The amphibians' preference is for clear rivers in forested areas: a good excuse to lace up your walking boots and do as the locals do – the Japanese love to hike. A good place to start is the mountainous, waterfall-strewn countryside around Maniwa, in Okayama prefecture, where the clean, glassy streams provide the perfect habitat.

To guarantee a sighting head to Asa Zoo, located in a suburb of Hiroshima, which runs a captive breeding program for giant salamanders, as well as rescuing at-risk individuals from the wild.

## Alternative Salamander-Spotting Experiences

Japan's giant salamanders may be rare, but there are more than 500 species of salamander in the world, some of which are significantly easier to spot.

✿ **Postojna** (Slovenia) For eyeless olm salamander, which live deep in the karst caves.

✿ **US eastern seaboard** (southern New England to northern Florida) For marbled salamander, which lurk in damp woodland.

✿ **Chilliwack River watershed** (British Columbia, Canada) For Pacific giant salamanders, one of the few species to produce sounds.

✿ **Warwickshire** (England) The most northerly populations of the Alpine newt.

# WHILE YOU'RE THERE

## Hiroshima, Western Honshū

As well as checking out Asa Zoo's giant salamanders, visit the Peace Memorial Park, a sobering reminder of the first atomic-bomb drop, in 1945, which flattened the now revitalised city.

## THE MOST GIANT GIANT OF THEM ALL

A 2m-long amphibian seems quite long enough but, according to one local legend, giant salamanders come in even greater proportions.

In the 17th century a 10m salamander prowled the countryside around Maniwa, Okayama prefecture, feasting on not just the odd fish, but also the townspeople's horses and cows. The townspeople did not appreciate this at all, so a local hero named Mitsui Hikoshiro stepped up to the plate, volunteering to let the beast swallow him (and his sword) whole. Once inside the salamander's belly, Mitsui sliced it open – mission accomplished!

However, after the salamander was slain the crops started failing, and people began dying in peculiar ways (including Mitsui himself). Clearly the spirit of the creature was not amused, and was wreaking revenge for its violent demise. The solution? To pacify the salamander's vengeful wraith, the citizens of Maniwa built a shrine – the Hanzaki Shrine, which you can still see in the city today. To pay your proper respects, visit in August when the annual Hanzaki Festival sees costumed locals parade through the streets pulling carnival floats decorated with – you guessed it – 10m-long salamanders.

## Tsuwano, Western Honshū

This 700-year-old mountain town has plenty of carp in its waterways, if not salamanders. Take the chairlift up to the castle ruins.

## Shimonoseki, Western Honshū

Salamander might not be for sale, but seemingly every other water-dwelling creature is at the Karato Ichiba fish market. Get up early (it opens at 4am) to watch the traders fling fish – both identifiable and not so – and to breakfast on couldn't-be-fresher sashimi.

## Usuki, Kyūshū

A collection of 1000-year-old Buddha statues sits in a ravine just outside the town of Usuki, while the town itself boasts fine old temples and reputedly the best *fugu* (poisonous pufferfish!) restaurants in the country.

## Matsuyama, Shikoku

Shikoku island's largest city is home to Dogo Onsen, a castle-style building of multilevel public baths – the perfect place to dip into Japan's hot-spring culture.

## GETTING YOU THERE

With Japan's super-efficient transport network, getting around the country is not a problem. Your giant salamander quest might take you all over, so consider an excellent-value Japan Rail Pass (www.japanrailpass.net), available for seven, 14 or 21 days; these must be purchased outside Japan.

## EXPLORING MANIWA

Head to Maniwa's Hanzaki Centre, where giant salamanders are studied, to learn more about the beasts; here, you'll find specimens in tanks and expert biologists who can give you more information. Specialist operator Inside Japan Tours (www.insidejapantours.com) has in-depth knowledge of the country and can give advice on visiting Maniwa and beyond.

## FAST FACTS

In Japanese the giant salamander is known as *osanshouo,* the 'giant pepper fish', on account of the milky substance it secretes when threatened – which smells like a Japanese pepper.

The Japanese giant is the only salamander species to practise external fertilisation. In autumn females lay between 400 and 500 eggs, which may be fertilised by several males; the eggs hatch in early spring.

Giant salamanders are not fussy eaters, happily feasting on anything they can grab, from insects to fish, mice and crabs.

Two species of giant salamander live in Asia – one in Japan and one in China.

The comparably huge, and excellently named, Eastern hellbender salamander species lives in eastern USA.

Giant salamanders are considered 'living fossils' because their skeletons today are almost identical to that of a fossilised specimen dating back 30 million years – a quite incredible absence of evolution.

# THE GREAT SALMON MIGRATION
## Knight Inlet, British Columbia, Canada

KNIGHT INLET ○

British Columbia

CANADA

USA

PACIFIC OCEAN

A wildlife spectacular follows the waterways through the Great Bear Rainforest, the world's largest intact temperate rainforest. As millions of salmon return to their spawning grounds, predators follow in hot pursuit: bald eagles, brown bears, grizzlies, spirit bears and, near the mouth of the inlet, orcas.

## On Screen

Following the largest freshwater fish migration in the world, *Planet Earth* takes you to the streams around Knight Inlet to watch as salmon struggle upstream towards their spawning grounds, zeroing in on the very location where they were hatched themselves. Exhausted and fighting the currents, they face the threat of a grizzly bear sow and her cubs picking off salmon for dinner.

## When

Around Knight Inlet the pink salmon begin their spawning run about mid- to late August, as hundreds of thousands of fish head for the rivers. A second run, of chum salmon, usually arrives around late September.

**(top) Spirit (Kermode) Bear**
Scientists estimate there are 1200 Kermode bears (including black ones and white ones) in the coast area stretching from around the northern tip of Vancouver Island northwards to the Alaska panhandle.

**(bottom) Pink Salmon**
The pink salmon is also known as the humpback because of the pronounced hump that develops on the back of the adult male before spawning.

# EXPERIENCE

The water seems to bubble and seethe like a cauldron, but not with heat. In the channels of the river bend hundreds of pink salmon writhe through the shallows, splashing, leaping, doing whatever it takes to continue the journey upstream to their spawning grounds. Instinct propels them, but not all will make it; occasionally a fish floats to the surface, dead from exhaustion.

There are other threats here, too. As you stand atop the wooden viewing platform, the biggest threat of all ambles into sight at a downstream bend, stepping beneath a fallen log and splashing through the shallow stream. From here it looks like a polar bear, only smaller, and you realise that you are looking at one of the region's great natural curiosities: a spirit bear.

Found only around the Great Bear Rainforest, the spirit (or Kermode) bear is a black bear that, due to a recessive gene, has cream-white fur. As it steps out of the stream, it disappears into the forest, and though you hear it stepping through the undergrowth on the opposite bank, it is gone from sight. It's been like a glimpse of ursine royalty. The splashing waters are momentarily forgotten.

Minutes behind the spirit bear there is further movement downstream. This time a black bear steps into sight, wandering upstream towards the shallow channels in front of you. This bear – a massive ball of muscle inside fur as dark as charcoal – stops no more than 5m from where you stand, looking your way briefly, but intent on the easy meals thrashing about in the water that barely rises above its paws.

Catching them is not as easy as it looks, though; the bear leaps about, swiping at its slippery prey. But finally the bear pins a salmon to the pebbly riverbed; this fish's long journey home will never be completed. The bear picks the salmon up in its teeth, where it hangs like a tongue, and carries it away to nearby rocks. There, the bear seems almost to sit on the rocks like a diner in a restaurant. It devours the pink flesh before returning to the braided stream for the next course in its meal.

For an hour it fishes right there in front of you, tolerating your presence. Eventually it continues upstream, wandering along a mossy log before disappearing around the next bend in the river. Before you, little appears to have changed: the river flows in one direction and the mass of salmon continues to flow in the other.

**An Orca in the Waters Around Vancouver Island**
The orca, also known as the killer whale, is the largest member of the dolphin family. There are thought to be around 300 resident and 200 transient orcas in the waters around British Columbia and Washington.

# TAKING ACTION

## As You Saw It

Feeding into Knight Inlet, the Glendale River is a major spawning river for pink salmon and draws dozens of grizzly bears to its banks and shallows. The river is remote and almost inaccessible, but there are three viewing platforms among the rainforest trees from which visitors can witness the spectacle of grizzlies snacking on salmon.

## Adding to the Experience

In the waters of Johnstone Strait, at the mouth of Knight Inlet, an even larger predator travels in pursuit of the spawning salmon. Through this narrow underwater canyon, 250 resident orcas hunt salmon and, uniquely, swim into the pebbly shores of Robson Bight to rub away old skin. Entry into the ecological reserve around the bight is banned, but kayak trips among the orcas operate through the strait and around the edges of the reserve.

## Alternative Bear-Watching Experiences

Continue north into Alaska and the McNeil River State Game Sanctuary and you have the chance to witness an even more spectacular scene in the bear-meets-fish game. It is here that many of the famous images were snapped of brown bears plucking leaping salmon out of the air as they attempt to hurdle to the top of a waterfall. Prime season for bear viewing on the McNeil River is July and August, but visits are by permit only – permits are issued by a lottery system. See p274 for more on the lottery.

# WHILE YOU'RE THERE

## West Coast Trail

Cross the strait to Vancouver Island and hike the wild west coast on one of Canada's best-known and toughest hiking trails. The 77km track was carved as an escape route for shipwrecked sailors, which ought to tell you enough about the nature of this coastline.

## Inside Passage Ferries

Taking an Alaska Marine Highway ferry or BC Ferries boat along the stunning Inside Passage and British Columbia and Alaska coasts almost guarantees sightings of marine life, including whales, dolphins and orcas. Also look for eagles overhead and bears on shore. This rugged coastline is largely part of the Great Bear Rainforest and you will spend hours passing deserted islands and rocky coasts.

# A FISHY TALE

It's a finely tuned instinct. Each year millions of salmon cross the Pacific to the western shores of North America, returning to the very spot from which they hatched, to lay their own eggs. How they retain this knowledge and navigate back to the same spawning ground is unknown.

In returning to their native streams, salmon have been known to swim more than 3000km, performing the unusual feat of leaving salt water to continue their journeys through fresh water. Once in fresh water the salmon do not feed, relying on the fat stores in their bodies, and their stomachs begin to disintegrate, creating more room for eggs and sperm. Their jaws also begin to change shape, becoming more hooked as a way for males to display dominance.

As they head upstream the fish begin to change colour, turning from silver to black (or, in the case of sockeye salmon, from silver and blue to red bodies with green heads). At the spawning ground the female salmon clears a space on the gravel riverbed and lays up to 10,000 eggs, which are then fertilised externally by a male. Pacific salmon die soon after spawning, usually within a couple of weeks.

## Khutzeymateen Grizzly Bear Sanctuary

This 45,000-hectare park is located about 40km northeast of Prince Rupert and is thought to be home to around 50 grizzly bears. It's set in a remote valley and the human presence in the park is heavily restricted, though you can join a boat tour or take a floatplane from Prince Rupert for a peek.

# GETTING YOU THERE

Access into spawning streams is difficult and will usually require joining a tour or staying at a remote lodge, usually at premium prices.

# EXPLORING KNIGHT INLET

There are a couple of tour options (August and September only) into Knight Inlet and its salmon-spawning streams.

✿ **Knight Inlet Lodge** (www.knightinletlodge.com) A fly-in lodge set on Glendale Cove in Knight Inlet. In August and September guests travel by boat and bus to Glendale River to observe grizzlies feeding on salmon.

✿ **Tide Rip Tours** (www.tiderip.com) Based at Telegraph Cove on northern Vancouver Island, Tide Rip runs day tours across the strait to Knight Inlet and the Kakweiken River.

✿ **King Pacific Lodge** (www.kingpacificlodge.com) This fly-in lodge on Princess Royal Island offers guest trips to nearby Gribble Island to view spirit bears and black bears along a salmon-spawning stream.

# THE COLORADO RIVER'S GRAND CANYON

## Arizona, American Southwest

Whether you consider it just the greatest hole on earth or one of the seven natural wonders of the world, you really have to see the Grand Canyon. This great desert chasm has taken eons to take shape, and even the most jaded travellers come away with a touch more appreciation for our ancient, ever-changing planet.

## On Screen

Upland rivers carry very little life, yet these stretches have more power to shape the landscape than any other stage in the river's journey. Driven by gravity, they're the most erosive force on the planet. For around five million years Arizona's Colorado River has been eating away at the desert sandstone and has carved the world's longest canyon system – a 1600km scar, visible from space.

## When

June is the driest month here, July and August the wettest; while January generally has overnight lows of -11°C to -7°C and daytime highs around 4°C, summer temperatures inside the canyon regularly soar above 40°C.

The South Rim is open year-round; the North Rim only from mid-May to mid-October – so most visitors come between late May and early September.

**Cathedral Rock**
The most-photographed formation in the area, Cathedral Rock is one of four rock formations in Sedona believed by New Age adherents to contain a power vortex.

# EXPERIENCE

You've seen all the slick brochures and adventure mags urging you to set out for the wilds, test your limits, ponder the big picture. Indeed the American Southwest is an awe-inspiring place of plunging canyons, colossal buttes, towering mountains and verifiable cowboy country.

But what strikes you more than anything else upon arrival in the desert is the space – bushes, trees and cacti in all sorts of gnarly shapes and colours spread out across rolling sandy hills that stretch as far as you can see. Armies of saguaro cacti stand along sun-parched highways looping lazily to nowhere, beckoning the start of your great American road trip.

*"It's more than a mile deep. At its widest, 17 miles across. Truly, the Grand Canyon."*

As you push the accelerator to the floor, the engine screams in protest. With the top down and the wind racing past your ears, the kilometres rack up on the odometer, edging you ever closer to your destination.

Arriving at the edge of the South Rim, you ditch the car keys, shake the dust from your hair and lace up your trusty hiking boots. Leaving the thronging tourist crowds well behind, you hit the backcountry trails – carrying an ample supply of fresh water and rations, a tent, an ultralight sleeping bag and the requisite permit.

With each passing hour the backpack grows heavier, beads of sweat pool at your temples and blisters burst forth from your toes; but you've got to press on while there is still daylight. Fortunately the stunning views and scurrying lizards at every turn are able to divert your attention from your discomfort; and the campsite lies just beyond the next mesa, just a couple of kilometres ahead as the buzzard flies.

The air grows cool and quiet as night falls over the desert. Up above, the sky is pixelated by countless bursts of celestial brilliance; with no city lights to pollute the view, soaring meteorites leave flaming trails across the irises of your eyes. Somewhere in the distance you can hear the growling of the hungry coyotes, but there is no more green-chilli stew left to share. Zipping up the door of your tent and crawling into your fluffed-out sleeping bag, you're grateful that sleep quickly takes hold – by early morning the mercury will already be starting to soar and it will be time to get moving again.

**Grand Canyon by Horseback**
There are many, many tour companies geared up to indulge your inner cowboy with a horse ride in the Grand Canyon.

# TAKING ACTION

## As You Saw It

The Colorado River snakes along the floor of the Grand Canyon; it has been carving out this natural monument for the past six million years, exposing rocks up to two billion years old – half the age of the earth. Taken together, the two rims of the Grand Canyon offer quite different experiences, but since they lie more than 300km apart by road they are rarely visited on the same trip.

Most visitors choose the South Rim, with its easy access, wealth of services and awesome views. But the quieter North Rim has its own charms – higher elevations and cooler temperatures support wildflower meadows as well as tall, thick stands of aspen and spruce.

## Adding to the Experience

To really appreciate a natural feature as large as the Grand Canyon, you need to get right in there and hike through its vast expanse. On the South Rim, the Rim Trail is the most popular – and easiest – walk in the park; while the South Kaibab is arguably one of the park's prettiest trails, combining stunning scenery and unobstructed 360-degree views with every step. The North Kaibab Trail is the North Rim's only maintained rim-to-river trail and connects with trails to the South Rim.

All overnight hikes in the park (as well as backcountry camping) require a permit. The Backcountry Information Center (www.nps.gov) accepts applications for permits for the current month and following four months only. Your chances are decent if you apply early (four months in advance for spring and autumn).

## Alternative American-Views Experiences

The neighbouring state of Utah is home to some natural vistas of classic Americana worth checking out.

❁ **Bryce Canyon National Park** Home to hoodoos: distinct formations of red, white and orange rock carved by the elements.

❁ **Zion National Park** This national park boasts rich species biodiversity, as well as a history of human occupation dating back eight millennia.

❁ **Monument Valley Navajo Tribal Park** A world-famous cluster of sandstone buttes that has graced the silver screen in nearly every classic Western movie.

# WHILE YOU'RE THERE

## Las Vegas

This is the only place in the world where you can see ancient hieroglyphics, the Eiffel Tower, the Brooklyn Bridge and the canals of Venice in a few short hours. Sure, they're all reproductions, but in a slice of desert that's transformed itself into one of the most lavish places on earth, you can bet that the fakery is slicker than a card shark dealing from the bottom of the deck.

A neon-clad metropolis catering to unruffled high rollers, college kids in search of cheap debauchery, and just about everyone in between, Sin City aims to infatuate. Hollywood bigwigs gyrate in A-list ultralounges, while grandparents whoop it up at the penny slots with the little ones in tow. You can sip designer martinis as

## POTTED HISTORY OF ARIZONA

The Pueblo, Mogollon and Hohokam tribes inhabited Arizona for centuries before Spanish explorer Francisco Vásquez de Coronado launched an expedition here from Mexico City in 1540. Settlers and missionaries followed in his wake, and by the mid-19th century the USA controlled Arizona. The Indian Wars, in which the US Army battled Native Americans over settlers and to claim land for the government, officially ended in 1886 with the surrender of Apache warrior Geronimo. Railroad and mining expansion grew after the war, and Arizona became the 48th state in 1912.

you sample world-class cuisine or wander the casino floor with a 1m-high cocktail tied around your neck.

## Sedona

Native tribes have long considered the Sedona area a sacred place, with its spindly towers, grand buttes and flat-topped mesas carved in crimson sandstone. Today it's one of the top New Age destinations in the world, and supposedly a hot spot for spiritually charged vortexes. Regardless of what you believe, Red Rock Country is one of the most beautiful places in Arizona, full of art galleries, gourmet restaurants and resorts, and with many a New Age healer.

# GETTING YOU THERE

Crowning the northern edge of the state, the Grand Canyon is Arizona's star attraction. The park's most developed area is Grand Canyon Village, 10km north of the South Rim entrance station. The only entrance to the North Rim lies 50km south of Jacob Lake on Hwy 67. The North Rim and South Rim are 300km apart by car, 35km on foot through the canyon, or 17km as the condor flies.

# EXPLORING THE GRAND CANYON

The main Grand Canyon visitor centre (www.nps.gov/grca) is accessible by the free shuttle bus that runs along the main roads inside the park, a 2km walk or bicycle ride from Market Plaza on the Greenway Trail, or a short walk from Mather Point (you cannot drive to the visitor centre).

More accessible, Verkamp's Visitor Center (www.nps.gov/grca; in Grand Canyon Village) has an information desk, exhibits on the history of Grand Canyon Village, maps for self-guided walking tours of the village, a bookstore and a meeting point for ranger-led walks and talks.

## METEOR CRATER

More than 1km across and 200m deep, the second-most impressive hole in Arizona was formed about 50,000 years ago, when giant sloths roamed these parts. In contrast with the Grand Canyon's slow-and-steady method of creation, Meteor Crater (about 60km east of Flagstaff) is, as its name suggests, the massive impact scar of a fiery meteor.

# LAKE MALAWI
## Great Rift Valley, Malawi, East Africa

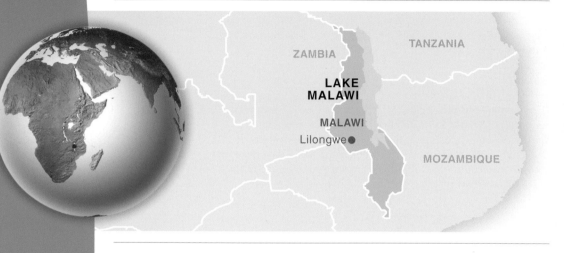

Lake Malawi is a shimmering mass of crystal water, and its shores are lined with secret coves, pristine beaches, lively fishing villages and dark, forested hills. Diving, snorkelling and kayaking can all be had here, and when you're done there's everything from backpacker-friendly beach huts to glamorous five-star resorts in which to lay your head.

## On Screen

The Great Rift Valley holds three of the world's largest lakes: Malawi, Tanganyika and Victoria. Malawi, the smallest of the three, is bigger than the US state of Massachusetts. We watch as *Planet Earth*'s divers descend into the waters to film a few of the 850 different species of cichlids that live here, all of which evolved from a single ancestor stranded eons ago.

## When

The best time to visit Malawi is during the dry season from May to October – October and November are the best times for wildlife viewing, but temperatures can be uncomfortably hot. Malawi has a single wet season, from November to April, when daytime temperatures are very warm and conditions humid.

**(top) Lake Fly Swarm Cloud**
While annoying if you get caught in a swarm, lake flies are extremely high in protein, calcium and iron, and are sometimes eaten in Malawi pressed into patties and fried, hamburger-style.

**(bottom) Cichlids**
Most of the cichlids in Lake Malawi are *mbuna,* a colourful fish that lives in rocky areas and is aggressive and territorial.

"Malawi's tropical waters teem with more fish species than any other lake."

# EXPERIENCE

You've heard the expression at least a dozen times before: 'Malawi is Africa for beginners.' But it wasn't until after you transited Lilongwe (Malawi's capital) and took the bus out to Cape Maclear that you really understood its significance. Compared with neighbouring destinations, Malawi's compact size, decent transport links and relative safety have made it a breeze to get around. Add to the mix legendarily helpful locals and stunning backdrops, and suddenly it's hard to even consider crossing the border.

The country of Malawi may be small, but Lake Malawi's magnitude is on another scale. This Unesco World Heritage Site makes up over 75% of Malawi's eastern boundary with Mozambique and Tanzania. Impressive to say the least, but knowing this fact wasn't enough to prepare you for the sheer beauty of the prime beachfront now lying before you.

Cape Maclear, a long piece of golden sand shielded by granite hills and thick green brush, sits on a slender finger of land at the southern end of Lake Malawi. It's also one of Africa's legendary backpacker hangouts, and the kind of place where onward plans are quickly forgotten. You've already travelled more than halfway from Cape to Cairo, but it looks like you're about to get sidetracked.

It doesn't take long for you to sink into a daily rhythm of sunbathing, snorkelling, chilling in the village and crashing in reed huts on the beach. Onward plans be damned – living doesn't get much better than this. So you give in, and sign up for an open-water scuba course, which in the end turns out to be the best decision you make all trip.

Cape Maclear is not only one of the most famous freshwater diving areas in the world, it's also one of the cheapest places to learn how to dive. Beneath the lapping waves of Lake Malawi, a blissful silence takes hold as all manner of wild and bizarre fish dart and dash before your eyes.

Your instructor holds the postdive debrief in a local fish restaurant on the beach. Lunch is barbequed *mpasa* (lake salmon) and *kampango* (catfish) served on banana leaves. The salty fish is washed down with a locally brewed Carlsberg lager. The sun is beating overhead, and all you can think to do is bask in the warmth and smile with glee.

**Beach at Chintheche**
The Chintheche area has some of the best beaches on Lake Malawi, with long stretches of white sand.

# TAKING ACTION

## As You Saw It

If you're after a face-to-face encounter with the famous cichlids of Lake Malawi, all you really need to do is don a mask, fins and snorkel, and then jump right in. For a more detailed look at these colourful critters, it pays to strap on a tank and maximise your bottom time, which is a fairly easy prospect given the abundance of dive centres surrounding the lake. The Aquarium at Cape Maclear is the lake's most famous dive spot. As for the lake flies, if you do happen to find yourself in these parts during the rainy season, it's best to pack plenty of potent bug spray.

## Adding to the Experience

The Shire River dominates the 548-sq-km Liwonde National Park, a wide, meandering stretch lined by thick undergrowth and tall, statuesque palms. Surrounding it are flood plains, woodland and parched scrub that is prime hippo- and croc-spotting territory – you shouldn't let a trip here pass you by without canoeing on the river. Waterbucks are also common near the water, while beautiful sable and roan antelopes, elephants, zebras and elands populate the surreal flood plains to the east. Night drives can reveal spotted genets, bush babies, scrub hares, side-striped jackals and even spotted hyenas.

## Alternative Freshwater-Lake Experiences

Oceans are overrated, at least in comparison to some of the world's behemoth freshwater lakes.

✿ **Lake Michigan-Huron** (North America) The largest of the Great Lakes straddling the US–Canadian border, Michigan-Huron is the largest freshwater body in the world by surface area.

✿ **Lake Victoria** (East Africa) Africa's largest lake, and the largest tropical lake in the world.

✿ **Lake Baikal** (Siberia) Although it is frozen for most of the year, Baikal is the most voluminous freshwater lake in the world. See p60 for more on Lake Baikal.

# WHILE YOU'RE THERE

## Senga Bay

North of Cape Maclear, this attractive bay is where beginner divers often pursue their open-water training. Islands in Senga Bay harbour are also home to monitor lizards, African fish eagles, and breeding colonies of white-breasted and reed cormorants. Thirty kilometres north is Mbenji Island, a target for more experienced divers, particularly when underwater visibility peaks in August and September.

# HERO & REVOLUTIONARY

John Chilembwe led Malawi's first serious fight against colonial rule. Born in 1871, he attended the Church of Scotland mission, and later worked for Baptist missionary Joseph Booth, with whom he travelled to Virginia in 1897. A spell at an African American theological college lit his revolutionary spark, and when he returned home as an ordained Baptist minister in 1900, Chilembwe set about establishing independent African schools and preaching self-reliance and self-respect. When famine struck in 1913, causing immigrants to pour in from Mozambique, Chilembwe was disgusted by the way plantation owners exploited refugees in the fight to secure land. Shortly afterwards, when the British conscripted local men to fight against the Germans in Tanzania during WWI, Chilembwe decided to 'strike a blow and die, for our blood will surely mean something at last'. On 23 January 1915, he and 200 followers attacked local plantations. When the uprising failed to gain local support, a distraught Chilembwe tried to flee to Mozambique, though he was captured and killed by soldiers 10 days later. Today, John Chilembwe is immortalised on Malawi's banknotes, and John Chilembwe Day is commemorated on 15 January every year.

## Nkhata Bay

Far north on the lake, this bay has a stepped shoreline that rapidly drops off to 150m, so dives here are shore-hugging. In addition to cichlids, there are catfish and crab, while night dives reveal schools of dolphin fish and, occasionally, eels. Just south, the Chintheche Strip has superb birdwatching – green coucals, Gunning's robins, narina trogons and palm-nut vultures are all seen at camps here.

## GETTING YOU THERE

Air Malawi (www.airmalawi.com) has a decent regional network, with flights connecting Dar es Salaam (Tanzania), Johannesburg (South Africa), Nairobi (Kenya), Lusaka (Zambia) and Harare (Zimbabwe) to Lilongwe. Commuter buses leave from Lilongwe's main bus station, and service towns and villages along the shores of the lake.

## EXPLORING LAKE MALAWI

The following can help you navigate Lake Malawi's shores:
✿ **Budget Safaris** (www.budget-safari.com) Based in Nkhata Bay, this wallet-friendly operator organises a wide range of individually tailored tours.

✿ **Land & Lake Safaris** (www.landlake.net) This excellent company runs tours across Malawi to suit all budgets. It also offers highly specialised birding and hiking excursions.

## CICHLIDS BY THE MOUTHFUL

To attract mates, male cichlids build either rocky territories or sandy courtship sites; rival suitors are then grappled, tossed and chased away. Females are attracted by the males' brilliant colouration, and shepherded in. Females lay their eggs one at a time (up to 200), grasping each in their mouth and nuzzling the genitalia and anal fins (which look uncannily like fish eggs) of several males. The males release sperm, which she sucks into her mouth where the eggs are fertilised and develop. When hatchlings leave the mouth they stay close to their mother, darting back into the mouth of the nearest female if danger arises – juveniles of several broods and even different species can end up in the same mouth. But some predatory species have successfully overcome this defence and are able to knock eggs out of the mouths of cichlids.

# LAKE BAIKAL
## Russia

RUSSIA

LAKE
BAIKAL

Listvyanka

MONGOLIA

CHINA

The world's largest lake combines with one of the planet's most evocative locations – Siberia – to create one of Earth's most fascinating ecosystems. Eighty percent of the wildlife species living in Lake Baikal are found nowhere else in the world, including the planet's only completely freshwater seal, the nerpa – of which the lake has a population of around 60,000.

## On Screen

*Planet Earth* unveils the world's largest, deepest and oldest lake – so big it holds around 20% of the world's fresh water (and 80% of Russia's fresh water) – taking you beneath the winter ice to the hardy creatures that flourish there.

## When

Lake Baikal can be a place for all seasons – a huge body of water in summer; it freezes into a massive ice block from around January to May. March is arguably one of the best times to visit, when the scenery is pristine white and there's no need to charter expensive excursion boats as (in places) you can hop in a taxi and drive across the lake – a thrilling proposition.

OLIVIER RENCK/GETTY IMAGES

KONSTANTIN MIKHAILOV/NATURE PICTURE LIBRARY

# EXPERIENCE

You've never imagined so much fresh water or ice – a vast white expanse laid out to the horizon, reminding you of the view from an aeroplane window as it flies above a mass of cumulus cloud. Far away, on the opposite shore, a mountain range looms, its white peaks rubbing against the sky.

You take a step onto the lake. Your feet sink through the snow banked on its surface, making you wonder briefly if you might be falling through the ice – you are literally walking on water, after all. Somewhere the ice flexes, issuing a frightening groan, and you wonder, again, if you're about to plunge right into the largest lake on earth, with its water so cold that you would probably survive less than a minute. But it holds firm. As

**Ice Fishing on Lake Baikal**
Fed by more than 300 rivers and streams, Lake Baikal boasts at least 50 species of fish.

you ponder the wisdom of what you are doing, a truck motors past, atop the ice – several tonnes of metal supported by 1m of frozen water. You walk on, feeling a little safer.

At intervals the ice is dotted with hatches. Popping one open, you see a fishing hole yawning deep. Peering through the hole you can clearly see the bottom of the lake; you can even make out individual pebbles and the marinelike sponges that grow on the lake bed. They look as though they are within reach, but the water here might actually be 30m deep. You are looking into one of the clearest bodies of water on earth, cleansed by small crustaceans that eat the algae and bacteria that would usually cloud the water.

As you watch, a fish swims into view through the ice hole and you remember why you are here. You drop a line and fish for a while, pulling in just enough omul – Baikal's endemic fish treat – for a meal. You close the hatch and look to the mountains across the sealike lake. The idea of walking to them is compelling, but who can tell the distance and effort required? To reach them would entail camping out on the ice for a night. But you have these omul to cook, so you turn back towards the village of Listvyanka – its log cottages a short walk across the ice, past the lake-top hockey goals and the birch trees with their trunks as white as the snow. It's like Narnia, but really it's Siberia.

*"Baikal is 400 miles long, and more than a mile deep. It holds one-fifth of all the fresh water in Earth's lakes and rivers."*

# TAKING ACTION

## As You Saw It

Lake Baikal is a long way from almost anywhere, but has been made accessible by air travel and the Trans-Siberian Railway. The days-long rail journey from Moscow, Vladivostok or Beijing will only increase the expectation of something wonderful.

You can see beneath the ice, as on the *Planet Earth* series, only if you are a certified diver – agencies in Irkutsk offer winter and summer diving trips.

## Adding to the Experience

The lake opportunities on Baikal are almost as deep as the water itself: there's boating and kayaking in summer; ice trekking, ice fishing, diving, dog sledding and even ice mountain biking through winter. Most winter traverses of the ice will require camping out, so come well prepared.

## Alternative Deep-Water Experiences

If you're collecting the world set of deep lakes and inland seas, you might want to visit some of the other deepest bodies of water.

✿ **Lake Tanganyika** (Tanzania, Democratic Republic of Congo, Zambia, Burundi) Reaches a depth of 1435m.

✿ **Caspian Sea** (Iran, Russia, Turkmenistan, Kazakhstan, Azerbaijan) 1025m

✿ **Lago O'Higgins/San Martin** (Chile, Argentina) 836m

✿ **Lake Malawi** (Tanzania, Malawi, Mozambique) 706m; see p54 for more on Lake Malawi.

✿ **Issyk Kul** (Kyrgyzstan) 668m

✿ **Great Slave Lake** (Canada) 614m

✿ **Crater Lake** (USA) 594m

✿ **Danau Matana** (Indonesia) 590m

✿ **Lago General Carrera** (Argentina, Chile) 586m

# WHILE YOU'RE THERE

## Baikal Museum

This museum in Listvyanka exhibits fish samples and seal embryos in formaldehyde, as well as tanks containing two frolicsome nerpa seals and various Baikal fish that you'd otherwise only encounter on restaurant menus.

## Olkhon Island

Halfway up Lake Baikal's western shore and reached by a short ferry journey from Sakhyurta (the town is also commonly called MRS), this 72km-long island is serenely beautiful. It boasts unparalleled lake views from sheer cliffs that rise at its northern end, culminating in dramatic Cape Khoboy. If Baikal proves too cold for a dip you can cool off in the small Shara-Nur Lake, where naturally occurring (harmless) chemicals in the water dye your skin red if you wallow too long.

## Barguzin Valley

This stunning valley, accessible from Ust-Barguzin, opens out into wide lake-dotted grassland, gloriously edged by a vast Toblerone of mountain peaks.

## THE GREAT BAIKAL TRAIL

Inspired largely by the Tahoe Rim Trail (a 246km hiking path encircling Lake Tahoe in California and Nevada), a small band of enthusiasts began work in 2003 on the first section of what is grandly named the Great Baikal Trail (GBT; in Russian, Bolshaya Baikalskaya Tropa). The GBT organisation's stated aim is the creation of a 2000km-long network of trails encircling the lake, passing through three national parks and three wilderness reserves – the first such trail system in Russia. About 400km has been completed so far.

## Circumbaikal Railway

Ride this scenic, lake-hugging branch line between Slyudyanka and Port Baikal, or – in winter – drive alongside sections of the route on ice roads from Kultuk. Hiking the entire route, or just sections of the track, is also popular; walking a couple of kilometres from Port Baikal leads to some pleasant, if litter-marred, beaches.

The most picturesque sections of the route are the valley, pebble beach and headland at Polovinnaya (around halfway), and the bridge area at Km 149. Views are best if you can persuade the driver to let you ride on the front of the locomotive.

## GETTING YOU THERE

The village of Listvyanka is the most popular visitor base on the lake. Daily buses (1¼ hours) run to Listvyanka from the city of Irkutsk, and from mid-May to late September daily hydrofoils stop at Listvyanka port between Irkutsk and Bolshie Koty. Irkutsk is on the route of the Trans-Siberian Railway and connected by air to cities throughout Russia.

## EXPLORING LAKE BAIKAL

For underwater exploration Aqua-Eco (www.aquaeco.eu.org) and SVAL (www.svaldiving.ru) are two professional Irkutsk dive operators; or atop the ice, from December to March, multiday cross-Baikal expeditions are possible with the Baikal Dog Sledding Centre (www.baikalsled.ru) in the lakeside village of Listvyanka.

# BOTOS & THE RIVER

## Amazon River, The Amazon, South America

Rivers are roads in Amazonia, and riverboat trips are a uniquely Amazonian experience: the slow pace, sleeping in hammocks, watching the river and forest and local life glide by...

### On Screen

The river itself is massive and unrelenting, as much a living thing as the plants and animals that depend on it. At its height, the Amazon can measure 40km across and dump 300 million litres of fresh water into the ocean per second. Its waters are so rich that they support more than 3000 species of fish – more than in the entire Atlantic Ocean – as well as freshwater dolphins, known as botos.

### When

Heavy rains fall from December to June, cooling the tropical air; July to November is drier and much hotter, with temperatures reaching 40°C. Travel during the dry season is more popular for tourists, though the wet season does bring lusher vegetation and fuller rivers.

**Boto (Amazon River Dolphin)**
Botos figured prominently in the folklore of South American Indians, who believed killing them would bring bad luck and misfortune. These taboos offered some protection to the species, until settlers arrived in the area.

"Planet earth's mightiest river is the Amazon. It carries as much water as the next top 10 rivers combined."

# EXPERIENCE

At an altitude of around 10,000m, you look out the window of the plane and finally get a true sense of scale. Indeed, flying over Brazil is really the best way to appreciate the full length of the country's iconic river. Rising in the Peruvian Andes, the main trunk of the Amazon flows east, draining more than a third of South America. Eventually, more than 6000km from its source, it empties into the Atlantic Ocean.

The Amazon has a population density half that of Mongolia, yet Manaus (an entry point for the Amazon) is a sprawling city of two million souls. Your hotel room is a cramped shoebox on a congested urban street that bustles all hours of the night. But the city does have its merits, especially when it comes to stocking up on last-minute supplies (hiking boots, two-ply toilet paper, and industrial-strength mosquito repellent of questionable health safety), getting your beer and internet fix and spending a last night in a proper bed before embarking on the long journey ahead. The morning that your adventure is to start, you awaken in a hot sweat, only to find that the electricity is out and your fan has stopped spinning – no bother, as it's almost time to head down to the bustling docks to meet your river captain.

It takes only a few hours for the Amazon River to start weaving its mystical spell over you. Sprawled out in a woven hammock, swinging back and forth in rhythm with a tropical breeze, you close your eyes and indulge in a relaxing nap. When you awaken, your eyes turn to the front of the boat where your berth mates are congregating in vigour.

In the murky waters below, a pair of botos is frolicking carelessly about. Surfing in the wake of the riverboat, their pink skins are shining luminously in the midday sun. While they might be cute and cuddly looking, those long, thin beaks are outfitted with up to 35 pairs of razor-sharp teeth, enabling them to slaughter prey with ruthless efficiency. Keeping your hands and feet inside the boat was never a better idea.

Before too long the botos lose interest in the boat and swim off in search of supper. You take heed and head down to the galley to see what's cooking. Lucky for you the catch-of-the-day is pan-fried piranha. You steer clear of the teeth and bones, but otherwise the meat is soft, flavourful and wholly exotic.

**(top) Squirrel Monkey**
Squirrel monkeys use a wide range of calls, from chirps and peeps for keeping in contact and raising alarms, to mating squawks and purrs, and threatening barks and screams.

**(bottom) Boats on the Amazon**
The Amazon and Nile Rivers have long been in competition for the title of world's longest river. The rivers vary over time and reputable sources disagree on their actual length.

# THE WILDEST WETLAND
## Pantanal, Brazil

PERU

BRAZIL

BOLIVIA

Cuiabá

Corumbá

PANTANAL

PACIFIC
OCEAN

CHILE

PARAGUAY

ARGENTINA

ATLANTIC
OCEAN

**(left) Piranhas**
The legend that piranhas will skin and eat a human alive is said to have started from an account by Theodore Roosevelt of seeing a cow stripped to its skeleton while he was in Brazil. It is also said that, to produce such a spectacle, local fishermen caught and dumped hordes of starving piranhas into the water, creating an unnatural feeding frenzy.

**(right) Toucans**
Surprisingly, the toucan's bright colours provide good camouflage in the dappled light of rainforest canopies. But the amount of noise they make commonly counteracts any camouflaging!

Like the Amazon, the Brazilian Pantanal is incredibly biodiverse. It's home to many of the same creatures as found in the Amazon, but in more viewer-friendly terrain. Watch spectacled caymans prowl the waterways, giant river otters frolic like schoolboys and monkeys swing in the trees. This is also the very best place to spot that elusive big cat, the jaguar.

## On Screen
The Pantanal is the world's largest wetland – a grand claim, but easy to comprehend as the *Planet Earth* team glides over flooded plains seeming to stretch to infinity. At closer quarters the volume of life supported in the region becomes clear, from the baby fish leaving the safety of their nurseries to the monstrous caymans lying in wait.

## When
The wet season (October to April) is when the Paraná River bursts its banks. It can be difficult to get around at this time and temperatures are high. May to September is the dry (and cooler) season; the Pantanal is less flooded and therefore more accessible. Also, the dry is better for wildlife viewing, as animals are concentrated around diminishing water sources. August and September are the peak months for jaguar sightings.

PETER SCOONES/BBC

JANE SWEENEY/LONELY PLANET IMAGES

# EXPERIENCE

The Pantanal is wilderness at its most alive. You can hear its pulse – the buzz of insects, calls of howler monkeys and trickle of around 230,000 sq km of waterways; you can see it flex – a river splash here, a quiver of scrub there; you can practically feel the warm breath of the trees.

From above it resembles a blue-green jaguar's coat – raised *cordilheiras* (vegetation islands) splotch the swamped land like the big cat's rosettes. And as you fly over you can appreciate how and why – with the Pantanal so low-lying (just 100m to 200m above sea level) – when the rains come they thunder down the surrounding highlands and end up here, bursting riverbanks, and keeping flood-averse humans out and wildlife very happy indeed.

Back on land (well, actually, water) as you paddle gently along a silk-smooth tributary, it's hard to tell where the water stops and the land begins – the wagon-wheel-sized lily pads and purple blooms of the abundant water hyacinth blur the distinction. But if you could see below, there would be no such confusion – down in the stream a hierarchy of fish is flitting amid the underwater forests: the disco-ball shimmer of thousands of tiddlers, the razor jaws of red-bellied piranha, the meaty mass of the dorado (known locally as the river tiger) and the prehistoric cayman, the Pantanal's crocodilian king.

The smaller fish thrash over falling fruit, the bigger fish munch the smaller fish and the piranhas hoover up the leftovers – reducing a fish corpse to nothing but skeleton in a matter of minutes. The caymans, floating on the surface amid water-hyacinth leaves – Pantanal camouflage – ignore it all. Their beady black eyes, you can tell, are scouting for a literally higher prize.

The trees by the riverbank are heavy with birds, thousands-strong squawking colonies nesting side by side. Prettiest in pink is the roseate spoonbill, all blush plumage and long spatula beak. The youngsters look ungainly as they wobble from the nests – and the opportunist cayman is waiting below. You hold your breath as a spoonbill trips, stumbles, does the splits – but somehow manages to stay on its branch. For now.

However, a wood stork – equally unsure of foot – is not so lucky. As you watch, the unfortunate bird, which doesn't have space to unfurl its massive wings as it drops clumsily between the boughs, lands on the ground with a flap. The cayman, coolly waiting for his takeaway to be delivered, makes a lunge; his order is ready. With a minimum of fuss he shakes his feathered feast and glides back into the water, the stork's wing hanging from his mouth like an unfurled sail. You slide further into the centre of the boat – there's no question about who rules this river.

**Pantanal Flood Plains**
Although not as celebrated as the Amazon, the Pantanal boasts similarly rich ecosystems – around 3500 species of plants, 1000 types of birds and 300 species of mammal flourish here.

"*Each wet season the Paraná River overflows its banks and floods an area the size of Arkansas.*"

# A WHOLE LOT OF WATER
## Sundarbans, Southern Bangladesh

INDIA

BANGLADESH

Dhaka●

INDIA

MYANMAR
(BURMA)

**SUNDARBANS**

Bay of
Bengal

---

The Sundarbans mangrove forest at the mouth of the delta of the Ganges and Brahmaputra Rivers is barely fit for human habitation. This makes it challenging to travel around, but all the more pristine for it. Man can't tame the wilderness here, so you'll see trees, insects, herds of deer, leaping monkeys, myriad birds and, if you're lucky, seriously big cats behaving just as nature intended.

## On Screen

It's no wonder the *Planet Earth* crew uses aerial shots to best show the delta of the Ganges and Brahmaputra Rivers – this is the planet's most widespread outpouring of water, saturating the spongy coast of Bangladesh; it's only from above that you can truly appreciate the effect this has on the land. Rather than forming a distinct coastline, Bangladesh and the Bay of Bengal merge in a mass of finger-like tributaries, swampy jungle and 2 billion tonnes of river-carried sediment.

## When

Bangladesh has three main seasons: monsoon (from late May to October); cool (late October to February); and hot (March to mid-May), during which temperatures can soar to a sticky 40°C. The cool is the best time to go – the temperature is much more bearable (averaging around 25°C) and it's dry and sunny.

Ganges Delta
View of the Ganges Delta from the space shuttle *Columbia*. The Sundarbans Biosphere Reserve is visible as the dark area at the edge of the Bay of Bengal.

*"The Ganges and the
Brahmaputra Rivers
join to form the world's
biggest delta."*

# EXPERIENCE

To be a drop of water in the Bay of Bengal…now, that's having travelled. That drop, an infinitesimal molecule freshly spewed out via the world's largest delta, has completed an epic journey of thousands of kilometres to reach its resting place in the sea.

If you wanted to trace that drop you would need to start in the world's highest mountain range, perhaps with a flake of snow melted into the course of the River Ganges or the Brahmaputra. This peripatetic globule gathers pace on its downward trajectory out of the chill heights of the Himalayas (narrowly avoiding being drunk by a yak), passing foothills and farmers, temples and time zones, to play out its later days in a land utterly unlike that of its beginning.

While high altitude and cold climes characterised its early days, by the time our droplet reaches the home straight, it must negotiate flat, sodden and sultry Bangladesh. To gaze down on the country with a satellite's all-seeing eye, it barely looks like a country at all. A pink-brown land riven with silvery fissures, its coast gives up the fight and disintegrates into the sea. These fissures, from above like shards of land-cracking lightning, are ever-changing river courses, wending through jungly swamps, creating a new island here, erasing one there. The water in these meandering tributaries is extremely determined – it will make its way to the sea, and there's little that can be done to stop it.

The last stand of solid(ish) land in this vast delta region is the Sundarbans, the world's largest mangrove forest. Few people live here – the terrain is too shifting, too saturated, too inhospitable. But animals thrive.

You can see them, if you look hard; leave your aerial overview and delve into the mangrove thickets aboard a simple vessel – for boat travel is the only sensible way of getting around hereabouts. The heat is oppressive – even your sweat is sweating; the buzz of insects is deafening (and their hunger insatiable if you're foolish enough to have forgotten industrial-strength repellent...). But between ducking under branches and floating amid the mangroves' tangled, subaquatic root systems, you are awed. This is one of the planet's most pristine environments. Wildlife sightings don't come easy amid this dense vegetation, but keep looking – on that branch over there, a snipe? A sandpiper? A gold heron? And swinging between those branches – a family of macaques, who seem (like you) a little hot and bothered. Screeching uncontrollably, they appear to be raising the alarm – what have they spotted in the forest? Perhaps they are alerting any other monkeys in the vicinity that a tiger – the majestic and terrifying Bengal tiger, undisputed king of the Sundarbans – is on the prowl…

**(top) Chital Deer**
The chital is also known as the axis axis or spotted deer. The small white spots covering its body provide extra camouflage in the dappled lighting of the Sundarbans' mangrove forests.

**(bottom) Mowalis (Honey Collectors)**
*Mowalis* gather with their community in Burigoalini to pray before embarking on a dangerous journey into the Sundarbans forest to gather honey.

# TAKING ACTION

## As You Saw It

Short of blasting into the upper atmosphere on a space flight (if you can spare the fare), you're not going to get such an all-encompassing view of the land-vs-water makeup of Bangladesh as the spectacular satellite imagery of *Planet Earth* provided.

To see the country from ground level, however, is much more straightforward, though Bangladesh is not the easiest country to travel in – buses and trains are cheap, but uncomfortable. Use the local ferry network for the best view – the country has more kilometres of river than road. Boat travel, while often painfully slow, will give you a great idea of life in the land of the largest delta.

## Adding to the Experience

Delve into the Sundarbans by boat with an experienced and knowledgable guide – essential for gaining access to the region and for standing any chance of seeing the delta's tricky-to-spot wildlife. Most people come hoping to catch a glimpse of a Bengal tiger – the Sundarbans boasts the densest tiger population in the world. To maximise your chances of seeing wildlife, head to the southeastern section of the Sundarbans; here, biodiversity is highest and visibility is best, thanks to the open meadows.

## Alternative Delta Experiences

The Sundarbans may be the world's largest delta, but it's not the only one.

✿ **Danube Delta** (Romania) Home to masses of migratory birds.

✿ **Nile Delta** (Egypt) Boasting traditional villages and red lotus flowers.

✿ **Mekong Delta** (Vietnam) Barter over fresh fish at floating markets.

✿ **Mississippi Delta** (USA) The home of the blues.

# WHILE YOU'RE THERE

## Burigoalini

This village on the edge of the Sundarbans is home to many of the region's fearless *Mowalis* (honey collectors), who brave swarming bees and man-eating tigers to collect their liquid gold. Guide Tours (www.guidetours.com), based in Khulna, runs trips into the forest with the *Mowalis*; the season runs from April until around June.

## Bagerhat

Set within rolling green hills and tropical trees, Bagerhat is home to some of Bangladesh's most fascinating architecture. You'll find a clutch of many-domed mosques, a crocodile-guarded

# THE BLESSING OF BONBIBI

The Sundarbans is a dangerous place: the tides are treacherous, the lands shifting and the tigers man-eating. So you need a reliable deity to see you safely through. Bonbibi ('lady of the forest' in Bengali) is worshipped by both the Hindu and Muslim residents of the Sundarbans, who believe she will protect them against big-cat attacks.

Legend has it that Dokhin Rai, the demon king, once ruled the jungles and delighted in devouring humans, in tiger form. The goddess Bonbibi was sent to earth to make this land of tides fit for human habitation. She managed to get the better of Rai and negotiated a truce, enabling man to enter areas of the forest. However, one greedy merchant ignored the boundaries and went searching for treasure in Rai's territory. Rai pounced and was about to slaughter one of the trespassing party when the youngster called on Bonbibi to help him. She appeared in a flash and the boy was saved.

Rai was beaten that day, but he's still on the prowl in the Sundarbans. And this is why no local would ever enter the forest without first paying their respects to the goddess.

tomb and the 20m-high Khodla Math Temple, the country's biggest Hindu monument.

## Swatch of No Ground
This wonderfully named deep-water canyon just offshore from the Sundarbans attracts Bryde's whales and bottlenose dolphins from December to February. Guide Tours arranges trips on scientific boats to see the marine life and watch the researchers at work.

## Karamjal Forest Station
If you don't have time to delve into the Sundarbans proper, arrange a day trip from Mongla to Karamjal, which has raised walkways, viewing platforms, a small zoo and a wild tiger that has taken to stalking the vicinity. No permits are required.

# GETTING YOU THERE

Most travellers will fly into capital Dhaka or cross the border from neighbouring India. The nearest border crossing to the Sundarbans is at Benapole, which is on the overland bus route from Kolkata to Dhaka. As for getting into the Sundarbans, you need to book an organised boat trip with operators based out of Khulna, Mongla or Dhaka.

# EXPLORING THE SUNDARBANS

Guide Tours (www.guidetours.com), based in Dhaka, runs small boat trips in the Sundarbans. The company has extensive knowledge of the area and is involved in local conservation and research projects. It will also organise all your permits, which are necessary for visiting the Sundarbans. For more information on the region's most famous inhabitants, consult the Sundarbans Tiger Project website (www.sundarbanstigerproject.info).

## FAST FACTS

Around 5000 wild tigers remain worldwide; it's estimated that 200 to 450 live in the Sundarbans.

Sundarbans tigers are thought to be responsible for around 120 fatal attacks on humans each year.

The Sundarbans is named after the straight, 25m-tall Sundari tree – a type of mangrove – that grows here; it survives well in water and is good for shipbuilding.

Four species of dolphin and porpoise have been recorded in the Sundarbans: the Ganges River dolphin, Irrawaddy dolphin, Indo-Pacific humpbacked dolphin and finless porpoise.

The Sundarbans forest is around 4000 years old.

The water levels in the Sundarbans rise and fall with the Bay of Bengal tide; high tide is reached every 12 hours and 50 minutes.

# CAVES
## *Planet Earth, Episode Four*

In the deep, shadowy underbelly of the earth, something stirs… Incredibly, despite dark, dank and unremittingly hostile conditions, our planet's caves play host to a range of wild (and often odd) life. Some creatures are merely visitors to this underworld – birds seeking a cosy roost in a cathedral-like cavern, for example. But others, from luminescent larvae to a strain of bacteria that glitters like diamonds, have learned to thrive here…and only here. It's a hardy traveller who joins them – our caves are one of our least-explored ecosystems – but a richly rewarded one, for they'll discover that some truly fascinating life lies beneath.

# LEAPING INTO THE UNDERWORLD

## Cave of Swallows
## (Sótano de las Golondrinas), Mexico

**This is the ultimate adrenalin high; if you're into flinging yourself into caves, there's nowhere better. But even the less suicidal will be awed by the fern-dripped setting, the inky depths and the raucous avian swarms.**

## On Screen

Claustrophobes and the vertigo prone, look away now... As the *Planet Earth* cameras focus on a cave shaft plunging nearly 400m down from a hole in the jungle floor, a BASE jumper – looking as serene as a jumpsuit-clad angel – silently plunges in. For these thrill-seekers, who find joy in freefalling relatively close to terra firma, with only precious seconds to deploy their parachutes, Mexico's Sótano de las Golondrinas (Cave of Swallows) is just about heaven.

## When

Mexico's central Gulf Coast is generally warm and humid – hottest from April to September (when temperatures exceed 30°C) and wettest from June to September. The cave can be visited (or jumped into) year-round, though when it rains water plummets through the opening like a waterfall.

Whatever the month, visit the cave at dawn or dusk to see its bird inhabitants make their en-masse exodus (at dawn) or return (at dusk).

**BASE Jumping into the Cave of Swallows**
Carl Boenish is credited with coining the term BASE jumping, together with his wife Jean and friend Phil Smith, in 1981. He also began issuing the sequential BASE numbers awarded to individuals completing a jump from all four categories. Phil Smith is BASE No 1; Carl and Jean are No 4 and No 3, respectively; and Phil Mayfield is No 2.

*"Thirteen-hundred feet
to the bottom – deep
enough to engulf the
Empire State Building."*

# EXPERIENCE

It makes your skin go clammy and your heart race just to look into the circular abyss that is the Cave of Swallows. You know it's named after the agile birds (actually white-collared swifts) that roost inside, but it could just as easily have an alternative meaning: the Cave of Swallowing – an open mouth, agape, waiting to consume you whole.

It's not the only such cavern in this region of Mexico. Large swaths of the country's Gulf Coast are bored and burrowed beneath the surface like a geological Swiss cheese, the result of subterranean water gnawing away at the limestone over millennia. Forest-set, vertical sinkholes dot the landscape, but this is a particularly excellent erosion – at 376m it's the second-deepest pit in the country, and the world's largest cave shaft. Beneath the surface opening, a dark and relatively narrow gash in the jungle floor, the cavern widens into a huge domed grotto – as great and glorious as a cathedral.

Obviously to see this you need to head inside – if you dare. You can perch on a rock by the rim, listening to the cackles and calls of the forest, glimpsing the odd green flash of a passing parakeet; but there are some for whom just sitting is not the ticket. Dressed in neon, looking brighter than the parrots they seek to emulate, a clutch of BASE jumpers are poised by the edge of the hole, waiting to dive in.

The jumpers look curiously peaceful as they plummet. The way their arms are outstretched looks faintly religious, a splayed-limb surrender to the forces of gravity and nature; the BASE jumpers' faith is not so much in God, perhaps, as their own skills in parachute packing. After dropping like stones for a few heart-stopping seconds, their canopies are wrenched open and they float to the cavern floor, drifting in and out of the lone shaft of dusty sunshine that spotlights their descent.

You can breathe a sigh of relief – they made it! (Though, as payoff for this instant of elation, they now have an hour-long rappel back to the surface.) It looks so easy, just to jump, to fly like a bird – albeit briefly; but there's real skill to controlling this death-defying manoeuvre. These extreme sportspeople must be extremely experienced – one wrong move, a spin too far to the side or a tangled cord, and the cave will swallow them for good.

**Rappelling into the Cave of Swallows**
Rappelling to the bottom of the Cave of Swallows typically takes just a few minutes; ascending back out takes an hour or more.

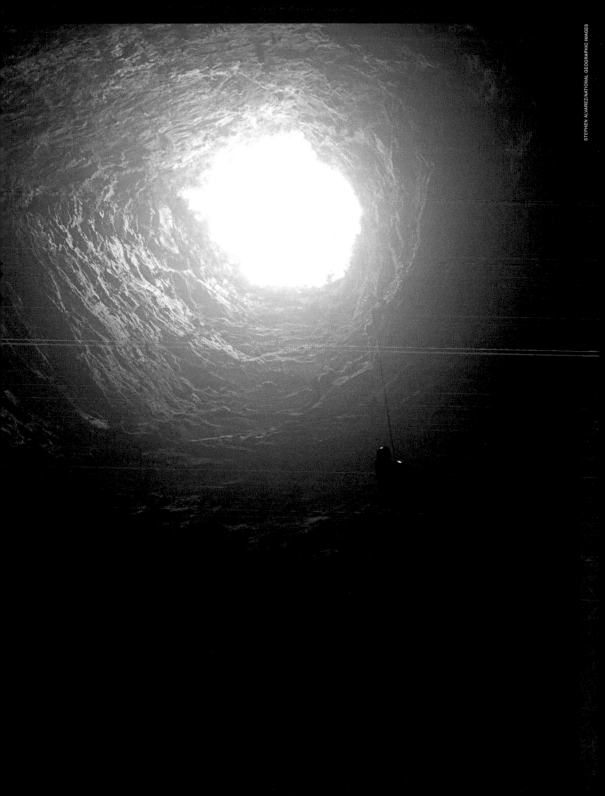

# UNDERWATER CAVES
Yucatán Peninsula, Mexico

**Look past spring break in Cancún, and the Yucatán Peninsula offers a wonderland of ancient Maya sites and around 3000 cenotes (flooded caves), including the three largest underwater caves in the world. The most famous Maya settlement of all, Chichén Itzá, with its famous Sacred Cenote, combines the two. But you'll need to head to others, such as Cenote Dos Ojos, to don air tanks and experience the cenotes as you saw them in *Planet Earth*.**

## On Screen

In *Planet Earth* you watch as divers explore water as clear as air in the Yucatán's seemingly endless system of cenotes, introducing you to a world of watery tunnels and freshwater aquatic life. More than 500km of these underground caves has been mapped, with countless more kilometres of the realm of Ah Puch (the Maya God of the Underworld) perhaps yet to be explored.

## When

The Yucatán's dry winter season, from around November to March, means there's little run-off into the cenotes, keeping the waters at their cleanest and clearest.

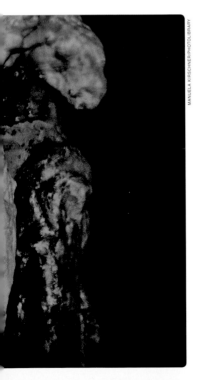

MANUELA KIRSCHNER/PHOTOLIBRARY

JOHN ELK III/LONELY PLANET IMAGES

# EXPERIENCE

As you slip into the water at the flooded entrance to a massive cave network, about the only difference in your surroundings you can discern is the ripples. The water is like air, filtered unbelievably clean by the limestone through which it has seeped to reach the cave. It's as though the water has been polished, and floating feels like flying. Even the temperature feels deceptively like air, with the water at a warm 25°C.

You think back to your adventure in the Bat Cave at Hidden Worlds, where you swam off into the darkness towards the faint light at the end of the cenote, angling yourself to try to catch the perfect reflection of stalagmites and stalactites on the surface of the water. Overhead, between the formations, the eponymous bats had flown about as others roosted on the ceiling. In Dos Ojos you'd been able to simply kick about, crossing from one *ojo* (eye) to the other, savouring the

**Cenote Azul**

According to Maya tradition, caves and cenotes are the home of Chac, the Maya god of rain. In times of drought or stress, Maya leaders would appeal to Chac by making offerings to him in cenotes. Mexico's National Institute of Anthropology and History (INAH) is concerned with protecting cenotes from looting by sport divers.

crystalline waters, the shafts of sunlight that cut through the water like blades and the milky blue light – as inviting as any tropical postcard. It felt as though you could see forever, if only the cave walls hadn't been there.

And here, today, in the Gran Cenote, a cavern near Tulum, you begin to swim again, descending, your light playing ahead of you across the guiding line of string that leads you down and away from the cave entrance. You kick gently, not wanting to stir any sediment and disturb the clarity of the water, drifting airily past stalagmites and stalactites that reach into the cavern like straws into a giant glass of water. Through a cave wall, the roots of a tree wave about like hair, the tree, many metres above, using the water in the flooded cave as its life source.

The rope leads you through narrow spaces for about 1km. As you head deeper into the cenote there's a change as abrupt as a shift in a vegetation zone. Down here, heavier salt water flows beneath the fresh water pooled above. Visibility and sensation change, as do the life forms. Few creatures live below the halocline, where the fresh and salt water meet, because the salt water carries little oxygen. But you do see remipedes, one of the world's most ancient crustaceans, swimming shrimplike on their backs.

Eventually you turn back towards the surface, rising through the halocline and once again into the gin-clear fresh water. The bubbles from your mouthpiece swim up ahead of you, stirring the surface and again reminding you that you are in water, not air.

# TAKING ACTION

## As You Saw It

To really explore the cenotes and their depths you need to dive. To plunge deep into caves, like you saw in the *Planet Earth* series – pushing through squeezes and exploring great depths – you need to be a certified cave diver.

It's more likely that you'll get to experience cavern diving, which is defined as being in a space where there is light at least every 60m; these dives make up the bulk of the peninsula's cenote experiences. Cavern dives must be made with a certified cave guide and require an open-water diving certificate – if you've come to the Yucatán uncertified, the island of Cozumel, south of Cancún, is a good place to correct things.

## Adding to the Experience

While diving offers the most intimate look at the freshwater world of the Yucatán Peninsula, snorkelling offers a surface look and is as simple as grabbing a mask, snorkel and fins. As the tourist industry develops around the sinkholes, new activities arise and it's now also possible to zipline and rappel around some cenotes, and even pedal a SkyCycle along a wire through a cavern.

## Alternative Underwater-Caving Experiences

Australia's 'Limestone Coast' and its Nullarbor Plain – the largest block of limestone on earth – are pitted with underwater caves. To dive at the following requires membership and qualifications with the Cave Divers Association of Australia (www.cavedivers.com.au).

✿ **Piccaninnie Ponds** (Mt Gambier, South Australia) With visibility of up to 40m in the Cathedral and Chasm.

✿ **Ewen Ponds** (Mt Gambier, South Australia) A shallow (10m) cave with freshwater crayfish and eels.

✿ **Cocklebiddy Cave** (Western Australia) A 6.5km-long wet cave beneath the Nullarbor.

# WHILE YOU'RE THERE

## Mesoamerican Reef

If you're diving the cenotes, you'll probably also want to sample the ocean's treasures. The Mesoamerican Reef, running along the Yucatán Peninsula shore (and all the way to Honduras' Bay Islands), is the world's second-largest barrier reef, featuring around 65 species of coral and 500 species of fish, most notably the whale shark. Between mid-May and mid-September you can snorkel with these gentle giants – the world's largest fish – just off Isla Holbox.

## Isla Mujeres Turtle Farm

For marine creatures of a different shell, visit the Isla Mujeres Turtle Farm, which protects

# AIN'T NO RIVER...

A curious feature of the Yucatán Peninsula is that it contains no streams or rivers, at least above the ground. Below the earth it's a different story. Around 65 million years ago a huge meteor struck the peninsula, leaving a 284km-wide crater on the land's surface. Millions of years later cracks formed just below the crater's limestone surface and rainwater began filling the cavities created by these fissures. Eventually the surface layer around the underground chambers began to erode and crumble, revealing the intricate vascular system of underground rivers and cenotes that lay beneath.

The Yucatán is now pitted with around 3000 cenotes, creating a honeycomb of caverns and sinkholes burrowed into the limestone like gigantic wells. In the absence of any other fresh water, it was the cenotes that sustained the Maya civilisation, which boasted accomplished astronomers and mathematicians, and some of the grandest monuments ever built.

the breeding grounds of sea turtles, including placing wire cages around their eggs to protect against predators.

## Maya Sites

The Maya were accomplished astronomers and mathematicians, and architects of some of the grandest monuments ever known. One of world's great ancient civilisations, they once had around 550 city-states in southern Yucatán, so there are a variety of sites to visit in the area. Check the ancient settlement at Chichén Itzá, which has been called the seventh modern wonder of the world; or scale the massive pyramid of Calakmul with toucans flying past. And the 32m-high pyramid at Ek' Balam is every bit as impressive as Chichén Itzá.

# GETTING YOU THERE

Cancún and Tulum make good bases for exploring the peninsula's cenotes. There are flights into Cancún – the busiest airport in southeast Mexico – from around Mexico and the USA. There are frequent buses (around three hours) from Cancún to Tulum.

# EXPLORING THE CENOTES

To get underground in safety, seek out the following sites and caving companies.

✿ **Hidden Worlds Cenotes Park** (www.hiddenworlds.com) With its access to the spectacular Cenote Dos Ojos – the third-largest underwater cave in the world – this park offers dives, snorkelling and such add-ons as ziplining and a SkyCycle. The park offers a transport service from Cancún, Tulum and stops in between.

✿ **Maya Diving** (www.dosojos.info) This Tulum-based company offers dives into Cenote Dos Ojos and the adjoining Bat Cave.

✿ **Cenote Dive Center** (www.cenotedive.com) This Tulum company offers cavern and cave dives at various cenotes around the area.

# FAST FACTS

The Yucatán Peninsula comprises 43,380 sq km.

........................................

The meteor that crashed into the Yucatán Peninsula 65 million years ago is believed to have caused the mass extinction of dinosaurs. Exactly how this may have occurred is still unknown.

........................................

There are around 3000 cenotes on the Yucatán Peninsula.

........................................

There are 17 known types of remipede and they are found only in halocline cave systems.

........................................

# THE CAVE OF A THOUSAND LIGHTS

Waitomo Caves, New Zealand

Auckland

**WAITOMO CAVES** ● Rotorua

Tasman Sea

**NEW ZEALAND**

PACIFIC OCEAN

Glow-worms exist in other parts of New Zealand, but the luminescent larvae at Waitomo put on the best show – conditions for their growth are just about perfect so they shimmer in extraordinary numbers. Waitomo also offers a range of viewing options. If you tend towards cave claustrophobia there are sedate tours of large caverns, to help you experience the worms without the fear. If you want to get wet, squeeze through tiny holes and jump off waterfalls in pitch-black nooks and crannies, you can do that too.

## On Screen

With the *Planet Earth* crew you descend into the bowels of New Zealand and meet the *Arachnocampa luminosa* – the glow-worm. These little larvae are both bug-ugly and gorgeously glowing: up close they're slimy customers that dangle silk lures to capture passing insects; turn off the lights and they glow like a subterranean Milky Way.

## When

Clambering through the caves of Waitomo is a year-round experience; the temperature remains pretty constant. The best times to visit the other delights of New Zealand depend on your interests. For hiking, February and March are ideal – school holidays have passed but it's still summery and warm. If you fancy skiing and snowboarding, come in July or August.

**Lost World, Waitomo**
The rappel down into the Lost World cave is 100m.

# EXPERIENCE

A distant drip echoes from the blackness, a solitary 'ploink' resounding off the increasingly narrow cave walls – which you can't quite see, but know are constricting around you. You can feel their damp, dank presence: 30 million years of creativity in limestone allowing you passage into the belly of the earth – welcome to the underworld.

It started alright: the outer chambers of Waitomo were welcoming in their cavernous proportions and glittering illumination; as the boat floated along the underground river through expansive Glowworm Cave, the resident larvae lit up the room like a starry night sky. You know the scientific reality: a chemical reaction in the glow-worms' bottoms produces a blueish glow for the sole purpose of luring insects to their deaths. But the effect is far less prosaic or gory – this is nature's version of Hollywood on Oscars night, star-studded and spectacular.

However, Glowworm Cave – and its relative spaciousness – is now a distant memory as you have walked, crawled and paddled deeper into this ancient abyss in search of more adventure. A 27m abseil, a cliff-climb up again, a squeeze through a tight tunnel – every sense and fear is being tested in this netherworld.

And now it's time for something completely different. You feel faintly ridiculous swaddled in the thick, clingy dry suit – but, hey, no one can see you in the darkness, and you're grateful for its warmth as you negotiate the chill streams. Especially when you reach the waterfall.

'Over you go!' says a voice, somewhere. Really? The water is churning, black and menacing, but you take the plunge, an exhilarating leap into the unknown – and into an ice bath. You yelp, at the cold and the thrill, but soon you're comfortably nestled into the ring of a rubber inner tube, gliding down the dark river as if it was the most normal thing in the world.

'Head torches off!' Another yelled instruction, which you obey as you and your tube float into a low-ceilinged tunnel. It's mesmerising: a billion (or so it seems) bottoms glowing in synchrony, a universe of constellations re-created in microcosm. You lean back in your vessel to stare upwards, in awe at the display, and at the tenacity of nature to find a way to survive even here, where light should never penetrate.

You float out of the cave, climb out of the tunnels, wind your way upwards and, finally, emerge into the blinding brightness of the real world – like an insect emerging from its cocoon. Soon enough, your eyes readjust to the daylight. But despite this sudden surplus of illumination, you won't forget the tiny magic of the glow-worms.

**Glow-worm Grotto**
In order to protect the glow-worms and cave formations at Waitomo, a scientific advisory group continually monitors the air quality (especially the carbon dioxide levels), rock and air temperature, and humidity. The information is used to establish how the cave should be managed: if and when air flow patterns should be changed and how many people are allowed to visit the caves each day.

"This galaxy of little lights is created by thousands of living creatures."

# THE CRYSTAL MAZE BENEATH THE DESERT

## Lechuguilla Cave, New Mexico

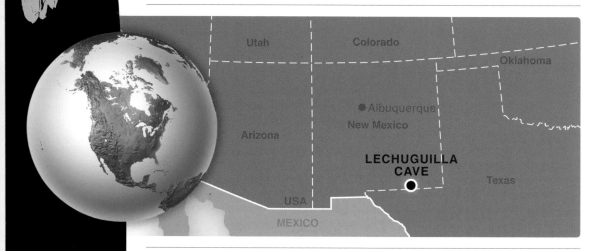

Utah
Colorado
Oklahoma
Albuquerque
New Mexico
Arizona
LECHUGUILLA CAVE
Texas
USA
MEXICO

**Lechuguilla Cave**
Lechuguilla is a warm, dry cave, which is almost unheard of and is why the breath-taking crystal formations have not dissolved in water.

**Six-metre-high gypsum chandeliers, 5m soda straws, hydromagnesite balloons, cave pearls, subaqueous helictites, rusticles... You don't need to know exactly what these mineral formations are to know that they sound impressive. And many haven't been found anywhere else on the planet. Lechuguilla, in Carlsbad Caverns National Park, is unique...and spectacular.**

## On Screen

Previously considered a rather run-of-the-mill hole in the ground, in 1986 a group of cavers dug through to a series of walkable tunnels at Lechuguilla. Since then nearly 200km of passages has been explored, plunging almost 500m deep – the fifth-longest cave in the world. And this subterranean labyrinth conceals some of the most spectacular and pristine geological formations ever seen.

## When

New Mexico is generally dry and clear – the state gets 300 days of sunshine a year – and Carlsbad Cavern is a constant 13°C. Thunderstorms are most likely to be encountered in late summer.

Cave tours run daily at Carlsbad Caverns National Park throughout the year. However, if you visit from April to October you can see some 400,000 Mexican free-tail bats roosting in the caves – come at sunset to watch their mass exodus, or predawn to see them return.

# EXPERIENCE

Helmet fastened, karabiners chinking, you lower yourself down the rope into the black unknown. This nondescript pit in the arid expanse of southeastern New Mexico looks like nothing at all – a dusty scar in the barren rock, a few shrubs on guard. Who would guess it's actually the entrance to the most magical of underworlds? Down and down you rappel, into the warm bowels of the earth. There's a whiff of something like rotten egg in the air. And there's obviously no light – this is one of the world's deepest cave systems, after all. But in the beam of your head torch you start to make out flashes of something sparkling in the gloom.

It seems, despite the lack of people – and very few people have ever set foot here – that all the caverns of Lechuguilla have been decorated for Christmas. Sparkling clusters of pristine crystals deck the floors, walls and ceilings; 5m-tall cone-shaped mounds – like freshly snow-dusted pine trees – rise up from the ground. As you scan your beam around the room it's as if the fairy lights have been switched on: almost every rock surface, thick with gleaming-white mineral formations – some bone-china delicate – is set a-glitter. In the so-called Chandelier Ballroom, nearly a mile underground, you gasp at the workings of nature. In this speleological palace, 7m-long and utterly untouched crystals hang from the roof like a frozen forest of tree roots, sparkling white tentacles reaching out to you from the darkness.

This festive geology is not the work of rain or underground streams, as is the case in many of the world's cave systems. The only water in Lechuguilla is a tranquil scatter of still pools, virginal in their purity. No, this network is the creative consequence of sulphuric acid nibbling at limestone over the millennia, leaving behind gypsum in the most exquisite formations. It is quite ludicrous in its beauty: as you crunch carefully through the galleries full of weird and wonderful formations you can't believe this place has lurked here unknown for several million years.

Perhaps even more unexpected than all this ornamentation, however, is the fact that something is actually alive down here. Feeding on the rock itself are innumerable battalions of extremophiles – a type of bacteria that survives without sunlight, using the very walls of its home for sustenance. Far from being a deserted, lifeless place, the dark, deep caves of Lechuguilla are thriving, in their own peculiarly spectacular way.

**Carlsbad Caverns National Park, Natural Entrance**
Beneath the arid New Mexico landscape lies a subterranean wonderland.

# TAKING ACTION

## As You Saw It

Sorry, access to Lechuguilla is limited to approved scientific researchers and exploration teams (and fortunate filmmakers). The *Planet Earth* team spent 10 solid days underground to get their footage – delving deeper than any previous camera crew – which required, in addition to expert caving skills, two years of permission negotiations.

## A More-Accessible Experience

Lechuguilla itself may be off limits, but you can explore other underground sections of Carlsbad Caverns National Park. There are two self-guided trails: the steep Natural Entrance Trail and the Big Room Trail, accessible by lift. Both trails lead to the Big Room itself – a vast 33,210-sq-metre cavern full of speleological curiosities; you can get an audio guide that explains the geology and history.

There are also guided tours to other parts of the park, which must be reserved in advance (go to www.recreation.gov). The two-hour Left Hand Tunnel tour is an easy stroll revealing Permian-era fossils and cave pools; the ½-hour Kings Palace trip descends to the deepest publicly accessible caves. For tight passageway crawls and ladder climbing, try the Hall of the White Giant or Spider Cave tours – more adventurous options (not for the claustrophobic) to give a taste of serious spelunking.

## Alternative Caving Experiences

Caves can be difficult to access, but there are several places worldwide where novices can still see fine rock formations.

✿ **Cango Caves** (Western Cape, South Africa) Multicoloured limestone and impressive stalactites.

✿ **Wind Cave National Park** (Hot Springs, South Dakota) Check out the boxwork, a bizarre honeycomblike calcite formation.

✿ **Cave of the Winds** (Colorado Springs, Colorado) Easily accessible and wonderfully decorated caverns.

✿ **Naracoorte Caves** (Naracoorte, South Australia) Limestone formations and fossils.

# WHILE YOU'RE THERE

## Living Desert State Park, Carlsbad

Walk the 2km trail around this park on the edge of town to learn about the Chihuahuan Desert's cacti, coyotes and other wildlife.

## White Sands National Monument

Huge, wavelike gypsum sand dunes have swallowed 710 sq km of New Mexico desert, creating an outdoor playground. Hike to a backcountry campsite for super stargazing, or try a ranger-guided full-moon bike ride.

# A FRAGILE WORLD

Lechuguilla Cave is within a national park and is thus fiercely protected, but the cave is very close to Bureau of Land Management land, where oil and gas are drilled. The ecosystems in Lechuguilla are extremely fragile and any gas or fluid leaked into the network could cause serious damage.

Inconsiderate tourists also pose a risk for the cave system – each year rangers have to remove bagfuls of litter, dumped by visitors, from the Carlsbad Caverns. This has contributed to contamination of the caves with fungus, which is eating away at the walls, turning them green or rust-coloured in places. If you visit the park, take your rubbish home with you, eat or drink only in designated areas and follow the rules laid down by park rangers.

## Lincoln National Forest

Mountains, rivers, sweeps of ponderosa pine, black bears and coyotes – Lincoln is a lush and varied wilderness, perfect for hiking. There are some impressive caves (permits required).

## Guadalupe Mountains National Park, Texas

Actually the remains of an ancient limestone reef, the Guadalupe Mountains rise over 2500m from the desert. Hike along McKittrick Canyon, which is arguably one of the most beautiful spots in Texas. The best time to visit for blazing autumn colours is late October or early November.

# GETTING YOU THERE

The town of Carlsbad is a five-hour bus ride from Albuquerque, but the best way to explore the state is to hire a car and drive one – or even a selection – of New Mexico's 24 scenic byways (see www .byways.org). The 48km Guadalupe Back Country Byway links Lincoln with the Guadalupe Mountains, with an easy detour to Carlsbad. For outlaw history, follow the Billy the Kid Trail; Lincoln was once home to both Billy and lawman Pat Garrett.

# EXPLORING THE CARLSBAD CAVERNS

There are many guided tours on offer in the Carlsbad Caverns. For more information go to www.nps.gov/cave.

## A NEW FORMATION

Most caves are formed by the erosive action of water – underground streams wear away at the subterranean rock, carving out caverns and tunnels. Lechuguilla and the caves of Carlsbad had a rather different genesis: between four and six million years ago hydrogen-sulphide-rich waters began to seep through fissures in the area's limestone. These waters mixed with oxygen-carrying rainwater, and the two substances combined to form sulphuric acid. This acid dissolved the limestone, forming the caves and leaving behind huge gypsum deposits – the magical crystalline sculptures that can be seen today.

# DESERTS

*Planet Earth,* Episode Five

Deserts the world over share one particular characteristic: rainfall – or extreme lack thereof. By definition, they are areas receiving less than 250mm of precipitation a year. Yet, though similarly arid, there is much variety in these parched places, and much life. The near-infinite, endlessly romantic rolling dunes of the Sahara are the most iconic, but the category encompasses such disparate spots as the icy Gobi and the red hot Australian outback. And in each you'll meet unique species that have somehow adapted to survive amid the sand and scrub, even if you have to look that little bit harder to find them. Think water equals life? Think again.

# THE SHIPS OF THE FROZEN DESERT

## Gobi Desert, Mongolia

OK, so it's not easy to get to the Gobi, and even less so in winter. And it's cold, really cold. And rather forbidding. But to walk on landscapes rarely trodden even by the sparsely spread local nomads, let alone by other travellers, is a special experience. Plus deserts are surprisingly varied – far from being monotonous sand, the Gobi has mountains and valleys, fossil cliffs and grassy steppes, all visitable from welcoming *ger* (traditional tent) camps where the stove will be lit and the *airag* (fermented mare's milk – an acquired taste) flowing freely.

## On Screen

The *Planet Earth* team battles for two months to film one of the Gobi's hardiest – and rarest – inhabitants: the two-humped bactrian camel. These shaggy beasts roam a vast and vicious land that, come winter, is whipped by icy winds and coated in snow, the camels' only water source. Yet still, somehow, they survive.

## When

The Gobi is a harsh mistress: summer temperatures soar to 40°C; winters plummet to -15°C and below. The best time to visit is September or October, when the climate cools a little but the tourist *ger* camps are still open. To see the bactrians nibbling snow you'll need to come from December to March or April – just make sure you pack your thermals (and someone else's).

### Domesticated Bactrian

To find out more about the relationship of surviving bactrians, scientists sampled the DNA of 18 domestic and three wild camels from different regions. Their research confirmed that all domestic camels originated from the same population, but not from the group that still survives in the wild.

# EXPERIENCE

It's hard to imagine anywhere bleaker. Vast ripples of tan steppe are dusted with snow, sparkling under a pale blue sky; creased folds of foothills – a landscape unironed – seem to stretch to infinity and beyond. The odd spiky tree does its best to cling on but, leafless and alone, looks like a symbol of decay rather than a living organism. The wind is fierce – 80km/h gusts direct from Siberia ensure it feels even colder than it looks (which is pretty cold); your exposed extremities are soon bitten by the blasting, which stirs the white powder into shimmering eddies of snow dust. In this environment you need to be well equipped to survive – like those beasts in the distance, for example.

The shaggy shapes of a herd of bactrian camels break the silhouette of a hill ridge; 20, maybe 30, of the creatures pressing against the gale. You're immediately envious – despite the chill they look toasty in their thick brown fur coats, though the wind is playing havoc with their styling: their hair pokes this way and that like they've been pulled through a hedge backwards. Not that there are any hedges here to be pulled through.

The camels' wide, two-toed feet move expertly across the snow, cracking the icy crust as they wander around looking for sustenance. And this sustenance comes in an unusual, and rather unappealing, form: snow. With no water available – the air is too cold and too dry for the snow to melt – the camels must nibble the white stuff itself, a flavourless Slush Puppy their only means of hydration. This creates its own dangers: filling the stomach with frozen snacks can be fatal, but the camels know this and limit themselves to around 10L a day, walking a fine line between hydration and death.

They're making quite a racket – the air is filled with plaintive moan-barks, like a desert full of Chewbaccas. It's mating season, and the males are doing their best (poor, ill-kempt creatures that they are) to impress the girls. You see one trying – this is sexy? The stocky fellow is performing an inelegant crouch, back legs bowed and splayed – more like he's answering a call of nature than on the pull. He's also slapping his rump with his own tail, the camelid equivalent of shouting, 'Look at me, ladies!' With such an ungainly mating display, you think, it's not hard to see why this species is so critically endangered. But each to its own – female bactrians probably lap it up. But with that Siberian wind still blowing, you can't stay long enough to find out.

Tony Wheeler climbed to the top of Khongoryn Els (Singing Dunes), some of the largest and most spectacular sand dunes in Mongolia.

The wild one-humped dromedary camel is already extinct, making the remaining wild bactrians the last-known wild camels.

"It's the biggest desert in Asia, one of the biggest in the world – and one of the harshest."

# TAKING ACTION

## As You Saw It

You're going to need time, transportation, luck and many pullovers to see snow-munching camels like those filmed by the *Planet Earth* crew. The Gobi covers somewhere in the region of 1,295,000 sq km; in it there are estimated to be just 350 wild bactrians. Poor *Camelus ferus* is rated Critically Endangered on the International Union for Conservation of Nature Red List.

## A Less-Intense Experience

While the plight of the wild bactrian is as bleak as the Gobi in winter (though the charity Wild Camel Protection Foundation is trying to help; see www .wildcamels.com), there are many domesticated animals: it's reckoned there are 1.4 million domesticated bactrians in Mongolia and China in total, vital beasts of burden for the local people.

While this is not ideal, it does mean you can get up close to a bactrian fairly easily – if, indeed, you want to; they are prone to barking, spitting and emitting pungent body odours. If you take a trip out into the Gobi you'll very likely come across a farmer's herd galloping or grazing in the distance. Or you can arrange more personal encounters: at Terelj you can hop aboard for a photo op, while *ger* camps at Ongiin Khiid can arrange multiday camel expeditions.

## Alternative Camel-Spotting Experiences

Camels are employed as ships of the desert by peoples worldwide – but there are still a (very) few places where you can see them roaming wild(ish).

✿ **Lop Nur Wild Camel National Nature Reserve** (Xinjiang province, China) China's remaining wild bactrians.

✿ **Northern Territory** and **South Australia** (Australia) Australia boasts one million feral dromedaries.

✿ **Baynunah** (western Abu Dhabi) The skeletal remains of 40-plus 6000-year-old wild camels were discovered here in 2007.

# WHILE YOU'RE THERE

## Bayanzag

Also known as the Flaming Cliffs, Bayanzag is an area of classic red rock, sand and sweeping emptiness in the central Gobi. It is one of the world's dinosaur-fossil hot spots, where heaps of prehistoric bones and eggs have been discovered. Hire a local guide to lead you there – it can be tricky to find.

## Khongoryn Els

Fulfil your desert fantasies at this patch of towering dunes, 100km long and up to 300m high. Climb the sand hills for magnificent views, or explore by camel – locals will be able to arrange this for you.

## Yolyn Am (Volture's Mouth)

Dispensing with the myth that deserts are always hot and sandy, Vulture's Mouth is a curious valley in the middle of the Gobi, encrusted with metres-thick ice practically year-round. Walk or camel trek the 2km trail from the car park to the gorge.

# WILD VS DOMESTIC CAMELS

There are more than one million domesticated bactrians – so why the fuss about conserving the puny population of wild ones? Sure, wild bactrians look only a little bit different – they have smaller, more slender bodies, trimmer legs and lower humps – but when scientists compared the DNA of both types they found that the two groups first diverged some 700,000 years ago, and that the wild ones are so genetically distinct from their domesticated brethren they are considered a separate subspecies.

The two are difficult to interbreed, which should help preserve the wild camels' genetic integrity – if they can establish a large enough population to survive at all.

## GETTING YOU THERE

Buses regularly leave the capital, Ulaanbaatar, for the main cities of the Gobi region; planes fly to a few of them. The Gobi has few proper roads, but the rock-hard jeep tracks are good enough to allow hardy vehicles to get around. Breaking down here is a serious business; never set off without water, supplies, maps, maybe a GPS – passing traffic is almost nonexistent.

## EXPLORING THE GOBI

One of the best ways to get acquainted with the Gobi and its hardy inhabitants is with Ger to Ger (www.gertoger.org). This Ulaanbaatar-based company arranges multiday treks in the desert, educating travellers in Mongolian etiquette before they set off to walk or yak-cart between *ger* camps, staying with local families en route. On arrival at the camps each day, activities – ranging from traditional archery to wrestling and horse riding – are on offer, as well as the chance to witness real nomadic life. The host families are well paid, and some of the proceeds go towards community development.

## FAST FACTS

Though this is undeniably desert, sand dunes cover only 3% of the Gobi.

In the 1920s Roy Chapman Androws discovered more than 100 dinosaurs on a two-year excavation in the Gobi; in 2006 scientists found 67 skeletons in one week.

Not only are bactrian camels excellent transporters of goods, they provide wool (5kg a year), milk (600L a year) and, as a last hurrah, a hefty amount of gamey meat.

Do not approach a bactrian camel during January and February – mating season – the males can get a little tetchy.

The Zoological Society of London ranks bactrian camels as among the 100 most evolutionarily distinct but globally endangered animals.

# A SEA OF SAND
Sahara Desert, North Africa

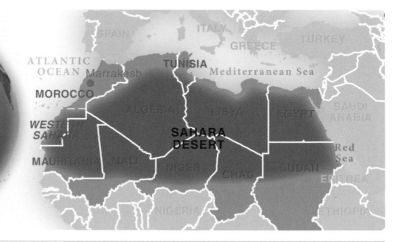

"*Sahara is the largest desert of all: the size of the United States, and the biggest source of sand.*"

**(left) Saharan Dunes near Chinguetti, Mauritania**
Chinguetti was founded in the 13th century as the centre of several trans-Saharan trade routes.

**(right) Leptis Magna, Libya**
Leptis Magna is a testament to Roman extravagance, with examples of lavish decoration, grand buildings of monumental stature, indulgent bath complexes and forums for entertainment.

**To truly unfurl the mysteries of the Sahara, you will have to surrender time: a quick foray into the dunes may satisfy shutterbugs, but it will take more time to explore the full extent of the world's greatest desert. Climb the dunes, feast on dried dates and quench your thirst with spring water, but don't forget to also slow down and talk to the various peoples that call the Sahara home.**

## On Screen

Capturing footage of enormous sand storms, and documenting the lives of fennecs, pale foxes and locusts, the *Planet Earth* team helps to demystify the great sandy expanse that is the Sahara Desert. The largest non-Arctic desert, the Sahara stretches more than 9 million sq km across most of North Africa.

## When

The Sahara has one of the harshest climates in the world, with surface temperatures reaching upwards of 50°C in the summer months (June to August), and annual rainfalls of less than 20mm in parts. Conversely, if you visit in the winter months (January to March), you need to be prepared for night-time temperatures that can drop well below freezing. Seasonal winds vary in different regions of the Sahara, causing a variety of secondary weather phenomena, including ferocious sand storms and swirling dust devils.

FEARGUS COONEY/LONELY PLANET IMAGES

PATRICK SYDER/LONELY PLANET IMAGES

# EXPERIENCE

With world map unfurled before you, suddenly the scale of the Sahara becomes brutally apparent. From east to west, the Sahara encompasses virtually everything between Morocco and Egypt, and is bounded from north to south by the Mediterranean Sea and the Sahel. With this diversity of destinations and potential experiences on offer, planning an itinerary across the sands is certainly not an easy task.

You pride yourself on being a purist at heart, which means there is only one way to penetrate the interior of the Sahara – by camel, the ship of the desert. Your port of entry is Marrakesh, a great Islamic city of antiquity. It has been a centre of scientific and religious scholarship for centuries. Your arrival on the continent is celebrated in true North African style as mint tea is poured in volumes, and sugary dates of the *deglet noor, medjool* and *khadrawi* varietals are consumed en masse.

A couple of days' travel out from Marrakesh you find yourself on the fringes of civilisation, stocking up on essential supplies in the string of market towns bordering the Sahara. And then with seemingly the last remnants of humanity at your back, your caravan turns with purposeful resolve towards the sands. Despite a surprising measure of initial hesitation, you take comfort in the fact that your trusty camel seems content to follow the path ahead.

You've always been captivated by dunes, and this is one department that the Sahara has well staffed. All around are perfect specimens reaching heights of nearly 200m from base to crest. In these great ergs (sand seas), dunes stretch for hundreds of kilometres, constantly shifting direction and changing shape at the mercy of the winds.

For human life to thrive in the arid zone, water is vital. Fortunately the Sahara is dotted with lush oases, enabling life to take hold even in this most extreme of environments. You gracefully dismount and lead your camel to drink. Overhead a date palm (planted alongside oases on trade routes in times gone by to provide valuable sources of food to caravans) is burdened by ripening fruit, providing strong evidence that you are not the first human to pass this way.

As you're surprised to discover, the Sahara is anything but a lifeless expanse of harsh sterility. On the contrary, the selective force of adaptation has resulted in a whole slew of dramatic wildlife. All around you, lesser creatures – such as the lowly locust – arise from the desert sands in tremendous swarms. And this bounty fuels the lifeblood of desert canines; pausing to catch your breath, you admire the gentle form of the fennec as it emerges from its lair to feast on a bounty of desiccated insect corpses. Taking a cue from the fennec, you search the bottom of your rucksack for a handful of dried dates, and use the sugary boost to press on.

Djemaa el Fna, Marrakesh, Morocco
Adjacent to Marrakesh's medieval medina (old city), Djemaa el Fna is one of the busiest market squares in North Africa. By night it turns into a riotous cacophony of merchants, performers and food stalls.

# TAKING ACTION

## As You Saw It

To see the Sahara as it was in the *Planet Earth* series, all you really need to do is go. From any of the classic oasis towns (some of the more famous include Merzouga in Morocco, Tamanrasset in Algeria, Ghadāmis in Libya, Douz in Tunisia and Siwa in Egypt) tour operators can have you out in the desert in no more time than it takes to saddle up a camel. Of course, what you see while you're out wandering the sands is subject to chance; you never know what will be waiting for you beyond the next dune.

## Adding to the Experience

No two dunes are alike, which is why you should try your best to experience the Sahara from all of its various corners. The flaming orange dunes of Erg Chebbi in Morocco and the chalky mineral deposits of the White Desert in Egypt are as geographically proximate to one another as New York is to Los Angeles. And if you fly over the desert's great interior you'll see Roman ruins in Libya, the Ahaggar Mountains in Algeria and date palmeries in Tunisia.

## Alternative Desert Experiences

If you want to explore some of the world's other monumental desert landscapes, pack your bags and head to the following.

✿ **Namib Desert** (Namibia) Stretches for 1600km along the Atlantic coast of southwest Africa. See p142 for more on the Namib.

✿ **Gobi Desert** (Mongolia) The fifth-largest desert in the world is a rain shadow, blocked from receiving precipitation by the Himalayas. See p112 for more.

✿ **Atacama Desert** (Chile) This virtually rainless plateau in South America is the world's driest place. See p130 for more.

# WHILE YOU'RE THERE

## Leptis Magna, Libya

Located along the Mediterranean coast in Libya, Leptis Magna is one of the best-preserved, most evocative Roman cities in the whole of North Africa.

## Luxor (Thebes), Egypt

Ancient Thebes, the capital of the New Kingdom, gave rise to the greatest Egyptian pharaohs

# THE SAHARA IN ANTIQUITY

The ancient Egyptians understood the nature of the desert, which they saw as being synonymous with death and exile. Seth, the god of chaos who killed his brother Osiris, was said to rule here. Despite their fears, it is believed that the ancient Egyptians maintained nominal links with the Western oasis towns throughout the Pharaonic era. And with the accession of a Libyan dynasty (22nd dynasty; 945–715 BC), a vast network of caravan routes extending outwards from the Nile Valley emerged, linking together far-flung population centres and facilitating the movement of trade goods across the continent.

The oases enjoyed a period of great prosperity during Roman times, when new wells and improved irrigation led to a vast increase in the production of wheat and grapes for export to Rome. Provincial army units, usually consisting of non-Romans serving under Roman officers, protected the oases and trade routes. (Garrisoned fortresses can still be seen in the desert, and Roman-era temples and tombs lie scattered across all the oases.) But when the Romans withdrew from Egypt, the trade routes became unsafe and were a target for attacking nomadic tribes. Trade suffered, the oases went into gradual decline and the population of settlements shrank.

To retrace those caravan routes by camelback is to quite literally retrace the footprints of history.

including the Rameses dynasty and Tutankhamen. Today the modern city of Luxor lures countless travellers to the site in search of rock-hewn temples, subterranean tombs and the mighty Nile.

### Marrakesh, Morocco
Known as the 'Red City of the Maghreb', Marrakesh lies in the foothills of the snow-capped Atlas Mountains.

## GETTING YOU THERE

Capital cities throughout North Africa are served by most of the world's major airlines, though depending on your point of departure, you may need to transit in either Western Europe or the Middle East.

## EXPLORING THE SAHARA

The following tour companies can help you access the Sahara's seemingly limitless expanse.

✿ **Camel Trekking Morocco** (www.cameltrekking.com) These expert camel jockeys will guide you through the dune sea as if it were a mere walk in the park.

✿ **Dabuka Expeditions** (www.dabuka.de) This German-based operator specialises in camel expeditions and 4WD courses across North Africa.

✿ **Pan Arab Tours** (www.panarabtours.com) Used by archaeologists as well as tourists, this company has more than 30 years' experience in Egypt's deserts.

✿ **Sea & Desert Tours** (www.sea-desert.net) Based in Libya, this tour company can help you arrange Libyan visas as well as onward travel across the Sahara.

## THE SAHARA: GREAT SAND SEA

The Great Sand Sea straddles Egypt and Libya, stretching over 800km from its northern edge near the Mediterranean coast south to the Gilf Kebir plateau in southwest Egypt. Covering a colossal 72,000 sq km, it contains some of the largest recorded dunes in the world, including one that is 140km long. The Persian king Cambyses is thought to have lost an army here, while the WWII British Long Range Desert Group spent months trying to find a way through the impenetrable sands to launch surprise attacks on the German army. Aerial surveys and expeditions have helped the charting of this vast expanse, but it remains one of the least-explored areas on earth.

## FAST FACTS

The Sahara covers large parts of Algeria, Chad, Egypt, Libya, Mali, Mauritania, Morocco, Niger, Western Sahara, Sudan and Tunisia.

With a natural history of more than three million years, its desert landforms, shaped by wind and rain, include ergs (sand seas), hamadas (stone plateaus), regs (gravel plains), wadis (dry valleys) and chotts (salt flats).

Oases in the Sahara are fed by a deep underground system of flowing rivers. In the winter time, mountains in the Sahara are snow-capped; the springtime melt sustains the flow of these underground rivers.

The widely spoken Arabic language unites the great diversity of peoples and countries that call the Sahara home.

# THE OUTBACK
## Central Australia

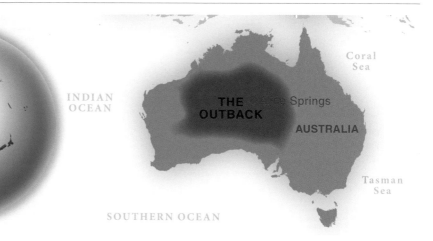

Coral
Sea

INDIAN
OCEAN

THE
OUTBACK

Springs

AUSTRALIA

Tasman
Sea

SOUTHERN OCEAN

If Australia is defined by any one natural feature it is the outback, which covers around 6.5 million sq km of its vast and empty interior. Within it are treasures such as the world's most recognisable rock, as well as the world's longest sand dunes, stretching in lines across the Simpson Desert. Here, red kangaroos as large as men roam, and the sense of space can be almost crushing.

## On Screen

*Planet Earth* takes you through a shimmering heat haze and over parched sands into the unforgiving Australian outback. You watch as red kangaroos ingeniously battle the heat – using the evaporation of their saliva, and the cooler sands just below the scorching top soil.

## When

It's blazingly hot in Australia's outback throughout the summer; the best time to visit is in winter (around May to September) for comfortable daytime temperatures, if freezing nights.

**(top) Section 8 of Larapinta Trail, West MacDonnell Ranges**
Hiker at Count's Point looking at Mt Giles (middle distance), Mt Sonder (far horizon), Chewings Range (right) and Heavitree Range (left).

**(bottom) Red Kangaroos**
To keep cool in the deadly desert heat, red kangaroos stay in the shade and lick their forearms, which contain a network of blood vessels near the skin – as their saliva evaporates, the blood cools.

# EXPERIENCE

The ghost gum offers little shade – it's like sitting in the shadow of somebody's finger – but it's all there is, so you drop your backpack and rest for a few minutes. You have been walking for almost a week now on the Larapinta Trail – the most intimate of introductions to the Australian outback – following the line of the West MacDonnell Ranges from Alice Springs towards their end 223km away atop Mt Sonder. The daytime scenery is gallery quality, as if straight from an Albert Namatjira painting; at night the stars are so bright it's as though you're falling asleep inside a cave of glow-worms.

This day will probably be the most memorable of the 16 days you will walk the trail. You begin by winding through Spencer Gorge; it's tight and straight, with a tangle of boulders, ancient cycads, river red gums, melaleucas and ghost gums that grow in any space and at any angle. Soon you begin climbing, up through Windy Saddle and onto the inevitably named Razorback Ridge, with its sharp spine of red rock and orange termite mounds.

You are at the heart of the West MacDonnells now, and though they are a popular tourist spot, there is nobody about for kilometres; it is too rugged here, too tough, too far from the road, too much work – for most people. Too bad for them because this ridge offers stretches of what might be among the best walking in this vast and varied country, at times right atop its very knife edge.

From the end of the ridge the only way to go is down, winding into Linear Valley before emerging in Hugh Gorge – another gorge to bookend your day, as is so often the case along this desert trail. The track turns south, towards the gorge entrance, but you head the other way; in this direction the platelike escarpments all but close together, the gorge seeming to narrow with each step.

Finally you can walk no further, the way blocked by a waterhole pinched between the cliffs. You strip off and plunge into the water, washing off a day of heat and red dust. Hidden from sunlight, the water is like ice, making your feet ache with the cold. It's a welcome pain compared to the jarring of walking on uneven, unforgiving rock for the last few days.

You dry off and return through the gorge, scrambling around small waterholes until the way opens up, the gorge becoming wide and wooded as you near the entrance. Here you will set up camp, no doubt listening once again to the howl of nearby dingoes as you drift into another well-earned sleep.

**Mt Sonder at Dawn**
One of Albert Namatjira's favourite land-scapes was that depicting Mt Sonder, known to the Western Arrernte Aboriginal people as *Rwetyepme*.

*"Of all the inhabited continents, Australia is the most arid. Without water, you could die of thirst within hours."*

# TAKING ACTION

## As You Saw It

The red kangaroo – the patriarch of Australian marsupials – roams freely throughout most of rural Australia, so expect to see them anywhere as you travel through the vast outback. They tend to do what all visitors to the outback should do: sit out the heat of the day in a welcome piece of shade; so the best time to see the animals active is around dawn and dusk. Be careful if driving at these times – the roadkill count on outback roads should give you some idea of the possible consequences.

## Adding to the Experience

If you want the rare combination of outback and water, head into Nitmiluk National Park (just outside Katherine), hire a canoe and head up through the 13 interconnected gorges along the Katherine River. If you spend a night or two out camping, you can make it deep into the gorge, although you will need to portage between sections. There are campsites located at the fifth, sixth, eighth and ninth gorges.

## Alternative Kangaroo-Watching Experiences

To shatter a myth... you won't see kangaroos bounding through the streets of Sydney and Melbourne; but they are abundant across much of the country. To see a few of the lesser-known kangaroo species, try the following locations.

❀ **Simpsons Gap** (West MacDonnell National Park, Northern Territory) For black-footed rock wallabies.

❀ **Brachina Gorge** (Flinders Ranges National Park, South Australia) For yellow-footed rock wallabies.

❀ **Mt William National Park** (Tasmania) For forester kangaroos.

❀ **Kangaroo Island** (South Australia) For tammar wallabies.

❀ **Daintree National Park** (Queensland) For Lumholtz's tree-kangaroos.

❀ **Rottnest Island** (Western Australia) For quokkas.

# WHILE YOU'RE THERE

## Uluru

The most famous of Australian rocks sits like a giant red paperweight at the heart of the country. Wander the 9km around its base, admire it from the various roadside vantage points, or climb to its top (but note that the local Aboriginal people request that visitors do not climb the rock).

## Kata Tjuta

Central Australia's *other* rocks. A striking group of 36 domed rocks, rising to 545m above sea level (around 200m higher than Uluru), sitting shoulder to shoulder, forming deep valleys and steep-sided gorges. The best way to view them is along the 7.4km Valley of the Winds walking trail.

# RED ALERT

The red kangaroo is the world's largest living marsupial and is abundant throughout the outback. It is capable of speeds of up to 60km/h, and can cover up to 8m in a single leap. Male reds can grow to 1.8m in height when standing upright, and if you look closely at these giants you will probably notice that many of them are battle scarred.

Part of the scarring will have come from the kangaroos' habit of 'boxing' with each other to assert dominance. When boxing, they rock back on their strong tails, kicking out with their hind legs, delivering jabs with their front legs, and often trying to wrestle their opponent to the ground. Such brawls can last for minutes and are one of the great sights of the Australian outback.

## Alice Springs Desert Park

Like a kind of Noah's Ark, the Alice Springs Desert Park has gathered up all the creatures and plants of central Australia and put them on display in one accessible location.

## Royal Flying Doctor Service Base

The famed and dedicated doctors of the outback make house calls in an area covering around 2.3 million sq km. Entry to Alice Springs' Royal Flying Doctor Service base is available on a half-hour tour; they run continuously all day.

## Kings Canyon

This yawning chasm is best seen on the Kings Canyon Rim Walk, which skirts the canyon's rim before entering the Garden of Eden: a lush pocket of cycads around a natural pool. The next section of the walk winds through a maze of giant beehive-shaped domes.

# GETTING YOU THERE

Alice Springs is at Australia's desert heart and makes a good base for exploring the outback. There are regular flights into Alice from cities around the country, while the Ghan (www.gsr.com.au) railway passes through Alice on its desert journey between Adelaide and Darwin. Greyhound (www.greyhound.com.au) buses between Adelaide and Darwin also stop in Alice.

# EXPLORING THE OUTBACK

There are any number of tour companies that can take you deep into the outback to experience the Australian desert.

✿ **Desert Tracks** (www.deserttracks.com.au) An Aboriginal tour company offering unique trips into the otherwise inaccessible Anangu Pitjantjatjara Yankunytjatjara lands of northern South Australia, including a visit to Cave Hill, central Australia's largest rock-art site.

✿ **Outback Spirit** (www.outbackspirittours.com.au) Runs trips into various parts of the Australian outback, including the Red Centre, Pilbara and Cape York.

✿ **Outback Track Tours** (www.outbacktracktours.com) Has a focus on birdwatching, taking you to some more unusual outback destinations, such as the Darling River, the Corner Country and the brutal Canning Stock Route.

# FINDING A DRINK IN THE DRIEST DESERT

## Atacama, Chile

PERU

BOLIVIA

BRAZIL

**ATACAMA DESERT**  San Pedro de Atacama

PARAGUAY

PACIFIC OCEAN

**CHILE**

ARGENTINA

Santiago

URUGUAY

ATLANTIC OCEAN

The Atacama Desert is an alien land – almost literally: in some areas its soil has been likened to that on Mars. To witness life thriving in such an inhospitable environment is a surreal surprise. Head to the coast to see the stoic guanacos, foxes and a flutter of birds slurping from the desert cacti, before heading inland to explore the scorched valleys, looming volcanoes and spewing geysers of the Atacama's dead-dry innards.

## On Screen

Officially the planet's driest spot, you'd expect this arid expanse of desert in northern Chile to be a lifeless place. But watching *Planet Earth* it becomes clear this isn't so. Along a slender coastal section of the Atacama, banks of fog roll in from the Pacific, condensing on the hills to form dew that waters a varied and tenacious group of plants and animals – including the lithe and lovely guanaco.

## When

You can visit any time; the moisture-laden clouds – known as *camanchaca* – occur regularly year-round. Also, temperatures vary little by month: days usually hover around 20°C to 25°C, with nights much colder, especially at higher altitudes.

**Salty Shores of Laguna Tuyajto, Atacama Desert**
Salt lakes are formed when more water is lost through evaporation than is replaced by rainfall – as the water evaporates, the mineral salts in the lake become more concentrated.

"In a land of almost no rain,
these precious drops are
lifesavers for many creatures."

# EXPERIENCE

The land is scorched and barren, a palette of pale yellows, dirt browns and dusky pinks, blurred by a heat-haze shimmer. You can see, feel and practically smell the rays pelting down from the cloudless sky, cooking this earth like a piece of toast.

It's far from boring, though – stark, but not boring. Looking west the Chilean Coast Range slides down into the deep-blue Pacific; looking east the rippling hinterland gives way to rising mountains – precursors of the Andes, which eventually peak at over 6000m. However, rein in your gaze a little and – what's that in the foreground? There's actually something moving in all that emptiness.

It seems incredible that anything could survive in such an outwardly hostile environment, but you've just focused on a guanaco – a whole herd

**El Tatio Geysers**
Plans have been in the works for several years to create a thermo-electric plant at El Tatio, where pressure-driven turbines would convert the geysers' steam into electric energy.

of guanacos, in fact – ambling across the horizon. Guanacos are to the plains of South America what the camel is to the Sahara – and rather pretty beasts: tan-brown, doe-eyed, llamalike but more elegantly proportioned. Their long, willowy necks swivel to survey their dusty domain; their bodies bounce gracefully into the distance when they get spooked by your company.

Sit quietly, though, and you can watch their antics, which largely involve eating – they spend 90% of their time foraging for food. Amazingly, a thin coastal strip of the arid Atacama supports a range of cacti and lichen, which the guanacos munch on for sustenance, bending to nibble the buds off floor-level scrub and rearing up onto their hind legs to reach loftier morsels.

Stay put long enough and how this unlikely vegetation survives is revealed. The clear sky is gradually obscured as a cold sea current cools the warm air above the water to produce first wisps, then thick billows of cloud, known locally as the *camanchaca*. An inshore breeze skims this cloud up over the hills to fill the valleys on the other side. Your previously far-reaching panorama is reduced to mere metres of visibility, the world shrouded in thick and, more importantly, wet fog.

Go back and reinvestigate the cacti you observed before. No longer desiccated, their spikes are dripping with water globules, as if a sun shower has just passed through. The lichen that cling to the cacti like shaggy beards have become soggy as a sponge. Soon birds are flocking: tiny swallows, ground-tyrants and sierra-finches perch on the needles to lap up the dew, twittering as they drink. The promise of water also brings out foxes, which you'll spot snuffling along the desert floor.

Of course the fog doesn't last. Stay longer still and the relentless Atacama sun burns off the cloud, returning the desert to its former thirsty state. But it's enough: as long as the mists keep rising the guanacos will survive to see another sun-baked day.

# TAKING ACTION

## As You Saw It

To see guanacos drinking their fill you'll ideally want some stop-motion photography to speed up that fog's inward roll. In the absence of this, employ a good guide and a light footstep: knowing where the creatures are most likely to be is key, and they can be flighty if they sense human presence. Take your time, and some good binoculars.

## Adding to the Experience

Probably the best place to see guanacos is Parque Nacional Pan de Azúcar, where the Atacama meets the more fertile Norte Chico region. Hike amid the thirsty cacti, but also head out with a local fisherman to the waters around Isla Pan de Azúcar (Sugarloaf Island), where otters, sea lions and 2000 Humboldt penguins lurk. There's a park information centre and cactarium at Los Piqueros beach; ask the rangers for their top tips. Immerse yourself in the mist by camping in the park: by the coast your tent may get as dew-dropped as the surrounding cacti. Just come prepared – it gets very cold at night, even in summer.

## Alternative Guanaco-Spotting Experiences

Big-eyed and adorably fluffy, guanacos are among the comeliest creatures inhabiting the open landscapes of South America, and are found across the continent.

✿ **Torres del Paine National Park** (Patagonia, Chile) For large herds in dramatic landscapes. See p22 for more on the Torres del Paine.

✿ **Tierra del Fuego** (Argentina and Chile) For guanacos at the end of the world.

✿ **Southwest Altiplano** (Bolivia) For a combination of camelids and pink flamingos.

✿ **Cotopaxi National Park** (Ecuador) For guanacos grazing under rumbling volcanoes.

# WHILE YOU'RE THERE

## El Gigante de Atacama

The biggest humanoid geoglyph in the world, this 86m-high giant reclines on a remote slope of Cerro Unita, 14km from Huara. Dating from AD 900, the mighty man can be seen on a tour from Iquique.

## Valle de la Luna

The striking dunes, lunarlike terrain and distant volcanoes of the Valley of the Moon, 15km west of San Pedro de Atacama, is the place for sunset, when the whole place glows pink. Book a basic tour, or explore by bike or horse.

## Laguna Chaxa

Spot three different species of flamingo at this crystal-crusty salt lake in the desert, 65km from San Pedro de Atacama. Come at sunrise to see the birds feeding.

---

# MAKING MUMMIES

The Chinchorro people, fishermen and hunter-gatherers who eked out a living along the northern Chilean coast, began mummifying their dearly departed two millennia before it occurred to the ancient Egyptians. Around 7000 BC these Chinchorro devised an elaborate burial process, which included removing the deceased's internal organs, drying the body with hot stones, reassembling the corpse using cactus-spine needles and painting it with ochre or manganese.

We know all this because many such mummies have since been discovered in the Atacama region – and the incredibly arid conditions have continued to preserve them to perfection.

See masses of mummies and Chinchorro-related paraphernalia on display at the Museo Chileno de Arte Precolombino in Santiago and the Museo Arqueológico San Miguel de Azapa, near Arica.

### El Tatio Geysers

Explosive spouts, bubbling fumaroles, hissing steam pools – yet freezing temperatures. At an altitude of 4300m El Tatio is the world's highest geyser field. For maximum drama visit at dawn, when temperatures are chilly despite the thermal rumblings. Tours leave San Pedro de Atacama at 4am.

### Star Tour

High altitudes, no clouds, no light pollution – the Atacama is out of this world for sky gazing. Join a Star Tour with astronomer Alain Maury (www.spaceobs.com); trips leave nightly from San Pedro de Atacama.

## GETTING YOU THERE

San Pedro de Atacama, the region's tourism hub, is a 20-hour bus ride (1670km) from Santiago (for timetables see www.turbus .cl, in Spanish). The Panamericana, a near-continuous highway stretching from Argentina to Alaska, dissects the region; self-drivers can use this to access side roads for further exploration.

## EXPLORING THE ATACAMA

San Pedro has a wide selection of agencies offering tours across the region – to the parks, geysers and valleys.

## MIST FOR THE MASSES

The wet-and-wonderful *camanchaca* isn't just handy for watering the Atacama's animal contingent. In the 1990s, in the village of Chungungo, Canada's International Development Research Centre instigated the hanging of fine mesh nets to harness the fog's water droplets for human consumption. Around 10,000L of water were captured in these nets each day, feeding gardens and filling taps. So successful was the relatively low-tech system that it was exported to other arid regions, including parts of Peru, Ecuador and Namibia.

Sadly, the fog-catchers of Chungungo have now largely fallen into disrepair, due in part to a lack of community involvement at the start of the project. But the methodology remains sound and has been used to irrigate parched places the world over.

# NUBIAN IBEX
## The Negev, Israel

LEBANON
SYRIA
Mediterranean Sea
IRAQ
**ISRAEL & THE
PALESTINIAN TERRITORIES**
Be'er Sheva
JORDAN
EGYPT **NEGEV
DESERT**
SAUDI
ARABIA

**While it tends to get less tourist billing than Israel's other natural attractions, the Negev is nothing short of a hiker's paradise, with an abundance of wide-open space and few other souls around to share it with. It is rich in desert-adapted wildlife, and one of the few remaining habitats of the Nubian ibex.**

## On Screen

When resources are scarce, conflict abounds. We watch as a young male Nubian ibex battles for access to breeding females. Such fights are rarely seen – even more rarely filmed – it took the *Planet Earth* crew three weeks to get this few seconds of truly remarkable footage.

## When

Average temperatures in July and August in the desert hover close to 40°C, and rainfall is nonexistent. Outside the summer months, however, cooler daytime temperatures and slightly chilly nights make for perfect hiking conditions.

**Nubien Ibex in Mitzpe Ramon,
Overlooking Maktesh Ramon**
To cope with the hot, arid conditions in which it lives the Nubian ibex has a light-coloured shiny coat that reflects sunlight.

"With little or no soil to
hold water, life struggles
to take root here."

# EXPERIENCE

Israel and the Palestinian Territories' complicated, volatile but intoxicating reputation far outstrips its diminutive geography. Of course, when you're by yourself in the middle of the Negev, the region's size takes on a far greater dimension. You've been hiking since morning, and even though the sun is already well past its apex, the only other signs of human life are the slowly disintegrating sets of footprints in the sand.

The lack of civilisation is precisely why you chose to spend your time in the Negev. That, and the fact that the desert is home to the Nubian ibex, a vulnerable species of goat antelope that numbers less than 2000 individuals in the wild. Standing 60cm tall at the shoulder, and weighing in at around 50kg, male Nubian ibexes are easily distinguished by their formidable horns, which can reach nearly 1m in length.

Spotting one is an achievement in itself, but you're out here roughing it in the hopes of catching a glimpse of their famous duels. Success! Up in the hills, two Nubian ibex square off like opposing generals, wrestling for control of the higher ground. Rare though they may be, these duels can last for up to an hour. And in this sweltering desert heat, you can only imagine how exhausted each of the combatants must feel right now.

For males fighting their way to the top of the hierarchy, everything is at stake. Losers may never get the chance to breed. An alpha male earns the loyalty of a harem of females, who will follow him in search of food and water. From this vantage point the competitors appear evenly matched, but you know that there are ways to turn the tide. 'No shame in fighting dirty,' you snicker to yourself.

It appears that one of the ibex was listening. A bold dash and thrash of the horns later, the challenger sinks to the ground in bitter defeat as the victor exhales a mighty breath. You feel a conflicting mix of empathy for both sides, but there's no sense in questioning the rules of Mother Nature. After all, the Negev demands that only the strongest survive, and this battle has ensured that the next generation will receive the choicest genes. As you zip your tent closed at the end of a long day, and wrap yourself into the comforting warmth of a sleeping bag, you're grateful about being in here – and not out there.

(top) Ein Avdat Canyon

The best way to reach Ein Avdat Canyon (part of the Ein Avdat National Park) is by the beautiful Wilderness of Zin nature trail. The long one-way hike through the canyon usually takes two to three hours.

(bottom) Wailing Wall, Jerusalem

Originally built as a retaining wall supporting the outer portion of the Temple Mount, upon which stood the Second Temple, the Western Wall (Wailing Wall) is often considered the most important religious shrine for the Jewish people.

# TAKING ACTION

## As You Saw It

If you want to see ibex duelling behaviour in the wild you need tremendous luck, as well as a slew of patience. But even if you don't have three weeks to dedicate to capturing a single shot, you stand a good chance of spotting a Nubian ibex in the rough mountainous terrain surrounding many of the region's hiking routes. The ibex is diurnal, and thus active throughout the day – if you keep an eye out for grassy patches in the hills, your odds of spotting one (or two) will increase dramatically.

## Adding to the Experience

Whether you're walking the trails of Sde Boker, the Wilderness of Zin, Ein Avdat National Park, Maktesh Ramon, Timna National Park or the Eilat Mountains, you're bound to be seduced by the magic of the barrenness of the desert. And then there is the Dead Sea, where you can float on your back with toes to the sky while leisurely reading the Sunday paper. After an obligatory float, don't miss the nearby ruins at Masada, as well as the natural springs of Ein Gedi nature reserve.

## Alternative Ibex-Spotting Experiences

If it's ibex you're after, consider the following locales for searching out some other subspecies.
✿ **Siberia** Siberian ibex: a cold-adapted ibex that is almost twice as large as the Nubian varietal.

✿ **European Alps** Alpine ibex: slightly larger than Nubians, Alpine ibex live at high elevations above the snowline.

✿ **Simien Mountains, Ethiopia** Walia ibex: an endangered species, there are an estimated 500 or so remaining in the wild. See p10 for more on the Simiens.

See p10 for more on the Simiens.

# WHILE YOU'RE THERE

## Jerusalem

Jerusalem, Israel's ancient, enigmatic and stunning capital, is without doubt one of the world's most fascinating cities, as well as one of its holiest and most oft disputed. Here you'll find a mix of religions, lifestyles and monuments to three of the world's great monotheistic faiths, with tension, turmoil and turbulence thrown into the mix. A trip here will challenge your preconceptions of this beautiful but deeply troubled land.

## Tel Aviv

A universe away from historical – and sometimes hysterical – Jerusalem, secular party-city Tel Aviv, barely a century old, is many things that Jerusalem is not: easy, breezy, sometimes garishly ugly, and open for business 24/7. It's a city of diners, drinkers and dog owners; here you'll find people out for a burger at 1am, doing their laundry at 3am, and taking an early morning dip in the sea at 5am.

## Eilat

Wedged between Jordan and Egypt, and separated from the Israel of international headlines by 200km of desert, Eilat is a resort

---

# BIBLICAL ORIGINS

Though the history of Israel and the Palestinian Territories is as fraught with disagreement as its troubled present, it's generally agreed that the first inhabitants of the land were the Canaanites, who migrated here as early as the 20th century BC. Around 2800 BC, Pharaonic Egypt claimed Canaan as part of its empire. It was still under Egyptian control when, 1000 years later, Abraham led his nomadic tribe – the Israelites – from Mesopotamia to the Judean Hills. Though Abraham's descendants were forced to move on to Egypt due to drought and famine, Moses (grandson of Abraham) led them back in 1250 BC via Sinai, thus ending their servitude under Egyptian rule.

town where glitzy hotels line an artificial lagoon, and glass-bottomed boats ply coral reefs. Its founding fathers, convicts sent here in the 1950s to build the city, have been superseded by holidaying spring break–style tourists intent on living it up.

## GETTING YOU THERE

As the largest city in the region, Be'er Sheva is the traditional entry point into the Negev. Buses run regularly to and from both Tel Aviv and Jerusalem, or from Be'er Sheva's central train station; you can travel comfortably to Tel Aviv roughly hourly from Sunday to Thursday.

## EXPLORING THE NEGEV

An amazing way to experience the wonders of the desert is on one of the Society for the Protection of Nature's (SPNI; www.aspni.org) Yarok Tours, which emphasise minimising our impact on Israel's wilderness (*yarok* means 'green' in modern Hebrew). One of the highlights is the Cold Nights on the Desert Heights tour, which encompasses a full-moon desert hike, camping, and t'ai chi in Maktesh Ramon.

# TRACKING DESERT ELEPHANTS

## Namib Desert, Namibia

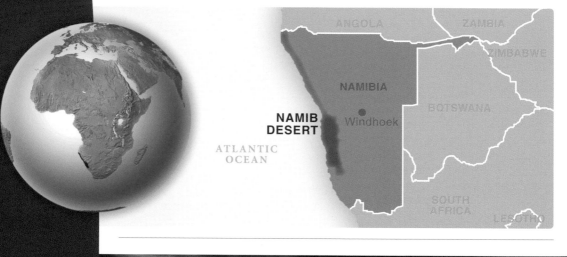

**(left) Deadvlei, Namib-Naukluft National Park**
Deadvlei, a white clay pan in Namib-Naukluft National Park, is surrounded by the highest sand dunes in the world. The highest, known as Big Daddy, is 350m high (on average).

**(right) Desert Elephant**
What little food exists in the Namib is so dispersed that desert elephants walk up to 80km a day following dry river channels in search of something to eat.

**While elephants are found throughout much of sub-Saharan Africa, only in the southwest arid zone can you encounter this increasingly rare desert subspecies. Sightings are never guaranteed, but tracking the herds through the shifting sands is a thrilling experience for anyone with grit and guts.**

## On Screen
*Planet Earth* highlights the plight of the desert elephants as they travel in herds across the Namib in search of meagre food sources and clean drinking water. With smaller bodies and larger feet for maintaining balance in the loose sands, these elephants are supremely adapted to life in one of the planet's harshest and most unforgiving ecosystems.

## When
Always on the move, the fate of desert elephants is inextricably tied to seasonal rains, which fall from January to April. Riverbeds turn a verdant green as long-dormant seeds erupt into bloom, providing essential nutrition for famished herbivores. Elephant sightings are never guaranteed, but your chances do increase after the rains have subsided and the herds become reliant on water holes.

# EXPERIENCE

Bouncing along gravel paths and barely visible trails in the sand, your guide scours the horizon for signs of the elephant herds. While they're surprisingly elegant, and even graceful at times, elephants display a tendency to bowl over obstacles rather than sidestep them. Broken limbs, trampled vegetation and shattered rocks are telltale signs that the herd has passed this way, as are the ubiquitous footprints and droppings in the sand.

Elephants are typically on the move during the day, when predators are sleeping and possibly digesting last night's kill. The desert sun is brutal even outside the summer months, so you've brought lots of sunscreen, some serious shades and your best safari hat. Lots of water is also a good idea as the mercury can soar out here.

**Sossusvlei, Namib-Naukluft National Park**
Despite being Namibia's number-one attraction, Sossusvlei (another pan set amid towering red dunes) still manages to feel isolated.

Your arrival is heralded by the trumpeting calls of protective parents, who quickly shift ranks and move their vulnerable young to safer positions. Weakened from lack of food and water, and constantly travelling towards the next uncertain destination, desert elephants are best given a healthy berth. If provoked, flared ears and mad eyes will accompany a mock charge – but keep your ground, don't panic and their bluff will be called.

With that said, heed our warning – an elephant is the largest land mammal on the planet, and they can flip even a large safari jeep with minimal effort. Fortunately you're travelling with trained professionals, who respect and admire the tenacity of these charismatic creatures. From the proper viewpoint, with binoculars in hand, you scope out the herd as it presses forward with singular purpose. The dramatic desert backdrop makes for some stunning safari photography.

Only the hardiest elephants can survive the elements for years on end, and the desert is one place where even the smallest mistake can end in total disaster. Seasonal rains bring with them a bounty of food and water, but irregular fluctuations make all the difference between life and death. The selective pressures wrought from this precarious existence have shaped the desert elephant into one of the most magnificent animals on the planet.

# TAKING ACTION

## As You Saw It

Tracking desert elephants is certainly not a walk in the park – you're going to need the services of an experienced guide, not to mention some serious wheels capable of tackling what pass for roads in these parts. Fortunately, however, there are two luxury lodges in northwestern Namibia, namely the Skeleton Coast Camp and Desert Rhino Camp, that are equipped to offer tracking expeditions along the Skeleton Coast (the northern part of the Atlantic coast of Namibia) and deep into the Namib Desert. Tracking expeditions aren't cheap, but you can't really put a price on adventure. And, even if the desert elephants don't make an appearance, you'll almost definitely spot oryx, and possibly even a black rhino or a big cat.

## Adding to the Experience

Further down the Skeleton Coast is Swakopmund, the adventure-sports capital of Namibia. Whether you hurl yourself out of a plane (with a parachute strapped to your back), or grab the handlebars of a quad bike and jump from dune to dune, this coastal town is the perfect accompaniment to a tracking expedition. In the evenings you can quench your parched throat with a few pints of Windhoek, a domestic lager that adheres to the German purity laws governing the brewing of beer.

## Alternative Elephant-Tracking Experiences

Southern Africa is home to some of the continent's largest elephant herds.

✿ **Etosha National Park** (Namibia) Centred on an enormous salt pan, Etosha is dense with wildlife, offering an extreme contrast to the Namib.

✿ **Chobe National Park** (Botswana) The heart of this national park is a permanent river system, which supports the world's largest elephant herds. See p182 for more on Chobe.

✿ **Kruger National Park** (South Africa) Southern Africa's most famous national park is home to the Big Five, namely lions, elephants, rhinos, buffalo and leopards.

# WHILE YOU'RE THERE

## Skydiving

Ground Rush Adventures (www.skydiveswakop .com.na) can provide the ultimate rush; skydiving in Swakopmund is sweetened by the outstanding dune and ocean backdrop.

## Quad Biking

In two hours, your Outback Orange (www .outback-orange.com) guide will take you over 60km across countless dunes, all the while enjoying panoramic views of sand, sea and Swakopmund.

## Scenic Flights

Pleasure Flights (www.pleasureflights.com.na), the most reputable light-plane operator in Swakopmund, has been offering scenic aerial cruises over the Namib Desert and Skeleton Coast for more than 15 years.

# SKELETON COAST

The name 'Skeleton Coast' is derived from its treacherous nature – it's a foggy region with rocky and sandy coastal shallows that has long been a graveyard for unwary ships and their crews. Early Portuguese sailors called it *As Areias do Inferno* (the Sands of Hell) – once a ship washed ashore the fate of the crew was sealed. This protected area stretches from just north of Swakopmund to the Kunene River, taking in nearly 2 million hectares of dunes and gravel plains to form one of the world's most inhospitable, waterless areas.

# GETTING YOU THERE

The Skeleton Coast Camp and Desert Rhino Camp are each accessed by a combination of private charter aeroplane and 4WD vehicle. Intercape (www.intercape.co.za) runs a daily bus service from Windhoek to Swakopmund.

# EXPLORING THE NAMIB

These two organisations are well equipped for tracking expeditions along the Skeleton Coast and into the Namib:

✿ **Skeleton Coast Camp** (www.wilderness-safaris.com) This private concession in the extreme northwest corner of the Skeleton Coast has the distinction of being the most remote property in the Wilderness Safari collection. Safaris include room, full board, transfers and activities.

✿ **Desert Rhino Camp** (www.wilderness-safaris.com) This mobile camp in the Palmwag Reserve in northern Damaraland monitors the movements of not only desert elephant herds, but also endangered black rhinos. Safaris include room, full board, transfers and activities.

## THE NAMIB

The Namib Desert is one of the planet's oldest and driest deserts. As with the Atacama in northern Chile, the Namib is the result of a cold current – in this case the Benguela Current – sweeping north from Antarctica and capturing and condensing humid air that would otherwise be blown ashore. As a result, there is virtually no rainfall in the Namib, though hardy life can sustain itself on the droplets of moisture that condense from the coastal fog.

## FAST FACTS

**Parabolic dunes** (otherwise known as multicyclic dunes) are found along the eastern area of the Namib's dune sea. They are the result of variable wind patterns and are the most stable dunes in the Namib, and therefore the most vegetated.

**Transverse dunes** are long, linear dunes found along the coast. They lie perpendicular to the prevailing southwesterly winds and, as a result, their slip faces are oriented towards the north and northeast.

**Seif dunes** (also known as linear dunes) are enormous all-direction-oriented sand ripples. With heights of up to 100m, they're spaced about 1km apart and show up plainly on satellite photographs. They're formed by seasonal winds: during the prevailing southerly winds of summer, the slip faces lie on the northeastern face; in the winter, the wind blows in the opposite direction, which causes slip faces to build up on the southwestern faces.

**Star dunes** appear in areas where individual dunes are exposed to winds from all directions. These dunes have multiple ridges, and when seen from above may appear to have a star shape.

# DEATH VALLEY

## California, USA

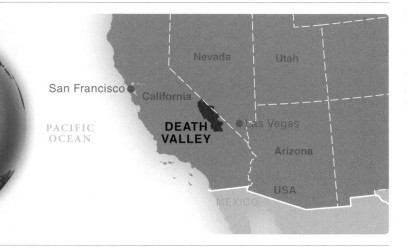

Nevada

Utah

San Francisco
California

PACIFIC
OCEAN

DEATH
VALLEY

Las Vegas

Arizona

USA

MEXICO

**It might not officially have the highest temperatures on record – Iran's Dasht-e Lut desert has cracked 70°C – but Death Valley is arguably the most consistently hot place on earth. It has the second-highest temperature ever recorded (56.7°C) and averages around 47°C in summer. Despite such brutal conditions, it's a place where life is abundant.**

## On Screen

On *Planet Earth* you see the hottest and driest place in North America burst into uncharacteristic colour after a hint of rain – Death Valley turning into 'life valley' as seeds that have lain dormant for three decades suddenly bloom.

## When

You can see Death Valley at its deadliest in the sulphurous heat of summer, when temperatures soar towards 50°C, or experience it more comfortably in the cooler winter months. Spring is the basin's most popular visitor time, with its wildflowers in bloom and its heat at a simmer.

**Devil's Golf Course**
Because it is elevated above the valley floor, the Devil's Golf Course (a large salt pan; not to be confused with the actual golf course at Furnace Creek) remains dry, allowing weathering processes to sculpt its salt into complicated forms.

# EXPERIENCE

Dawn's deceptive chill is lifting off the land and, at the edge of Hwy 190, a coyote trots away into the saltbush, seemingly as tame as a poodle. Summer is gone, but still the forecast is for a 40°C day – so you are out early, before the sun fries the valley, turning it as deathly as its name suggests.

From the highway's edge you walk out onto the Mesquite Flat dunes, the sand still mercifully cool, with the sun only now peeping over the crinkle-cut horizon of mountains. Sand ripples run like veins across the dunes, and with the sun so low they are tiger-striped with shade and light. It seems almost a pity to walk here and spoil the surface patterns. Atop these dunes Death Valley resembles the typical sandy image of a desert, though in reality only around 1% of the trough (this is not a true valley, it's a basin created by earthquakes) is covered in sand.

You turn your head to look up and down the 250km-long basin, framed by the brown, seemingly lifeless Panamint and Amargosa Ranges. To the south the basin trends downward, dipping to Death Valley's pin-up geographical feature: the vast salt flats of Badwater, as white as magnesium fire and beginning to feel almost as hot. From here, at North America's lowest point, it's difficult to believe that if you hop just one valley west you'll be at the foot of 4418m Mt Whitney, the highest peak in the USA's lower 48 states.

By now the earth is shimmering behind a heat haze. The mountains seem to belly dance and even the ever-present coyotes seem reluctant to brave the sun. It's a heat so intense you wonder how anything lives here, but you know that creatures do, adapting in their various ways. Such as the sidewinder rattlesnakes that never drink, instead eating the juiciest of small creatures. Or the kangaroo rats that also don't drink, their bodies instead metabolising the water they need from the dry seeds they eat. Death Valley even has a fish, the tiny pupfish, which is found in the rare permanent water sources, such as Devils Hole and Salt Creek.

Humans, rather than adapt, brought air-conditioning into the basin – cooling the settlement at Furnace Creek, with its preposterous green golf course (the only golf course inside a US national park). It's to Furnace Creek that you now head, following the animals' lead – escaping the midday sun for a feed and perhaps a sleep.

**Death Valley Landscape**
In spite of its ominous name, nature puts on a spectacular show in Death Valley, with water-sculpted canyons, singing sand dunes, palm-shaded oases, eroded mountains and plenty of endemic wildlife.

"*Death Valley is the hottest place on planet earth – yet even this furnace can be transformed by water.*"

# TAKING ACTION

## As You Saw It
To witness Death Valley in bloom, your best option is to come in spring, after the possibility of small winter rains. Rainfall is rare – the valley receives less than 5cm a year, and has twice recorded years without any – but even a sprinkle can bring a surprising number of wildflowers to life. Death Valley is home to more than 1000 species of plants, many with remarkable desert adaptations, such as root systems that extend up to 20m below the ground.

## Adding to the Experience
For the ultimate in Death Valley contrast, climb to the summit of the national park's highest mountain, Telescope Peak. The 22.5km round-trip takes you to the summit of the 3367m mountain named for the vastness of its view. From here the vertical drop to the depths of the valley floor at Badwater is the equivalent of two Grand Canyons.

## Alternative Low-Altitude Experiences
At 86m below sea level, Badwater is the lowest bit of land in North America, but there are lower places across the globe. To dip even closer to the earth's crust, check out the following.

- ✿ **Dead Sea** (Israel) -414m
- ✿ **Lake Assal** (Djibouti) -157m
- ✿ **Turpan Depression** (China) -155m
- ✿ **Qattara Depression** (Egypt) -133m
- ✿ **Laguna del Carbón** (Argentina) -105m

# WHILE YOU'RE THERE

## Racetrack Playa
At this mysterious site you can see large rocks that appear to have moved on their own across the mud flat, making long, faint tracks in the sunbaked surface. Scientific theories abound, but nothing has been proven. It is reached by a tire-shredding dirt road that requires 4WD.

## Scotty's Castle
Walter E Scott, alias 'Death Valley Scotty', was a quintessential tall-tale teller who captivated people with his fanciful stories of gold. His most lucrative friendship was with Albert and Bessie Johnson, insurance magnates from Chicago. Despite knowing that Scotty was a freeloading liar, they bankrolled the construction of this elaborate Spanish-inspired villa, now restored to its 1930s appearance.

# GOODBYE DEATH VALLEY

Death Valley. It's a name of biblical proportions that came from a biblical-sized epic in the desert. In 1849 a small band of pioneers wandered into the valley after separating from a larger emigrant group along the Old Spanish Trail to take a sensible southern route to avoid crossing the Sierra Nevada in winter.

Taking what they hoped would be a short cut to the California goldfields, the small party struggled across the Nevada desert for a month before entering the basin from the east. Exhausted and running out of food and water, they arrived near Furnace Creek on Christmas Eve of 1849, but couldn't get their broken-down wagons over the Panamint Range.

While most of the party sheltered near a waterhole, two young men were sent to scout for a route west over the mountains. Two families waited for the scouts, who eventually returned after 26 days in the wilderness. Near Stovepipe Wells, they slaughtered their oxen, burned their wagons and walked out of the valley through what is now called Emigrant Canyon. As they left, one woman reputedly looked back and uttered the words, 'Goodbye, death valley.'

## Badwater

Drop into the lowest bit of land in the USA, the salt-crusted Badwater, 86m below sea level. Nearby is the so-called Devil's Golf Course, a barren stretch of land covered with lumps of crystallised salt. Further north is the Artists Drive, a one-way scenic loop that passes alluvial fans (where streams have left deposits at the mouths of side canyons), and the Artists Palette, with colourful exposed minerals and volcanic ash.

## GETTING YOU THERE

To explore Death Valley you'll need your own wheels. Furnace Creek is about 180km (two to 2½ hours) north of Baker, or 230km (2½ to three hours) northwest of Las Vegas. Failing that, the Death Valley Bus (http://deathvalley-trip.com/death-valley-bus.html) makes summer runs into the national park from Las Vegas and San Francisco.

## EXPLORING DEATH VALLEY

From late October through to mid-April there are ranger-led programs, including walks and lectures, throughout the national park. For schedules and information, see the park website, www.nps.gov/deva.

Escape Adventures (www.escapeadventures.com) also offers hiking tours for an intimate look at Death Valley.

## FAST FACTS

Death Valley has the USA's highest recorded temperature – 56.7°C. This occurred in 1913, and for nine years it made Death Valley the hottest place on earth.

The highest ground temperature ever recorded in the valley was almost 94°C, on 15 July 1972.

In 1929 and 1953 Death Valley recorded zero annual rainfall.

In 1997 Death Valley recorded 15cm of rain – its wettest year on record.

# ICE WORLDS
## *Planet Earth, Episode Six*

Perhaps nowhere is more pristine yet more in peril than
the icy extremes of planet earth. It is here that humanity,
despite its exploratory tendencies, has failed to make
a lasting impact in terms of cities or settlements, yet
is having the most dramatic effect in terms of climate
change. Nothing sums up the tragedy of our meddling
like the sight of a polar bear – massive, magnificent,
imperious – stumbling on the Arctic pack ice, which
is melting to slush beneath his mighty paws. But the
Arctic and Antarctic are not done yet: their shimmering
wildernesses still offer some of the world's best wildlife
experiences – for now, at least.

# BIG BEAR, SHRINKING WORLD
## The Arctic

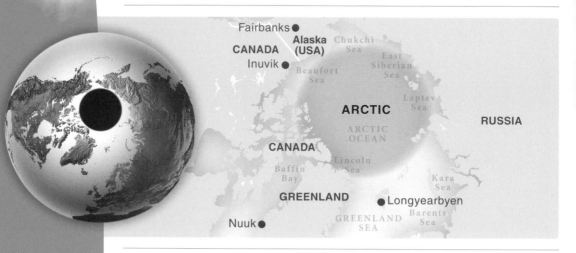

Fairbanks●
**Alaska** Chukchi
**CANADA** **(USA)** Sea
Inuvik ● East
Beaufort Siberian
Sea Sea

Laptev
**ARCTIC** Sea
ARCTIC
OCEAN **RUSSIA**
**CANADA**

Lincoln
Baffin Sea
Bay Kara
Sea

**GREENLAND** ●Longyearbyen
Barents
GREENLAND Sea
Nuuk● SEA

Polar bears are at the frontline of climate change. The chance to see one of these increasingly endangered creatures in its natural environment is a privilege future generations may not enjoy. And there is also much more to see in the Arctic realm – landscapes of glittering purity, with seas and skies full of life, including the supremely well-adapted mammals (Arctic foxes, caribou, muskoxen) that eke out an existence in this land of ice.

## On Screen

Awesome and heartbreaking, *Planet Earth* captures the fraying fortunes of the mighty polar bear. These beasts are among the world's most powerful – you watch their massive haunches striding across the icy vastness. But you also see the mighty bears stumble in puddles, fall through thinning ice and, ultimately, edge closer to losing the battle for survival in their climate-changed world.

## When

The Arctic in winter is a forbidding place: temperatures plummet to -40°C and 24-hour darkness descends. While February to mid-April is a great time to catch the northern lights, spring and summer (from March to August) are the best times to visit, as temperatures rise to a relatively scorching 10°C to 15°C, animals stir and the sun finally creeps over the horizon, staying put pretty much permanently from June to August.

Arctic National Wildlife Refuge
A polar bear cub scratches itself with a bowhead whale jawbone.

"Each year, as the climate warms, the Arctic holds less ice. Without its solid platform, bears can't hunt the seals they need to survive."

# EXPERIENCE

As you glide above the vast, icy expanse in a chopper, all you can make out in the white-on-white brilliance below is a pair of black eyes – no, two pairs – peeping out from a hole in the snow. As the Arctic wilderness wakes from its winter slumber, so too do two baby polar bears, perfectly camouflaged, emerging from their den to take a first look at the world.

To the inexpert observer there's little variety to their surrounds – a uniform icy glitter that somehow these fumbling cubs must master. Luckily mum is on hand to help. You gasp involuntarily when she appears: she's massive, an awesome powerhouse of white fur. And then she does something unbefitting her noble countenance: she slides down the slope like a child on a toboggan, powder spraying her muzzle, washing away the fug of her long hibernation. She's having a ball.

The fun must end, though. You can hear her cubs mewing for assistance as they slip on the unfamiliar terrain, wobbly as drunks. Mum dutifully returns, scooping them up oh-so-gently in her deadly jaws, and the trio stride – unsteadily – out into the wilderness. She will need to teach them how to survive in this hostile place; life is becoming increasingly difficult for the planet's polar bears.

**Aurora Borealis (Northern Lights)**
The northern lights is an atmospheric phenom-enon that occurs when particles of solar wind are directed towards earth's magnetic poles and collide with atoms in the upper atmosphere, emitting light.

Take him. The next bear you spot, this time from a rigid-hulled Zodiac, looks magnificent, but he stumbles and his bulk breaks the fragile crust of the fragmenting ice floes, plunging him into the inky water. Although he actually looks quite comfortable swimming in the open water – those huge paws make fine paddles – it's not his natural preference. He needs solid ice on which to hunt. When, after his long doggy paddle, he does reach land again he looks exhausted.

The island stinks, courtesy of the mound of gelatinous walruses snorting and farting to the right. You are incredulous – is the bear really going to try to catch one of these things? Has he seen the size of their tusks? But try he must – you can see the hunger-driven desperation on his pointed face. He makes his move.

The walruses are not stupid. They jelly-wobble into a formidable barricade of brown blubber, protecting their young. Even when the bear sinks his teeth into one mum, it's no more than a flesh wound – her hide's as tough as old boots. You watch as the bear tussles; he's getting nowhere, but has little choice – he has to make his kill before the walruses flee to the sea. This makes him reckless, and you flinch on his behalf as a long, white tusk pierces his furry flank. He limps away, defeated.

The bear scratches himself a shallow pit and curls up with a pained roar. He is starving, and now injured; there is nothing else to be done. You turn away, a lump in your throat as he rests his mighty head on his paws and closes his eyes, and the sun dips towards the horizon.

## TAKING ACTION

### As You Saw It

Polar bears are becoming increasingly rare – there are now believed to be no more than 25,000 left in the world, with the worst predictions suggesting the species could become extinct within 100 years. In the vastness of the Arctic they can be tricky to track down without the help of a helicopter and some powerful zoom lenses. However, there are hot spots for sighting the bears; head to one of these in the right season, with a good guide, and you should be able to see a white giant in action.

### Adding to the Experience

Expedition cruising around the Svalbard archipelago in the Norwegian Arctic is one of the best ways to spot polar bears; around 3000 of them survive here (which is more bears than people). Sturdy vessels allow access to remote bays, as well as keeping you at a safe distance. Cruises run in summer, so you'll be bathed in the midnight sun. You may also spot walruses, seals, reindeer and millions of migrant birds. The more adventurous can explore Spitsbergen by kayak, snowmobile or dog sled.

### Alternative Polar Bear–Spotting Experiences

Polar bear numbers are diminishing, but there are a few places where you might catch a glimpse.

✿ **Churchill** (Manitoba, Canada) For bear watching by tundra buggy.

✿ **Arctic National Wildlife Refuge** (Alaska) For polar bears plus muskoxen, grizzlies, wolves and huge herds of caribou.

✿ **Wrangel Island** (Russia) For really remote wildlife watching – it's accessible only by sturdy icebreaker or helicopter.

✿ **Grise Fjord** (Nunavut, Canada) For bear-watching boat trips with the locals of Canada's northernmost civilian community.

## WHILE YOU'RE THERE

### Longyearbyen

The capital of Svalbard, on the island of Spitsbergen, is a surprisingly cosmopolitan frontier town of 1700 souls. Visit the excellent Svalbard Museum (www.svalbardmuseum.no) for info on the whaling history, wildlife and geology of the region.

## FINDING A WAY THROUGH THE ICE

The Northwest Passage is an icon of exploration. This route across the top of North America – linking the Atlantic and Pacific Oceans via a network of waterways between craggy north Canada and the Arctic pack ice – became a holy grail for traders wanting to pass more quickly from Europe to China. The first recorded attempt to locate it was mounted around 1500 by John Cabot, under the command of Henry VII. Many subsequent voyagers followed, some probing the continent's rivers – the Hudson and the St Lawrence – hoping they were in fact making inroads towards the Pacific.

It wasn't until 1906 that Norwegian Roald Amundsen telegrammed from Alaska after three years at sea to report that he had successfully navigated the Northwest Passage – but that it was so full of ice it wasn't a commercially viable option.

Until now, that is. In 2007 satellite images showed that ice loss in the region had opened up the passage for the first time since records began. A tourist cruise liner has even made the journey. And as the globe continues to heat, the passage will become more easily navigable.

THE ARCTIC

## Land Expeditions

Spitsbergen Travel (www.spitsbergentravel.no) offers multiday snowmobile, dog-sledding and hiking trips into the wilderness. The Svalbard Wildlife Service (www.wildlife.no) leads summer ski trips and camping excursions.

## Magdalenefjord

Beautiful blue-green Magdalenefjord, backed by alpine peaks, is one of the most scenic spots on Spitsbergen's west coast.

## A Night on the Noorderlicht

In the winter months the two-masted schooner *Noorderlicht* is purposefully marooned in the pack ice to become one of the region's most atmospheric hotels (www.basecampexplorer.com). Transfer here by snowmobile, and look out for the northern lights.

## GETTING YOU THERE

Accessing any part of the Arctic is expensive. Useful hubs include Longyearbyen, Nuuk (Greenland), Inuvik (Northwest Territories, Canada) and Fairbanks (Alaska, USA). You will then need onward transport – possibly an expensive flight charter, a snowmobile ride or an expedition vessel – to delve into the region proper, for any chance of spotting bears (though hungry ursines have been known to wander into downtown Longyearbyen).

## EXPLORING THE ARCTIC

Many sturdy ships take travellers around the Arctic – these can be booked through a range of different specialist tour operators. Before booking consider what you want to see (remote fjords, big wildlife, abandoned whaling stations) and make sure your vessel of choice includes these; some boats offer extras such as expert marine biologists or kayaks.

The Arctic spans several countries, but the same rules apply wherever you visit. This is a pristine and fragile world and you need to tread as lightly as possible. Don't pick flowers, destroy vegetation, interfere with or feed wildlife, or leave any litter. Make sure any tour operator you travel with is environmentally sensitive.

# THE ICE CONTINENT
## Antarctica

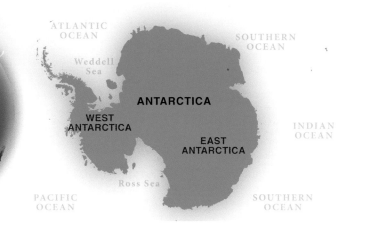

ATLANTIC
OCEAN

SOUTHERN
OCEAN

Weddell
Sea

**ANTARCTICA**

**WEST
ANTARCTICA**

INDIAN
OCEAN

**EAST
ANTARCTICA**

Ross Sea

PACIFIC
OCEAN

SOUTHERN
OCEAN

Visit one of the last – and by far the most demanding – wildernesses on earth, permanently packed in ice and brimming with storybook wildlife. Here penguins shuffle about the coast, seals surface offshore and a variety of whales cruise the chilly seas. Once tourism's final frontier, today the ice world at the southern tip of the globe is visited by growing numbers of cruise ships.

## On Screen

*Planet Earth* takes you through a year of seasons in Antarctica, from light-filled summer to the coldest, darkest winter on earth. In summer a host of birdlife – snow petrels, Adélie penguins, chinstrap penguins – seeks rocky nesting grounds, while winter brings the blizzard-battered march of the Emperor penguins.

## When

The Antarctic tour season is short – about four months (December to March), taking you to a world of 20-hour daylight.

**Tourists Checking Out a Glacier at Paradise Bay**
Paradise Bay is one of two ports used for cruise ships to stop at Antarctica (the other is Neko Harbour). An abandoned Argentine scientific base, Almirante Brown Antarctic Base, and the Chilean summer base, González Videla Antarctic Base, are located here.

"At the southernmost extreme of our planet, the continent of Antarctica is as large as the US... it holds 90% of the world's ice."

# EXPERIENCE

After four days at sea, the ice continent is finally here, bobbing about off the starboard. Behind you is the obstacle course through which you arrived: the Antarctic Sound, known as Iceberg Alley for reasons you now understand, with its croutons of floating ice, from chunks the size of a car to tabular icebergs as large as a city block – large enough to make even the occasional surfacing whale look small. You had expected bitter cold, but it is surprisingly warm – just above zero – reminding you that this is the mildest location on the continent.

From the ship that has been your home these last few days, you board the Zodiac and skim across the sea towards the shores of Hope Bay, an indent in the northern tip of the Antarctic Peninsula. At the bay's edges glaciers leak down into the sea, and the land ahead is streaked with snow, though it looks more like the reverse: like the earth is etched into the snow, like syrup. In the water, leopard seals swoosh about, seemingly at double speed.

Huddled at the foot of the mountains are the red container-huts of Esperanza, the Argentine research station. Here you see the curious sight of children running about – it was here that the first Antarctic birth took place in 1978, and today the station remains an Antarctic rarity, allowing researchers' families to live there. It even has a post office and school.

The Zodiac runs ashore on Hope Bay and you pile out, taking your first steps onto Antarctic soil – though it hardly qualifies as soil, with rock and ice crunching beneath your feet. The day is polar perfection – blue, clear, almost windless – and you are here less to see Esperanza than the Adélie penguins that nest here in massive numbers – up to 125,000 pairs plus their brown downy chicks.

From a distance you watch the Adélie penguins waddling about, arms held wide and pinned back, looking momentarily airborne as they leap into the sea. Nearby, a Weddell seal lies on the ice, moving gracelessly, laboriously, as it scratches its belly on the ground.

The animals and the researchers will not be the only things sleeping on the ice tonight, with the stable weather permitting you to stay ashore, camped on the frozen continent. As the day marches on towards continuing daylight, you slip on your eye mask inside your tent – how else are you going to sleep when the night is just four hours long? – and fall asleep to a soundtrack of moving ice and sea.

**Adélie, Chinstrip & Gentoo Penguin Rookery**
Adélie, chinstrip and gentoo penguins are of the same genus, and sometimes establish colonies within the same or overlapping geographical areas.

# TAKING ACTION

## As You Saw It

All of the animals seen on *Planet Earth* can be found around the Antarctic Peninsula, where the majority of Antarctica's exposed rock is found, creating nesting sites for a wealth of birdlife. Commercial trips to Antarctica focus on the peninsula, bringing you direct to the best wildlife.

## Adding to the Experience

If walking among the wildlife and ice isn't enough, try your paddling hand at a bit of polar sea kayaking. A number of Antarctic cruise operators now offer sea-kayaking options – you can cruise around icebergs and along the shoreline of penguin rookeries as you listen to the creak, groan and splash of calving glaciers. The rich Antarctic waters promise marine sightings, such as seals, penguins and even whales.

## Alternative Penguin-Watching Experiences

Penguins are synonymous with the Antarctic, but they are not limited to the southern ice. Here are a few other places that can provide you with penguin encounters.

✿ **Reserva Provincial Punta Tombo** (Patagonia, Argentina) Continental South America's largest penguin nesting ground, with a colony of more than 500,000 Magellanic penguins.

✿ **King Island** (Tasmania, Australia) Australia has numerous penguin-viewing opportunities, but in Grassy, on this Bass Strait island, you will have little penguins to yourself as they shuffle ashore on the breakwater.

✿ **Boulders Beach** (Cape Town, South Africa) A very personal experience with a colony of African penguins, as the birds wander about the beach among the sunbakers and swim unconcerned among human bathers.

✿ **Otago Peninsula** (Otago, New Zealand) From a system of hides and trenches at the private Penguin Place, you can watch rare yellow-eyed penguins trundle about the coastline.

✿ **Isla Fernandina** (Galápagos Islands, Ecuador) The largest population of Galápagos penguins, the world's only equatorial penguin.

# WHILE YOU'RE THERE

## Deception Island

Cruise into Pendulum Cove for the strange experience of swimming in the Antarctic – the sea is heated here by thermal waters from a volcano.

## Commonwealth Bay

Douglas Mawson's Australasian Antarctic Expedition was based at Commonwealth Bay from 1912 to 1914. The furious katabatic winds that

# PINK SNOW

Snow is not always white. Sometimes it has a pink, red, orange, green, yellow or grey cast, caused by snow algae, single-celled organisms that live atop snowfields around the world, including many places on the Antarctic Peninsula.

Snow algae have been remarked upon for at least 2000 years; Aristotle wrote about snow that was 'reddish in colour' in his *History of Animals*. Somehow 350 species of algae manage to survive in harsh, acidic, freezing, nutrient-starved, ultraviolet-seared snow environments. They tend to live in either high altitudes or high latitudes, and reproduce by remarkably hardy spores, which can withstand very cold winters and very dry summers. Researchers are investigating snow algae's pharmacological potential in the treatment of certain cancers.

Near penguin rookeries, of course, there's another reason for snow's pinkish-orangish tinge: guano (penguin excrement), as seen on the *Planet Earth* series.

caused Mawson to call this the 'Home of the Blizzard' often make landing here impossible, and have made conservation of Mawson's huts difficult. In 2007 a small laboratory was built here to help conserve artefacts.

## South Georgia Island

Combine your Antarctic visit with a stop at South Georgia Island, famed for Ernest Shackleton's epic 1916 walk across the then-uncharted island after the *Endurance* was crushed by Antarctic pack ice. The island is a good place for viewing king penguins, fur seals and elephant seals. Shackleton's grave is in the cemetery at Grytviken whaling station – he died in January 1922 aboard his ship moored off Grytviken.

# GETTING YOU THERE & EXPLORING ANTARCTICA

Nearly all visitors to Antarctica arrive on cruise ships (most leaving from Ushuaia in Tierra del Fuego, three days' sail from the Antarctic Peninsula), stepping onto the continent and its islands on day trips from the boat. The following are some of the oldest and most established companies cruising to Antarctica.

✿ **Abercrombie & Kent** (www.abercrombiekent.com) Charters *Minerva,* an ice-reinforced vessel that can carry 199 passengers.

✿ **Aurora Expeditions** (www.auroraexpeditions.com.au) Operates the 56-passenger *Polar Pioneer* and the 100-passenger *Marina Svetaeva,* which carries two helicopters. Aurora also offers scuba diving, kayaking, mountain climbing and camping.

✿ **Fathom Expeditions** (www.fathomexpeditions.com) Offers small-ship voyages to the Antarctic Peninsula.

✿ **Heritage Expeditions** (www.heritage-expeditions.com) Operates the 48-passenger *Spirit of Enderby,* which carries two hovercraft. Heritage offers trips to New Zealand's sub-Antarctic islands, Macquarie Island and the Ross Sea.

✿ **Lindblad Expeditions** (www.expeditions.com) Operates the 110-passenger *National Geographic Endeavour* and the 148-passenger *National Geographic Explorer* and offers kayaking.

✿ **Oceanwide Expeditions** (www.oceanwide-expeditions.com) Operates the 46-passenger *Grigoriy Mikheev,* the 46-passenger *Aleksey Maryshev,* the 52-passenger *Professor Molchanov* and the 52-passenger *Professor Multanovskiy.* Also offers scuba diving.

✿ **Quark Expeditions** (www.quark-expeditions.com) Offers trips to the Ross Sea aboard the powerful, Russian-flagged, helicopter-equipped, 112-passenger icebreaker *Kapitan Khlebnikov,* and a variety of trips to the Antarctic Peninsula and South Georgia on *Akademik Ioffe* (109 passengers).

## FAST FACTS

The coldest temperature on earth (-89. 2°C) was recorded at Vostok station, near the Geographic South Pole, in 1983.

The average altitude in Antarctica is around 2300m.

The Antarctic ice sheet has an average thickness of 2.7km.

Antarctica has 90% of the world's ice.

Nine species of penguin live in the Antarctic.

The largest animal that permanently dwells on land in Antarctica is a wingless midge that grows to just over 1cm in length.

# COUNTLESS HERDS ON THE ENDLESS TUNDRA

## Plains of Arctic Canada

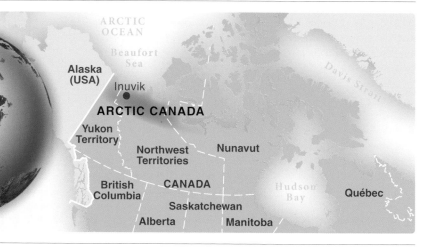

There are few wildernesses so open, so unpopulated by humans and so remote. Here life – for all creatures, including humans – is raw and primal. Getting here will be expensive and tough – but the chance of seeing one of the planet's epic migrations makes it more than worth the effort and outlay.

## On Screen

For so many months covered with snow and ice, the summer brings a thaw to the sweeping tundra – and sees millions of caribou congregate, calf and commute. *Planet Earth* uses groundbreaking aerial camerawork to capture the vastness of the migration, and the heart-bursting energy of a wolf hunt.

## When

Female caribou head north to the calving grounds in spring, to give birth in early June. July is the time to see the mass migration south, with the huge herds starting to disperse in August. July, unfortunately, is also when the biting insects get frisky – pack military-strength repellent.

ANN MANNER/PHOTOLIBRARY

ANN MANNER/PHOTOLIBRARY

# EXPERIENCE

You haven't slept properly in days. You never foresaw how disorienting you'd find the absence of darkness, but it's turned your sense of time and self topsy-turvy; you've been living through a morning that lasts for weeks, like a kind of reverse Groundhog Day.

So when the small plane you're peering out from swoops over the tundra, you've lost all perspective. The land seems unending: undulating plains stretching to the horizon in every direction, and the horizon further away than you'd imagined possible. Below, the brown-green moor is broken only by pools (seas? puddles?) and shallow waterways, creating geometric patterns like the tessellated skin of a Canada-sized giraffe.

You bank over a swarm – there's no other word – of caribou: thousands of white dots interspersed with the darker coats of infants. From on high they appear as insects, or birds, sweeping and turning like a starling flock coming to its evening roost.

You're gliding over the shore of a lake; the herd paddles across its shallow waters, all single-mindedly following a shared internal compass. The caribou never stop, not to suckle, not to graze; they bend to tear tussocks of grass as they pass and munch on the hop.

Another, smaller group of white shapes rounds the shore at a distance: wolves, perhaps ten of them. They approach the caribou, worrying the herd, like teasing a ball of wool, tugging and stretching it till it splits.

As you watch, enthralled, the herd divides; one calf, panicked, takes a wrong turn away from its mother. Instantly a wolf peels off from the pack and gives chase. It's a race, a gamble for both animals: will the wolf tire before the calf slips or loses speed? The wolf is hungry, and hunger feeds tenacity. He's not giving up.

For a mile, and another, your plane follows the chase. Moment by moment you try to second-guess the result. First the hunter loses ground, and seems to be fading; then the calf's pace falters. A glimmering puff flashes as the calf dashes through a puddle, then another a split-second later as the predator follows. Now the gap is noticeably shrinking. A twist, a final kick – and it's over. For this wolf, for now at least, the hunger is deferred.

**Porcupine Caribou Herd**
First Nation communities have hunted caribou for upwards of 20,000 years. In March 2010 representatives of several First Nation and Inuit communities and Canadian government bodies entered into a Harvest Management Plan for the conservation of the Porcupine caribou herd.

"This is the longest overland
migration of any animal."

# TAKING ACTION

## As You Saw It

Reaching the truly remote Arctic tundra isn't a simple undertaking (it's sparsely populated for a reason – well, several). Three Canadian provinces cross the Arctic Circle: Yukon, Northwest Territories and Nunavut, all with national parks that host calving caribou.

Yukon's adjacent Ivvavik and Vuntut National Parks host the 125,000-strong Porcupine caribou herd; the former is a major May-time calving ground for the herd, which migrates annually across the border into Alaska's Arctic National Wildlife Refuge. You'll be chartering a plane to spot and watch the caribou *Planet Earth*–style.

## Adding to the Experience

If you've come all this way, you might as well make the most of it. Canoeing and hiking are popular ways of exploring the wilderness; many visitors dip a lure and a line into the rivers while they're here, too, hoping to reel in Arctic char or trout. The icy waters of the Firth River gush through Ivvavik, offering some high-octane white-water rafting. The wetlands of Vuntut welcome some 500,000 migratory water birds in late summer, with correspondingly fine birdwatching.

## Alternative Migration-Watching Experiences

Mass migrations make for enthralling spectacles.

✿ **The Great Migration** (Tanzania, Kenya) Millions of wildebeest (and various herbivore hangers-on – plus hungry predators) cross the Serengeti National Park and Masai Mara National Reserve – arguably the world's most famous animal exodus.

✿ **Reindeer of Lapland** (Sweden, Finland) The reindeer can be tracked on trips with the indigenous Sami people.

✿ **Monarch butterflies** (USA, Mexico) Clouds of orange insects make an annual pilgrimage from the Great Lakes to Central America and back.

✿ **Sardine run** (South Africa) Shoals numbering in their millions, some 7km long, migrate northeast along the coast to the sea off Mozambique.

## WHILE YOU'RE THERE

You know what? What there is here is a lot of nothing – emptiness, void, nada. It's enthralling, but you can't pop to the cinema or go bowling if you fancy a change from hiking and wildlife watching. You'll need to head back south to do much else – but then that's really the point.

## GETTING YOU THERE

With the notable exception of the Dempster Highway to Inuvik – an epic drive through the Yukon and Northwest Territories, taking in some magnificent mountain and tundra scenery – there are no roads in Canada's Arctic regions. Air North (www.flyairnorth.com) serves Inuvik (which is in the Northwest Territories, 200km east of Ivvavik)

## JUST SO YOU KNOW THE DRILL

Each year on its migration through the Yukon's parks the Porcupine caribou herd also wanders through an environmental battleground: Alaska's Arctic National Wildlife Refuge (ANWR). This vast reserve – around 80,000 sq km, the USA's largest designated wilderness – is precious in more ways than one: the US Geological Survey estimates its limits contain oil reserves totalling between 5.6 billion and 16 billion barrels. Despite growing public support for drilling (on the US side of the border, at least), permission has yet to be granted. Given the soaring price of crude, it remains to be seen how long this remote wilderness can stave off the attentions of the big oil companies.

from Dawson City, while Canadian North (www.canadiannorth.com) has indirect flights from Yellowknife and elsewhere.

## EXPLORING ARCTIC CANADA

Inuvik has several fixed-wing and helicopter charter companies – see the Parks Canada website (www.pc.gc.ca) for details.

## FIRST NATIONS FACTS

Over a fifth of the Yukon's population is of indigenous ancestry, belonging to one of 14 First Nations; their ancestors probably arrived from Asia over a land bridge and inhabited an area around what's now Old Crow, more than 20,000 years ago. Thanks to the Yukon's relative isolation, many First Nation communities – particularly elders – still speak traditional languages such as Gwich'in and Han, and maintain lifestyles with elements unchanged for centuries. The tiny, remote settlement of Old Crow, Yukon's northernmost, still relies heavily on hunting the Porcupine caribou herd, using hide for moccasins and other clothes as well as eating the meat.

## FAST FACTS

Caribou are the only ungulates whose females and males both grow antlers.

Tuktut Nogait National Park takes its name from the Inuvialuktun words meaning 'young caribou'.

The species migrating through Yukon is called barren-ground caribou, which form five huge herds; the Porcupine herd numbers around 125,000 and covers upwards of 3000km each year.

Yukon Territory covers 483,610 sq km – just a little less land area than mainland Spain, but has a population of only 32,000 – compared with Spain's 40.5 million.

An adult caribou eats at least 3kg of vegetation each day; in summer they enjoy plant fodder, but in winter survive largely on lichen.

# GREAT PLAINS
## *Planet Earth,* Episode Seven

Space. Seemingly endless, unceasingly flat sweeping space, so far-reaching it monkeys with our sense of perspective: that's what defines the world's Great Plains. But plain they are not. Though difficult to get a handle on due to their gargantuan proportions, these areas – the African savannah, the Mongolian steppe, the North American prairie – are teeming with life. A safari to see a lion stalking his prey perhaps delivers the most iconic image of this landscape type, but there are many other kings to be found in the vastness, from the rhino tramping the Indian grasslands to the curious-looking foxes padding the high-altitude and highly remote Tibetan Plateau.

# GAZELLE MIGRATION
## Eastern Mongolia

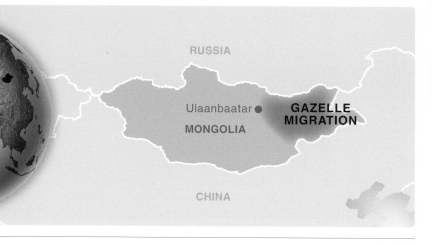

RUSSIA

Ulaanbaatar •
**MONGOLIA**

**GAZELLE MIGRATION**

CHINA

Eastern Mongolia is home to one of the last great, unharmed grasslands – a visually arresting landscape of great expanses that fosters enormous herds. It is also home to the Khan Khentii mountains – the legendary homeland of Temujin, the embattled boy who grew up to become Chinggis Khaan. So, for safari-goers and history buffs alike, eastern Mongolia is rife with opportunity for adventure.

## On Screen

The distant reaches of outer Mongolia, one of the most sparsely populated places on the planet, are home to one of the planet's greatest animal migrations. Few people ever see this extraordinary annual event, but the *Planet Earth* team is able to magnificently capture this wide-open terrain, and the movements of the Mongolian gazelle herds as they search for fresh grass and safe breeding grounds.

## When

For the majority of the year the Mongolian gazelle are scattered across this vast landscape, which covers 287,500 sq km. But every summer they gather together en masse to have their young.

**(top) Prayer Flags Outside Ulaanbataar**
Shamanistic and Buddhist practices (both of which are practised in Mongolia) use blue flags to represent sky. According to some lamas, Buddhist prayer flags date back to the shamanistic Bön tradition.

**(bottom) Golden Eagle**
Golden Eagle pairs, who are monogamous and may remain together for several years if not life, can maintain territories as large as 155 sq km.

# EXPERIENCE

Eastern Mongolia is where the heavens and earth fuse – a blank slate of blue sky colliding with a sea of yellow grass. The occasional wooden shack reminds you that humans do inhabit the region; but for the most part it's an unspoilt amphitheatre of bounding gazelle, scurrying marmots and jeep tracks that squiggle endlessly into the distance.

With no bushes or trees to hide behind, all inhabitants of the great plains are constantly exposed to danger. For the gazelles, communal calving is the safest way to have their young: with so many watchful eyes, it's harder for predators to sneak up. And so these herds of tens of thousands, currently bouncing and darting before you, gather here annually, at Dornod Mongol, a quintessential Mongolian steppe of pancake-flat grasslands.

Hunkered down in your old Russian jeep, you peer upwards into the heavens where golden eagles circle with devious intentions. In a quick burst of speed, an eagle swoops down in an admirable attempt to seize an unsuspecting gazelle calf. But even quicker animal instincts save the gazelle's life – it leaps and darts out of harm's way – forcing the eagle to return to the skies empty handed.

Mongolian gazelles are born to run, and young calves can out-pace even the fastest jeep driver. You see this fact evidenced when you shift into third gear, causing the diesel engine to rev and spurt with monster-truck force: a wave of panic ripples through the surrounding herd as frightened gazelles make mad dashes across the steppe.

You pull over and switch off the jeep, and eventually the gazelles appear to forgive you for your trespass, resuming their search for fresh grass, albeit now off in the distance. You make yourself what you consider a far more appetising lunch – steamed dumplings and fried mutton – and crack open a copy of *The Secret History of the Mongols,* in preparation for the next stage of your expedition. Although it served you well on your central Asia safari, it will soon be time to trade in the jeep and go full Mongol style – a trusty steed will better carry you deep into the Khan Khentii mountains. The location of the long-lost tomb of Chinggis Khaan has alluded archaeologists and historians alike for centuries, but that doesn't mean that you can't throw your explorer's hat into the ring.

**Mongolian Gazelles**
Newborn gazelles usually weigh about 3kg. They can keep up with their mother from just a few days after birth.

"Mongolian gazelle. Two million are thought to live here, but no one really knows. Most of the time they're scattered through this vast landscape – but once a year they gather to have their young."

# TAKING ACTION

## As You Saw It

To see the gazelles gather, head to Dornod Mongol, in eastern Mongolia. The government has designated it a Strictly Protected Area, which will ensure continued environmental protection, with limited infrastructure development.

## Adding to the Experience

Dornod Mongol is part of a much larger 1 million hectare international reserve, which links the Siberian taiga with the inner-Asian steppe. This area protects rare endemic species such as the Daurian hedgehog and white-naped crane, and is also worth exploring.

## Alternative Migration-Watching Experiences

There are many other great migrations around the world worth tracking down.

✿ **The Great Migration** (Tanzania and Kenya) Follow the wildebeest and zebra through Serengeti National Park (Tanzania) and Masai Mara National Reserve (Kenya).

✿ **The Great Salmon Migration** (Knight Inlet, Canada) See p42.

# WHILE YOU'RE THERE

## Khentii

Chinggis Khaan grew up in Khentii, established his empire on its grasslands and, from Delgerkhaan, launched his military machine to the heart of Asia. As a nomad empire the Khaans left few physical reminders of their existence, but so far researchers have identified more than 50 historical sites relating to Chinggis Khaan's life.

## Dadal

Dadal is a storybook village of log cabins that claims to be the birthplace of the great Khaan. The area is home to gorgeous lakes, rivers, forests and log huts reminiscent of Siberia, which is only 25km to the north.

## Choibalsan–Chuluunkhoroot Train

A direct rail line from Choibalsan to Russia was built in 1939 to facilitate the joint Soviet–Mongolian war effort against Japan. It still functions, albeit only twice weekly. As a foreigner, you can go as far as Chuluunkhoroot on the Mongolian side of the border, but the train no longer carries passengers across the border, and only travels to Russia to pick up fuel.

# PLIGHT OF THE GAZELLE

When pre-eminent biologist George Schaller first visited the region in 1989, he proclaimed the immense herds of Mongolian gazelle to be one of the world's greatest wildlife spectacles. Sadly, indiscriminate poaching (for both subsistence and sale) has reduced their numbers by as much as 50% in the past 10 years, and it's harder to find such large herds these days. Up to 200,000 of these creatures are illegally shot every year.

Gazelles are especially prized for their meat, skin and horns. Habitat loss to overgrazing, road construction and the erection of barriers puts their numbers at further risk. Mining is another threat: oil exploration in southern Dornod has brought large-scale infrastructure and thousands of workers into a once-uninhabited region.

But efforts are being made to protect the species. The Mongolian government has declared Strictly Protected Areas, and linked these spaces to other parks across the border in Russia to form bi-national conservation zones. The New York–based Wildlife Conservation Society (www.wcs.org) has been researching the migration habits and ecological needs of these animals for nearly a decade, and these findings have been provided to the government. Specialists are hopeful that the government will continue to endorse conservation plans and efforts to reverse the decline.

## GETTING YOU THERE

Most international arrivals in Mongolia touch down in the capital city of Ulaanbaatar. From here, a paved road between Ulaanbaatar and Öndörkhaan is nearly complete, allowing for relatively hassle-free entry into the region. Decent dirt roads connect other areas, although the far north can get boggy after heavy rains. With your own vehicle, it's possible to drive to eastern Mongolia from the Gobi; or you could even enter from Russia at the Ereen Tsav–Solovyevsk border crossing in Dornod province.

## EXPLORING EASTERN MONGOLIA

Hire a jeep, possibly with a guide, from Ulaanbaatar or from one of the regional capitals. Make sure your guide and driver have some experience in the region, as this will make navigation easier (a GPS is also a handy addition to your expedition party). Or go Chinggis Khaan–style and opt for horseback; there are tour operators in Dadal that rent horses, or just make arrangements with the locals.

## THE GREAT TABOO

For the Mongols, disposing of a corpse has always been tricky business. According to steppe tradition, a person was left exposed to the elements to be consumed by wild animals. In some cases, such as the deaths of ruling elites, a person would be buried; but the grave would be left unmarked – to thwart grave robbers, who it was believed (in addition to stealing possessions) would destroy the soul of the deceased in disturbing their remains.

When Chinggis Khaan died in 1227 his inner circle went to extraordinary lengths to ensure the secrecy of his grave. According to lore, a burial guard slew everyone en route to the grave. Then, at the grave site, thousands of horses were raced over the tomb to conceal its location. (Another theory states that a river was temporarily diverted and Chinggis was buried in the riverbed.) The burial guard was then killed by 800 soldiers, who themselves were massacred upon their return to the capital. The Mongols still consider the idea of disturbing the grave of Chinggis as the 'Great Taboo', an act that would invite a horrific natural calamity.

# LIONS ON THE HUNT
## Savuti, Chobe National Park, Botswana

Kasane
Savuti • CHOBE
NATIONAL
PARK
ZIMBABWE
NAMIBIA
BOTSWANA
MOZAMBIQUE
SOUTH
AFRICA
SWAZILAND INDIAN
OCEAN

Savuti's flat, wildlife-packed expanses are awash with distinctly African colours and sights. In addition to lions and elephants, the region is home to vast herds of buffalo, zebras, impala, wildebeest and antelope, as well as cheetahs, wild dogs and hyenas.

## On Screen

Arguably the most dramatic scene in the entire *Planet Earth* series is the coordinated hunting of an unfortunate elephant by hungry lions. One lion on its own would never stand a chance against such enormous prey, but this particular pride has adapted to harsh conditions in a marvellous way. For the first time on film, the *Planet Earth* crew captures this exceedingly rare hunting behaviour.

## When

The best time to visit Savuti is during the dry season (May to October) when seasonal waterways disappear and wildlife concentrates around a few scattered waterholes.

**(top) Lion with his Kill**
Lions are the only cats that live in groups. A pride will consist of related females and their offspring, and only a small number of males. Female cubs typically stay with the pride as they age.

**(bottom) African Bush Elephant**
African bush elephants are the largest living land mammals. The biggest ever recorded was a bull that weighed 10 tonnes and stood 4m at the shoulder.

FILMING VEHICLE DO NOT FOLLOW

# EXPERIENCE

You are awoken for your night safari – not by the sound of an alarm, but rather by the smell of percolating French-press coffee. You slide into your slippers, throw on a plush bathrobe and zip open the cavernous entrance to your canvas tent. Your caffeine fix lies waiting on a silver tray, along with what appear to be freshly baked chocolate-chip cookies. Camping has never been so glamorous.

A quick shower and change of clothes later, you greet your safari guide with a sleepy nod and jump into the sputtering Land Rover. Everyone is tired – there is no doubt about that – but when the engine roars to life and your guide shifts out of neutral, the adrenalin surges. In an instant, your eyes and ears sharpen, tuning in to the sights and sounds of the African bush.

Pulling out of camp you're immediately greeted by a herd of frightened impala. They sense danger, and the intrusion of your safari vehicle is most definitely the least of their concerns. Somewhere in the shadows, on this bright moonlit night, there is a pride of hungry lions stalking their next meal.

There they are. Evidence starting out as paw prints in the sand quickly gives way to the enormous feline that left them. A lioness scowls in your direction, but otherwise your arrival in their hunting grounds doesn't seem to cause the pride much alarm. Perhaps it's easy to forgive your human presence knowing that the main course is about to be served.

No matter how many safari videos you may have seen, nothing can prepare you for the raw display of nature that is a successful hunt. Often the prey is never aware that it is about to lose its life; other times the struggle to survive is fierce and inspiring. The hairs on the back of your neck stand at attention, and an emotional mix of awe and sympathy takes hold. On this particularly evening, the lions are intent on taking down an unsuspecting baby zebra. Despite the cries from its mother, the offspring's clumsy footing and weak defences prove no match for the seasoned killers.

When death comes in the wild, it is generally not pretty. The stillness of the savannah is punctuated by beastly screams and the sound of death throes. The lions waste no time, immediately gorging themselves in a fury of oozing blood, cracking bones and tearing flesh. Furry manes turn from a golden yellow to a deep cornelian. Your stomach turns, and the chocolate chip cookies are suddenly not sitting so well.

**Hippopotamus Amphibius**
Hippos spend the majority of their time in the water – including when giving birth, suckling their young and mating. They consume as much vegetation as they can during the night, and return to the water to digest when the sun rises.

# TAKING ACTION

## As You Saw It

Chobe National Park is home to the planet's largest concentration of elephants, numbering in the tens of thousands. Savuti is a section of the park with a unique hydrology and animals finding themselves here during the dry season have limited access to fresh water. The scarcity of resources that this results in drives lion prides to take on potentially dangerous animals, such as lone adult elephants.

While you should count yourself extremely lucky to witness an elephant-kill, lions on the hunt are a fairly common safari sight. There are a handful of luxury lodges in Savuti, any of which can arrange a guided safari. If you're sticking to a budget, cheaper mobile safaris pass through Savuti en route from Kasane to Maun.

## Adding to the Experience

The most famous stretch of the national park is the Chobe Riverfront, where you can abandon your 4WD cruiser in favour of a motorised pontoon. As you skim along the surface of the water, with crocs and hippos cruising alongside, you can watch as animals venture down to the river's edge to drink.

## Alternative Lion-Tracking Experiences

Southern Africa is lion country, particularly at the following national parks.

✿ **Etosha National Park** (Namibia) Centred on an enormous salt pan, Etosha offers the classic safari experience in arid surrounds.

✿ **Hwange National Park** (Zimbabwe) One of Zimbabwe's great safari parks, Hwange continues to offer stunning wildlife encounters despite the country's collapse.

✿ **Kruger National Park** (South Africa) The most famous safari park on the continent offers extremely well-developed tourist infrastructure.

# WHILE YOU'RE THERE

## Okavango Polers Trust

The Okavango Polers Trust (www.okavangodelta .co.bw) is a collective run entirely by the villagers of Seronga. All profits are shared by the workers, invested into the trust and used to provide the local community with better facilities. The main tourist activity on offer from the group is a guided tour of the Okavango Delta by *mokoro,* a traditional dug-out canoe. See p210 for more on this experience.

# THE SAVUTI CHANNEL

The Savuti Channel, which links the Savuti Marshes with the Okavango Delta, creates an oasis for thirsty wildlife herds and water birds. But, remarkably, this channel starts and stops flowing seemingly with lack of rhyme or reason; its flow appears to be independent of the Chobe River system. In 1925, when the river experienced record flooding levels, the Savuti Channel remained bone dry. At times the channel has even stopped flowing for years at a stretch (eg from 1888 to 1957, 1966 to 1967, and 1979 to the mid-1990s).

Some experts believe this phenomenon is due to plate tectonics. The ongoing northward shift of the Zambezi River and the frequent low-intensity earthquakes in the region reveal that the underlying geology is tectonically unstable. The flow of the Savuti Channel could therefore be governed by an imperceptible, gradual flexing of the surface crust. The minimum change required to open or close the channel is estimated to be at least 9m, and there's evidence that this has happened at least five times over the past century.

## GETTING YOU THERE

The traditional departure point for both overland and fly-in/fly-out safaris in Chobe National Park is the town of Kasane in northeastern Botswana. Several regional carriers, including South African Airways (www.flysaa.com), offer connections through regional hubs.

## EXPLORING SAVUTI

Savuti is accessed either by private charter aeroplane or specially outfitted 4WD vehicle – the operators listed here will arrange all of your transport.

✿ **Savute Safari Lodge** (www.desertdelta.com) The base camp in Savuti for Desert & Delta, which has been offering fully customisable safaris in Botswana for almost three decades.

✿ **Savute Elephant Camp** (www.orient-express.com) Savuti base camp for Orient-Express, an ultra-high-end operator offering specialised all-inclusive packages.

✿ **Dragoman** (www.dragoman.co.uk) This UK-based overland specialist offers numerous itineraries throughout the African continent.

## CHOBE NATIONAL PARK

Chobe National Park, which encompasses nearly 11,000 sq km, is understandably one of the country's greatest tourist attractions. After visiting the Chobe River in the 1930s, Sir Charles Rey, the Resident Commissioner of Bechuanaland, proposed that the entire region be set aside as a wildlife preserve. Although it was not officially protected until 1968, Chobe has the distinction of being Botswana's first national park.

## FAST FACTS

Chobe is one of the finest national parks for witnessing interactions between the super-predators. As competitors for the same resources, they share no affinity and encounters between them are typically hostile.

**Lions** By far the largest African carnivore, the lion sits largely unchallenged at the top of the pecking order. Lions usually kill anything they can, and that includes other large predators if they get hold of one.

**Hyenas** Adult lions in turn mostly only worry about other lions, but large hyena clans occasionally kill injured or young lions, and are certainly able to drive small prides off their kills. Hyenas also dominate the other hunters, often trailing lions on the hunt, hoping for a free meal.

**Leopards** Hyena clans dominate leopards, but individuals do so at their peril: leopards sometimes kill lone hyenas.

**Cheetahs** At the very bottom of the hierarchy, cheetahs have sacrificed brute force for speed and can't physically overpower the other super-predators; they cannot afford the risk of injury and invariably give way to other large predators, regardless of numbers.

# NORTH AMERICAN PRAIRIES

## Yellowstone National Park, Wyoming, USA

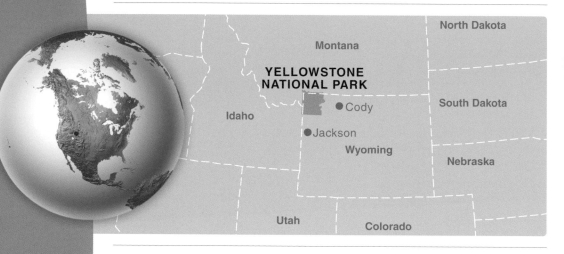

The state of Wyoming is an amazing natural healer – a few blissful days of road-tripping and your stress is swept away into the cloudless blue sky. For how can one stay depressed in a place where the snow-capped peaks, wildflower meadows and misty ponderosa forests are so beautiful they inspire artists to paint masterpieces and songwriters to pen classic tunes?

## On Screen

Sixty million bison once roamed the North American prairies. A century ago, however, rampant overhunting and uncontrolled loss of habitat shrunk the millions-strong herds to barely 1000. Today, thanks to rigorous governmental protection, the species is slowly but surely recovering. *Planet Earth* shows us dramatic aerial footage of herds on the move, as well as up-close shots of their courting behaviour.

## When

Yellowstone National Park is open year-round, but most roads close during winter. And when it comes to the park's bison, although they are there year-round, summer is the time for growth and reproduction. Weighing in at almost 1000kg, male bison in the high summer are fat from grazing and in top form; but only a few will mate, which is decided through dramatic courtship displays.

**Upper Falls, Yellowstone River**
As the Yellowstone River flows north from Yellowstone Lake, it plunges over the 33m-high Upper Falls and then, 400m downstream, over the 94m-high Lower Falls.

# EXPERIENCE

Cruising down Wyoming's backcountry roads, you momentarily give in to the temptation of song: 'Oh, give me a home, where the buffalo roam, and the deer and the antelope play. Where seldom is heard, a discouraging word, and the sky is not clouded all day'. Not your best performance by any stretch of the imagination, though fortunately there is no one around to criticise. Out here in the prairieland you're free to bask alone in the glory of wide-open space.

While human inhabitants may be in short supply, there are plenty of other mammals about. Several days of wildlife watching has thus far turned up sightings of rutting elk, pronghorn antelope and bighorn sheep – not to mention a whole lot of bison. They certainly grow their mammals big up in Yellowstone.

The 'American safari' experience certainly has its moments of excitement. Parked on the side of the road, taking a brief respite from driving, you scan the horizon. Success! A grizzly bear wanders into the viewfinder of your binoculars. And it looks like he (or she) is carrying lunch. As tempting as fresh rodent may sound, don't plan on sharing – grizzlies are formidable beasts that are best given a wide berth.

Minutes later you hear the bugle of a solitary male moose just before it dips its mighty head into the river for a drink. Feeling a fraternal connection with the largest extant member of the deer family, you take a swig of cold water from your canteen. The moose unfortunately doesn't seem to acknowledge your toast.

The main event out here, however, is the courting of the bison. At present they're hurling their massive bulk into one another in an attempt to garner the attention of receptive females. The deafening sound of muscled collisions echoes across the prairies, sending flocks of birds into the sky in search of cover. The bison momentarily pause to catch their breaths and regain their footing, only to once again slam heads and lock horns in combat.

You head on back to the visitors' centre to stretch your legs in relative safety, and tuck into a soft-serve ice cream cone. Just when you think life couldn't get any more fascinating, a low rumble followed by a violent eruption captures your full attention: cue Old Faithful, North America's most dependable geyser.

**Bison Bull Face Off**
Bison have very poor eyesight, but excellent hearing and smell, and can run up to 55km/h.

# TAKING ACTION

## As You Saw It

Yellowstone National Park boasts the lower 48 states' most motley concentration of wildlife, plus half the world's geysers. And when you factor in the plethora of alpine lakes, rivers and waterfalls, you'll quickly realise you've stumbled across one of Mother Nature's most fabulous creations.

Hayden Valley, at the heart of the park, is your best all-round bet for wildlife viewing. Get up early or stay out late, as dawn and dusk are the best times to see furry critters on the move. You can pull over anywhere off Grand Loop Rd and stage a stakeout.

Lamar Valley, in the north of the park, is ground zero for spotting wolves, as this is where they are being reintroduced. Ask rangers where the action is when you're there – catching a glimpse of these wild, shaggy giant dogs, previously pushed to the brink of extirpation, is an exhilarating experience.

## Adding to the Experience

Hikers can explore Yellowstone's back country from more than 85 trailheads giving access to 2000km of hiking trails. A free back-country permit, available at visitor centres and ranger stations, is required for overnight trips. Back-country camping is allowed in 300 designated sites, 60% of which can be reserved in advance.

## Alternative Great-Open-Space Experiences

The American West offers some of the grandest expanses of wide-open space.

✿ **Glacier National Park** (Montana) Home to more than 1000 different species of plants and animals, this is one of North America's most biodiverse areas. See p20 for more on hiking Glacier.

✿ **Grand Teton National Park** (Wyoming) This north–south range is an extension of the Rocky Mountains.

✿ **Rocky Mountain National Park** (Colorado) The Rocky Mountains comprises the tallest range in the continental US. For more on the Rockies, see p16.

# WHILE YOU'RE THERE

## Jackson

Jackson is as jet-setting as Wyoming gets. The handsome town – which many people incorrectly call Jackson Hole (the 'Hole' actually refers to the entire valley) – is set against a stellar backdrop of the Teton mountain range. It's the kind of place where cowboy meets couture: where moose, elk

## GEOLOGY OF YELLOWSTONE

Yellowstone National Park was established in 1872 to preserve the region's spectacular geography. The park itself is split into five regions (countries), representing the five distinct ecosystems found inside the boundaries.

✿ **Geyser Country** The most famous geothermal feature in Geyser Country is Old Faithful, which ejects 14,000L to 32,000L of water 30m into the air every 90 minutes or so.

✿ **Mammoth Country** Mammoth Country is North America's most volatile and oldest-known continuously active (115,000 years) thermal area.

✿ **Roosevelt Country** The highlights of Roosevelt Country, the park's most remote, scenic and undeveloped region, are the fossil forests and craggy peaks of the Absaroka Mountains and Tower Falls.

✿ **Canyon Country** A series of scenic overlooks and the 'Grand Canyon of the Yellowstone's' network of rim trails highlight the beauty of Canyon Country.

✿ **Lake Country** Yellowstone Lake, the centrepiece of Lake Country, is one of the world's largest alpine lakes.

and bison cruise the valley floor and powder hounds swish down world-class ski slopes. The vibe is playful and slightly glam, but never pretentious. Wander into the Mangy Moose Saloon, packed with ski bums, tourists, hipsters, ranchers and even the occasional movie star, and you'll get the idea. Jackson buzzes year-round; summer visitors can hike, bike, raft and roam to their heart's content.

## Cody

Cody, 84km east of Yellowstone, capitalises on its Wild West image (it's named after William F 'Buffalo Bill' Cody). With a streak of yeehaw, the town happily relays yarns (not always the whole story, mind you) about its past. Summer is high season, and Cody puts on quite an Old West show for the throngs of visitors making their way to Yellowstone. From Cody, the approach to geyserland is dramatic to say the least. US President Teddy Roosevelt once said this stretch of pavement was 'the most scenic 50 miles in the world'.

## Denver

Sitting at exactly 5280ft (1.7km) or one-mile high (hence the nickname 'Mile High City'), this one-time Wild West railway town is a cool place to acclimatise. Low on humidity and high on sunshine, the city is compact and friendly. Take a stroll down the pedestrian-only 16th St Mall or plop down at a chic sidewalk cafe in the trendy LoDo neighbourhood (which dates back to 1865) to soak up the effortless blend of cosmopolitan and Old West vibes.

## GETTING YOU THERE

The closest year-round airports to the national park are Yellowstone Regional Airport (COD) in Cody (90km) and Jackson Hole Airport (JAC) in Jackson (95km). However, it's often more affordable to fly into Salt Lake City, Utah (665km) or Denver, Colorado (955km), and then rent a car.

No public transport exists to or within Yellowstone, so touring in a private vehicle is best. But be warned – driving around Wyoming takes longer than it looks. Attractions are spread across long distances, and roads don't necessarily go in a straight line between points A and B. If there's a wilderness area or park – or a really long, deep canyon – in between, you'll have to go around. Services are also few and far between – when in doubt, fill up the tank.

## EXPLORING YELLOWSTONE

To explore the park you need an entrance permit, which can be obtained at the park's visitor centres and ranger stations and will be valid for entry into both Yellowstone and Grand Teton National Parks. Summer-only visitor centres are evenly spaced every 40km or so along Grand Loop Rd.

## FAST FACTS

Wyoming is nicknamed the Equality State, and the Cowboy State.

The population of Wyoming is 532,688, it encompasses 253,325 sq km and its capital city is Cheyenne (pop 55,314).

Wyoming is the birthplace of abstract expressionist artist Jackson Pollock (1912–56), and the home of former vice president Dick Cheney.

Wyoming is famous for Yellowstone National Park, agriculture and dude ranches, and is USA's biggest producer of coal.

# LIFE ON THE HIGHEST PLAIN

Tibetan Plateau

**(left) Trekkers Heading Towards Mt Everest North Base Camp**
There are two base camps on opposite sides of Mt Everest: South Base Camp in Nepal and North Base Camp in Tibet. North Base Camp is used when climbing via Everest's northeast ridge.

**(right) Plateau Pika**
Long considered a pest, scientists now believe the pika is a keystone species for the biodiversity of the Tibetan Plateau. A keystone species is one that has a disproportionately strong influence within an ecosystem, such that its removal results in ecosystem destabilisation and can lead to further species losses.

The Tibetan Plateau is inhospitable, stark and challenging; parts of it are only marginally more populated than Antarctica and Greenland. But these facts make it all the more impressive, in terms of both the truly wild landscapes and the hardy creatures that manage to survive in them.

## On Screen
Snow-dusted (even in summer), oxygen-starved and dry as a bone, the high plains of Tibet are hostile in the extreme. Yet the *Planet Earth* crew are able to find life – and plenty of it – in this parched brown land, from oddball wild asses to stoic yaks to one of the rabbit's fluffiest cousins – the pika.

## When
Visit the Tibetan Plateau in summer, when temperatures are not quite so chilly (in winter it can plummet to -40°C) and mountain passes are more likely to be open. Avoid travelling in March: the anniversary of the 1959 Tibetan uprising is a politically sensitive time, and could make entry into the region difficult.

IAN CUMMING/PHOTOLIBRARY

W K FLETCHER/PHOTOLIBRARY

# EXPERIENCE

You wheeze in the pathetically thin air; being transported to the Tibetan Plateau – average altitude around 4500m – is like aging overnight or trying to run after smoking a pack of cigarettes. And it's cold – barely above freezing – despite the fact it's summer. A chill mist rolls off the hills and, in places, snow still covers the ground, a sparkling carpet under which precious tendrils of grass quiver.

Precious because there are, remarkably, animals up here to eat it. You are watching a herd of yaks out on the plain, plodding in front of a meringue-whip of snowy mountains. The beasts bow now and then to nibble the scrub, and seem quite unperturbed by the harsh winds – well, why would they be? They're sporting great tufts of hair along their flanks, a woolly pelmet perfect for keeping the legs toasty.

And it's not just the yaks that like it here. In the distance, between the tornadolike swirls of a couple of dust devils, two galloping wild asses emerge from a puff of kicked-up earth. These rusty brown, flat-faced males are fighting it out for the best territory to entice the ladies, and biting lumps out of each other in the process. The females themselves don't look especially impressed as they roll in the dirt and clop along in a posse, like a band of girlfriends out on the town. Instead of showing the boys much attention, they head off to a nearby oasis for a quick drink, before tottering home again.

But what catches your eye most are the fluffy pikas – less rock rabbits than wigs with faces. They snuffle about the ground trying to graze, but looking generally too terrified to eat much – and justifiably so. For stalking along the sidelines is a Tibetan fox, looking rather arrogant and imperious as the wind ruffles his handsome russet-grey fur. His narrowed eyes are on his prey; gradually the fox lowers his stocky body and, with square head and back held straight and stiff, trots stealthily towards his hairy would-be lunch.

The poor pika. You're on its side – it looks so frightened. And just when you think it's got away from the hungry fox the resourceful predator digs into the rock rabbit's underground burrow and wrenches it out, legs still twitching, mouth emitting a pitiful squeak. As the fox pads off, mouth full, you feel for his victim. As if life on the barren and wind-blasted Tibetan Plateau wasn't hard enough.

That night, as you lay in your camp, safely inside your own human burrow, you can't get it out of your head: the poor rock rabbit's final cry.

**Yaks in the Lhasa River Valley**
*Bö cha* (yak-butter tea; made with tea leaves, yak butter and salt) is part of the staple diet for Tibetans. It's warming, provides lots of caloric energy and helps prevent chapped lips.

"*The great Himalayan range blocks clouds moving in from the south – casting a giant rain shadow that leaves Tibet high and dry.*"

# TAKING ACTION

## As You Saw It

In 2009 the European Commission's Joint Research Centre mapped the world's 'connectedness', based on how long it would take to travel from any given point by land or water to the nearest city with a population of 50,000 or more. The Tibetan Plateau was revealed as the planet's most remote location; the capital, Lhasa, is a three-week journey away. So, your first challenge in re-creating the *Planet Earth* experience is accessing this wilderness.

Pikas are extremely small compared to the plateau's enormity – it covers 2.5 million sq km, making a little pika like a needle in several thousand haystacks. However, they are many. So if you can get there, and brave the chill, finding pikas should be fairly straightforward. You're quite likely to see (and hear) these squealing fluff-balls perched up on the rocks. You will probably also encounter herds of domesticated yaks – not quite as big as their wild cousins, but impressive nonetheless.

## Adding to the Experience

Try to plan a multiday trek in Tibet to maximise your chances of seeing the wildlife. This will also give you time to visit some of the region's remote mountain monasteries and meet the hard-as-nails monks and nomads who live in this hostile environment. But do remember that trekking in Tibet requires good preparation – pretty much everywhere is remote, so you need adequate supplies and transport. Also, everywhere is high; you need to be physically fit and well acclimatised to the altitude before setting out.

Independent trekking is not permitted, but if you go to a local Tibetan operator and tell them what you want to do, they can arrange a bespoke guided itinerary for you.

## Alternative High-Altitude Experiences

The Tibetan Plateau is the highest and biggest great plain on the planet. But there are many other lofty wildernesses worldwide.

✿ **Altiplano** (Bolivia) Average elevation 4000m; with multicoloured lakes swamped with feeding flamingos.

✿ **Bale Mountains National Park** (Ethiopia) Average elevation over 4000m; with endemic species such as the mountain nyala (a type of antelope) and Simien fox.

✿ **Colorado Plateau** (USA) Average elevation around 1500m; with a bevy of brilliant rock formations, including the Grand Canyon, the hoodoos of Zion National Park and the cliff dwellings of Mesa Verde.

## THE GREAT TRAIN CONTROVERSY

The wild Tibetan Plateau was finally tamed in 2006 when the Qīnghǎi–Tibet railway line opened, trundling for 1956km across this harsh wilderness from Golmud to Lhasa. It's an engineering masterpiece: 86% of the track looms above 4000m, there are 160km of bridges and seven tunnels (including the world's highest), and a complex cooling system ensures the whole thing doesn't sink into summer-thawing permafrost.

The train is one of the easiest ways to get some grasp of the scale and drama of the Tibetan Plateau; you might even spot wild asses and foxes from your carriage window.

While the Chinese are rightfully swollen with pride over this engineering marvel, the Tibetans aren't quite sure what to think. The railway will bring cheaper goods and greater economic growth, but it will also increase Chinese Han migration. Symbolically it is also like a 'Made in China' label tagged to the Tibetan landscape.

# WHILE YOU'RE THERE

## Lhasa
Acclimatise in Tibet's capital, perched at a breathy 3595m. Enter the enormous, if soulless, Potala Palace; join the pilgrims at the Jokhang, the most revered religious building in Tibet; and barter for yak butter at Tromsikhang Market.

## Everest Base Camp
For sublime views of the world's highest mountain, trek to the Tibetan base camp (5150m). The hike in from Dìngrì takes three to four days; wild ass may be spotted en route.

## Nam Tso
This turquoise lake, backed by mountains and surrounded by the camps of Tibetan nomads, is 240km northwest of Lhasa. Acclimatise before you visit; the lake is at an altitude of 4730m and altitude sickness is common.

## Tashi Lhunpo Monastery
More a walled town than a simple monastery, Tashi Lhunpo (3840m) survived the Chinese Cultural Revolution fairly unscathed – an authentic insight into ancient Tibetan Buddhism.

# GETTING YOU THERE

Getting into Tibet can be tricky. Political machinations mean visa and permit regulations can change on a whim; always check the current situation before travelling. You will probably need to join a tour to get to Lhasa. Once in, independent travel may be possible. To get out to the wilder reaches of the plateau will require local knowledge and some sturdy boots – transport options are limited, co in many areas walking will be the only option.

# EXPLORING THE TIBETAN PLATEAU

Lhasa-based Shangrila Tours (www.shangrilatours.com) and Visit Tibet Travel & Tours (www.visittibet.com) offer various trips across the plateau. Another option is to hire a Land Cruiser and driver (foreigners are not allowed to drive in Tibet), enabling you to dictate your own itinerary. This can be economical if you join together with other travellers. Make sure you agree your route and the price, in writing, before you set off.

## FAST FACTS

An estimated one million wild yaks roamed the Tibetan Plateau around 50 years ago; today numbers have dwindled to just 15,000, due to a boom in hunting.

Yaks have three times more red blood cells than an average cow, and one or two more pairs of ribs; these adaptations allow the yak to breathe more easily in the thinner, high-altitude air.

The pika has been spotted living at over 5000m on the slopes of Mt Everest – the highest habitat of any mammal.

The Tibetan Plateau is bounded by desert to the north and the Himalaya, Karakoram and Pamir mountain chains to the south and west.

# MAKING A HOME IN A FOREST OF GRASS
## Himalayan Foothills, Northern India

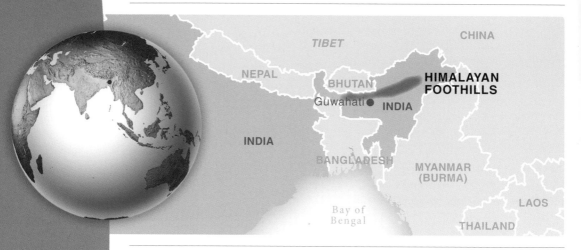

The adventure is in exploring near-blind – probing into an environment hosting some of the planet's rarest creatures, but being barely able to see the nose in front of your face. You might stumble upon a pygmy hog, an armoured rhino or a bird leaping in a bizarre courtship ritual; but the thrill is not so much in what you find as in getting lost yourself.

## On Screen

This is grass, but not as you know it. The clue's in the name: elephant grass. This Brobdingnagian plant forms dense, thick-pile carpets across swaths of the tropical plains of India and Nepal's southern Terai region. *Planet Earth* leads you among the long blades, uncovering the creatures great and (very) small lurking in the moist grasslands.

## When

The monsoon that sweeps across the region waters the grasses most heavily from late May to September, when florican courtship displays also peak. October and November are good times to delve in among the still-lofty grass, though wildlife is often more visible later in the cycle, because grass is burned off in December or January, and new shoots in February lure animals out into the open.

### Suru River Valley
The glacier-fed Suru River forms the western and northern boundaries of the Zanskar mountain range. The river's catchment has been carved by glaciers, both past and present.

# EXPERIENCE

The endless green around you is thirsty. Among the jungle of grass, soaring above your head and all around, the rain droplets play their percussive part in the symphony of the monsoon; the tapping of the beads as they patter on the long blades punctuates the steady hum of insects and birds.

Then, as suddenly as it broke, the storm moves away; birds break into energetic song as the downpour thins, and the sun burns through the haze to create a layer of mist that drifts over the emerald swaths. You dry off quickly in the powerful warmth of the tropical sun, and push ahead through the dense leaves, sniffing the steamy air as the droplets evaporate around you. In this extreme tropical climate, you're growing accustomed to the constant contrasts – drenched one moment, sweltering in the searing sun the next.

You halt abruptly as a violent rustle and guttural rumble ahead vaunt the arrival of the neighbourhood heavyweight: the elephant. And another; then two small-scale models – an idealised family unit of mum, dad and two kids. Veined ears flap as they amble in leisurely fashion through the leaves that also provide their picnic, plucked on the move. They vanish off into grass stands even higher than themselves, a swaying of the topmost leaves betraying their path. This tightly packed forest of grass hides everything.

But what if you don't want to be hidden? You're startled as a crazed-looking black-and-white bundle shoots vertically out of the undergrowth ahead, propelled by a brief, frantic burst of flapping before falling back into the sea of green. The male florican, delicate head-plumes splayed in a halo behind his swivelling head, is on the lookout for love. If a series of pronking leaps is what's needed to rise above the competition (and the camouflage), that's what he'll do. Sadly, no eligible ladies are on hand to be impressed by his aerial prowess. Instead it captures the attention – albeit momentarily – of a less-suitable mate: a rhino, wrinkled and myopic, watchfully guarding her young. A flick of her ears and a low grunt signal the end of the show, and normal masticating service is resumed; chewing endlessly, the rhinos lumber on to the next patch of verdant chow.

This much grass – and this big – feeds many huge animals, but it's more than mere fodder. A dark scuttling at the foot of a nearby stand catches your eye: a gaggle of pygmy hogs, no bigger than rabbits, chattering as they root around among the stems. One grabs a sheaf of dry leaves to extend her nest. Watch carefully and you'll see a pinkish-grey piglet, tiny enough to fit in the palm of your hand, totter out of the nest and along a fallen branch, sniffing inquisitively, before returning to mum and the safety of the litter.

**Elephant Safari, Kaziranga National Park**
A World Heritage Site, Kaziranga National Park is inhabited by the world's largest population of one-horned rhinoceroses.

*"The long-grass plains of tropical India are home to some of the largest grass-eating mammals on planet earth."*

# TAKING ACTION

## As You Saw It

The monsoon waters grass-clad plains across the north of the subcontinent. Manas National Park in Assam, northeast India, supports the world's only viable population of pygmy hogs, as well as Asian elephants, Indian rhinos and Bengal floricans. Rhino encounters are more likely in nearby Kaziranga National Park, home to around 1800 of the tanklike beasts – some two-thirds of the globe's total. Both parks also host tigers and a plethora of other animal and bird species. You're more likely to spot the endangered lesser florican displaying further west in Gujarat or parts of Rajasthan, Madhya Pradesh or Maharashtra.

## Adding to the Experience

As in most Indian parks, jeep safaris or elephant-back jaunts are the norm to reach the richest areas for wildlife spotting – book through your lodge or the park office. In Manas it may be possible (though not necessarily comfortable) to arrange multiday elephant-back safaris; rafting trips offer another perspective. You can undertake walking safaris in some parks, including Nameri National Park, where leopard sightings are possible.

## Alternative Rhino-Spotting Experiences

All species of Asian rhino are endangered; even if they weren't, an encounter with such a huge beast in the wild would be unforgettable. Other places to look out for them include:

✿ **Chitwan National Park** (Nepal) A population of over 600 rhinos offers a good chance of a meeting.

✿ **Jaldapara Wildlife Sanctuary** (West Bengal, India) A small reserve with a fairly good rhino density.

✿ **Endau-Rompin National Park** (Malaysia) An ancient forest with a small population of Sumatran rhinos – though you'd be incredibly fortunate to spot one.

✿ **Tabin Wildlife Reserve** (Sabah, Malaysian Borneo) There's a herd of Sumatran rhinos here – again, they're rarely seen, but an elephant encounter is possible.

# WHILE YOU'RE THERE

## Brahmaputra River Cruise

This vast, sacred river bisects Assam; take a luxurious cruise or just hop on a ferry to go with (or across) the flow. If you're really lucky you might spot a rare, blind Gangetic dolphin – January's the

## AND ALL BECAUSE THE LADY LOVES...RHINOS

Kaziranga National Park is one of the success stories of Indian conservation, and like so many great ideas its conception owes much to the influence of the woman behind a powerful man.

In 1904 Baroness Mary Curzon, American wife of the Indian viceroy Lord George Curzon, visited the Kaziranga area. Before the arrival of the British in the early 19th century rhinos were widespread in the region, but after decades of heavy hunting – some hunters reputedly shot over 100 animals each – only a handful remained in the district by the time of Baroness Curzon's visit. She failed to spot a single rhino; glimpses of footprints were the closest she came. Concerned for their survival, she pressed her husband to take action; the reserve that he subsequently proposed was created in June 1905, with an initial area of 232 sq km.

Despite sporadic poaching, rhino numbers have increased steadily, and it's now believed around 1800 roam the park.

best time.

## Majuli Island

The world's largest river island is a mass of shifting sandbanks, water meadows, rice fields and Hindu monasteries – visit at dawn or dusk for a chance of taking in some traditional dancing or chanting.

## Tea Plantations

Roam the tea plantations around Jorhat and experience colonial-style living at a heritage estate – try lounging on the antique furniture and verandahs of Sangsua (www.heritagetourismindia.com).

## Drive to Little Tibet

If you can wangle a permit, a visit to Tawang is a highlight of this area. Over the border from Assam, in Arunachal Pradesh state, Tawang is a restricted area for which all visitors (including Indian citizens) require a permit to visit. Buddhist gompas – especially the impressive medieval citadel Tawang Gompa – reflect the proximity of Tibet. Even if you don't swing the permit, the drive up to the border is picturesque.

# GETTING YOU THERE

Barpeta Rd, the most convenient point of entry for Manas, is on the train line to Assam's state capital, Guwahati (three hours). Buses from Guwahati reach Kaziranga in six hours; overnight or multiday tours to Kaziranga are easily arranged in Guwahati.

# EXPLORING KAZIRANGA

Wild Grass (www.oldassam.com) is an ecofriendly lodge with expert naturalists on hand to help plan your Kaziranga exploration.

## FAST FACTS

Elephant grass can grow several metres high.

Kaziranga's 430 sq km hosts over 450 bird species, as well as boasting what is reputedly India's greatest tiger density (roughly 30 per 100 sq km) and the world's longest venomous snakes – the king cobra, which grows up to 5.6m.

The Indian rhino can weigh up to 3500kg and has a gestation period of almost 16 months.

Assam has 655 plantations, from which over half of India's tea is produced – around 500,000 tonnes annually.

The pygmy hog is the world's smallest and rarest pig – there may be fewer than 150 surviving in the wild.

# GLIDE THROUGH AN INLAND ESTUARY
## Okavango Delta, Botswana

**(left) Navigating the Marshes**
*Mekoro* were introduced to the Okavango area by the people of the Bayei tribe, who used them as a traditional means of transport.

**(right) Botswana's Elephants**
Northern Botswana contains Africa's largest contiguous savannah population of elephants. In the dry season, the population concentrates near the main permanent water sources, including the Okavango Delta.

The Okavango Delta is unique in many respects, not least its wealth of wildlife. Here you can spot all of the Big Five (lions, leopards, buffalo, elephants and rhinos) as well as most of the other key game species and some specialities – the endangered African hunting dog roams protected areas.

## On Screen
The rainy season in Angola pumps huge volumes of water down the tributaries that feed the mighty Okavango River, and into the 16,000-sq-km expanse of this vast inland delta. *Planet Earth* showcases the wildlife that thrives in this verdant oasis in the Kalahari, from playful elephants and herds of rare red lechwe and sitatungas to the troupes of baboons for whom the flood brings soggy toes.

## When
There's no bad time to be in the Okavango Delta, though summer rains (late December to March) make road transport sludgy and see some protected areas closed. Floods, resulting from rains far upstream in Angola, sweep through the delta through the winter, which coincides with the dry season (July to October). Wildlife watching is at its best in September and October, which are also hot and humid; low-season visits can still be fruitful, though, and are significantly cheaper.

GUIZIOU FRANCK/PHOTOLIBRARY

GREGORY MD/PHOTOLIBRARY

# EXPERIENCE

You lower yourself gingerly into the *mokoro;* this simple canoe –
hewn from a single sausage-tree log – feels about as stable as
a greased barrel in the shallow waters. Your poler steps lightly
aboard, chuckling as you grip the *mokoro's* sides in panic at the
slight rolling motion. Then he dips his *ngashi* (pole) and pushes –
and away you glide. Instantly you relax – it's serenity redefined. It
even smells peaceful – like a riverbank on a still afternoon.

At first there's little to see above the tall reeds and grass stems,
but the very sensation of being afloat in this watery wonderland is
immersive in itself. You're mesmerised by the gentle, rhythmic splash
of the punting and the hypnotic trill of the ubiquitous frogs.

In low tones barely louder than a whisper, your laconic poler makes
observations, nodding his head to left and right as he speaks. What
you take at first to be a swaying palm breaking the flat of the horizon
proves to be the lolloping shape of a lone giraffe; in the distance you
hear the splashes of an elephant herd, while flashes of vivid colour
announce the swoops of lilac-breasted rollers. The heat rises as the
day builds and you're tempted to dangle your hand in the cool water –
till you're reminded that logs aren't always just logs: Nile crocodiles
(and their snapping maws) lurk among the papyrus and reeds.

To starboard – you're thinking in nautical terms, even though the
water is only half a metre or less deep – a group of small, dark shapes
splashes into view: a troupe of chacma baboons. Paddling through
the shallows, they're hilarious. Arms held high, bobbing up and down
as they pick their way between the reeds, they look like *Thunderbirds*
puppets, or prim Victorian ladies holding up their skirts to keep the
hems from getting wet. As they splash towards you the baboons reach
out to pluck blossoms and tender grass shoots, eating on the move.

A tiny infant clings to its mother's belly; as she lopes forward, its
back is dipped in and out of the water. Tired of the repeated dunkings,
the baby hauls itself up mum's flanks to find a drier perch on her back;
from there it can reach down and pick the tips of stems, while mum
munches on a juicy snail she's found among the rushes.

It's feast time in the delta. Even if living high means getting your
paws wet.

**Okavango River**
In 1994 Angola, Botswana and Namibia entered
into an agreement for the establishment of
the Permanent Okavango River Basin Water
Commission (Okacom), committing the member
states to promote coordinated and environmentally sustainable regional water resource
development.

# TAKING ACTION

## As You Saw It

*Mokoro* safaris can be arranged independently, either with agents in Maun (the main town to the southeast) or, in the northwest of the delta, through the Seronga-based Okavango Polers Trust (www.okavangodelta.co.bw), a cooperative organisation benefiting local communities.

If you're staying at one of the upmarket accommodation options in the delta itself, *mokoro* trips are usually arranged by your lodge or camp as part of the (inevitably expensive) package.

## Adding to the Experience

*Mokoro* trips aren't the only way of exploring the delta; indeed, most *mokoro* safaris include stretches of walking on the palm-shaded islands and dry patches rising above the floods, enabling you to get closer to species less keen on damp feet. Horse-riding safaris into the delta can also be arranged – try African Animal Adventure Safaris (www.africananimaladventures.com). You'll also want to take at least one scenic flight over the delta to grasp the scale of the flooding. If you're staying in the delta itself, chances are you'll be flying in anyway; otherwise, there are numerous operators at Maun's airport offering scenic flights.

## Alternative Wetlands Experiences

Wetland regions around the planet offer a range of wildlife-watching opportunities.

✿ **Pantanal** (Brazil) For capybara, profuse birdlife and a (relatively) high chance of spotting a jaguar. See p72.

✿ **Sundarbans National Park** (Bangladesh) Mangrove swamps with a population of notorious man-eating tigers. See p78.

✿ **Esteros del Iberá** (northern Argentina) Wetlands with coypus, caymans and dizzying birdlife.

✿ **Camargue** (southern France) For wild horses and flamingos.

✿ **Mai Po Marshes** (Hong Kong) For the spectacle of thousands of birds taking off simultaneously at high tide.

# WHILE YOU'RE THERE

## Chobe National Park

Famous for its vast herds of elephants, Chobe National Park is also home to most other big game animals – hippos, cheetahs and lions are common sights along the river. See p182 for more on Chobe.

## Kalahari

Known to the Tswana people as Kgalagadi (Land of Thirst), the desert that defines this region is arid, empty and mind-expanding. Head into the 52,000-sq-km Central Kalahari Game Reserve, and keep an eye out for brown hyenas.

## WHAT'S IN A NAME?

The systems of names, peoples and languages in Botswana are, to say the least, tricksy. Here's a quick primer – try to keep up…

The people of Botswana, of whatever tribal or ethnic background, are known as Batswana (that's the plural, a single person from Botswana is Motswana). The word means 'people' *(ba)* of Tswana, which is both the dominant tribal group and the most common language (also known as Setswana). So Batswana can mean either 'people of Botswana' or 'people from the Tswana tribe'.

All clear? Good. Now, just bear in mind that almost 30 other tribal tongues, as well as languages imported with immigrants, are spoken around Botswana – we won't even start with the click languages of San peoples such as the !Kung, G||wi and !xo…

### Tsodilo Hills

The ochre and white rock paintings here were created by ancestral San artists in the late Stone Age – or, according to legend, even further back in the mists of time.

### San People

The raw wilderness dominating Botswana's interior is a harsh, extreme environment; meet the San people of D'kar to learn more about how this ancient culture has adapted to the habitat.

### Makgadikgadi Pans

The planet's largest area of salt pans is a mesmerising landscape of dazzling white patches. Surprisingly, game populations inhabit the seemingly inhospitable environment; spot ostriches, elephants and much more as the spring rains arrive.

## GETTING YOU THERE

Maun (pronounced Mau-UUn) is the main town serving as an access point for the Okavango Delta. You can fly to Maun from Botswana's capital, Gaborone; or fly from Kasane, on the border with Zimbabwe and Zambia near Victoria Falls, with Air Botswana (www.airbotswana.co.bw). Alternatively, get to Maun by bus or combi – from Gaborone you'll need to change at either Francistown or (for a longer route) Ghanzi; the journey takes upwards of 11 hours. Air Botswana also links Maun with Johannesburg (South Africa), while Air Namibia (www.airnamibia.com.na) flies between Windhoek (Namibia) and Maun.

## EXPLORING THE OKAVANGO DELTA

The Okavango Delta is one of the planet's finest wildlife-watching spots, partly because it's neither easy nor cheap to reach – certainly not both. The most straightforward way to access the really wild wildlife hot spots is also the most expensive: book a package with one of the lodges or camps in the Inner Delta or Moremi Game Reserve. Packages usually include (very good) food, wine and beer, activities such as *mokoro* safaris and extremely luxurious accommodation in game-rich areas. Independent travellers can arrange *mokoro* trips from Maun or Seronga, explore the eastern delta by 4WD (your own or through a tour agency) and settle in at camps run by the Department of Wildlife & National Parks (DWNP), which also takes daily park entrance fees.

# JUNGLES
## Planet Earth, Episode Eight

Welcome to the planet's wildest wildlife party, where
the dress code errs on flamboyant, and your chances
of getting any sleep are slight – the chirruping, howling,
hissing and buzzing will go on all night long. This is
nature's biggest bash: jungles cover around 3% of
the planet yet contain 50% of its species, a heaving
menagerie ranging from microscopic bugs to massive
cats via a rich profusion of plants. Though the wealth of
life is astonishing, it can be hard to see through all that
green – but when you do glimpse a bird of paradise
flaunting its feathers or a chimp levelling its so-human
gaze at yours, you'll feel like part of the party.

# BIRDS OF PARADISE
## New Guinea

In the dripping highlands of New Guinea, the hirsute mess of forest provides a stage for one of the most colourful and striking wildlife courtship rituals. The males from almost 40 kinds of birds of paradise dance, sing, strut, flare and flounce to impress potential mates. Just as impressive is the rainforest itself – a single hectare of forest here contains up to 250 different plant and tree species.

## On Screen
On *Planet Earth* you watch birds of paradise perform their ritual rhythmic mating dances, and see rainforest plants race to make use of a brief intrusion of sunlight in the wake of a fallen giant.

## When
The one guarantee in a highland rainforest is rain – in extreme rainfall areas, such as West New Britain province or the northern areas of the Gulf and Western provinces of Papua New Guinea (PNG), the annual rainfall can average more than 8m a year. New Guinea's driest season is from May to October. The birds of paradise are best seen between July and October when their plumage is at its zenith.

**Sepik River**
There are no major urban settlements or mining and forestry activities in the Sepik River catchment area, allowing the river to remain largely unpolluted. The river is a source of food and transport, and part of the culture of local villagers.

# EXPERIENCE

In the highland dawn, the forest chorus has started; the mountainside rings with birdsong. Pockets of warm mist rise like steam from the valleys below, and the sky is heavy (as always) with the promise of rain. In the natural enclosure of the rainforest, the song makers are rarely visible, hidden among the tangle of shrubs, creepers and 50m-high hardwoods.

You stop and wait, as patient as nature itself, for only this way might you witness the ornithological dances you have trekked to see: the courtship rituals of the birds of paradise – birds flashier than a flamenco dancer and with more mating moves than a Rio nightclub.

If you are lucky, the show will come to you. Your fingers are crossed that you might see a six-plumed bird of paradise displaying on the forest floor in a space cleared specially for the show, its body turned out like a skirt as its performance begins. Or a Magnificent bird of paradise, which might be glimpsed in the lower branches, its love song ticking through the forest, its yellow belly proudly puffed out for its more immediate audience – a female of its species.

Most activity, however, is taking place frustratingly out of sight, high in the canopy – a thick ceiling of leaves and branches that allows little more than 2% of the available sunlight to reach the forest floor. As you walk on, stepping around the arms of vines and creepers, a tall hardwood tree lies fallen and broken on the ground. You blink in the sunlight that suddenly streams through the hole created in the canopy by this stricken giant.

Around it the race for life has begun, with vines and other climbers scrambling and groping towards the light, seedlings suddenly sprouting from the forest floor. Stand for a few minutes and it seems almost as though you can see the macarangas – the racing cars of this forest – expanding, for they will grow around 8m a year, or about 2cm a day, while this light pours in.

Eventually the slow-growing hardwoods will emerge victorious, their tops closing in the canopy once again. And up there, out of sight but in earshot, you just know the aptly named birds of paradise are preparing for another courtship performance.

**Goldie's Birds of Paradise**
Discovered by Scottish collector Andrew Goldie in 1882, the Goldie's bird of paradise is classified as Near Threatened on the IUCN Red List of Threatened Species, due to ongoing habitat loss, limited range and hunting.

*"The island of New Guinea
harbours nearly 40 varieties
of birds of paradise – each
with a display more bizarre
than the last."*

# TAKING ACTION

## As You Saw It

To see the mountain forests, a crash course in local language will be handy, because you will need to enlist the skills of an experienced New Guinean bushman. Such guides are often men from the older generation who speak no English, with the younger generations spending less and less time in the forest. One of the best places to spot birds of paradise – and first brought to world attention by the 1990s BBC series *Attenborough in Paradise* – is the Tari Basin.

## Adding to the Experience

To add an adventurous edge to your bird search, try a journey along the 1126km-long Sepik River in a dugout motor-canoe. One of the world's great rivers, the trip along the Sepik will introduce you to complex local cultures and potent imagery, such as the towering facades of spirit houses, all as you keep an eye out for birds of paradise along the banks.

## Alternative Bird of Paradise Experiences

New Guinea is ground zero for birds of paradise, but they can also be found in parts of Australia and Indonesia. Australia's three species are known as riflebirds, with Victoria's riflebird the most commonly sighted; in north Queensland riflebirds sometimes visit cafes near rainforest for handouts. The Atherton Tableland and the Paluma Range and Daintree National Parks are among the best spots in north Queensland for sighting riflebirds.

# WHILE YOU'RE THERE

## Goroka Show

The Goroka Show is held over the Independence Day weekend (mid-September) at the National Sports Institute in Goroka, PNG. The show attracts *singsing* groups, bands and other cultural activities, as well as having some elements of an agricultural show. It is the glamour event on the

## WIGMEN

The area around Tari is one of the few in Papua New Guinea where some people still wear traditional dress, including the famous Huli wigmen, whose traditional dress is very distinctive. The Huli are the largest ethnic group in the Southern Highlands, with a population of around 55,000 and territory exceeding 2500 sq km. Huli don't live in villages, but in scattered homesteads dispersed through immaculately and intensively cultivated valleys. Their gardens are delineated by trenches and mud walls up to 3m high, broken by brightly painted gateways made of stakes. The women do most of the work, while men concentrate on displaying their finery, plotting war and growing their hair.

Traditional Huli culture is highly developed and strikingly executed in dress and personal decoration. Huli men wear decorative woven wigs of human hair. The hair is the wigman's own, grown before he is married, while living for months with other unmarried men in isolation from the rest of their community. Under the tutelage and guidance of a master wigman, spells are cast, diets are restricted and rituals adhered to – all to ensure a healthy head of hair. Many Huli wigmen have more than one wig, but all must be grown before the man marries. Designs are indicative of a wigman's tribe. The Huli cultivate yellow, everlasting daisies that are used to decorate their wigs; they also use feathers and cuscus fur.

Huli men also wear a band of snakeskin across the forehead, and usually a cassowary quill through the nasal septum. Their faces are decorated with yellow and red ochre; kina shells are worn around the neck; a decorative belt and *bilum* cloth cover the privates; and the rear is covered by a bunch of leaves attached to a belt (known collectively as a *tanket* or *arse gras*).

social calendar for many performers – it's extraordinary how many feathers one person can squeeze onto a headdress.

## Crater Mountain Wildlife Management Area

This is one of the best places in PNG to experience the spectacular countryside, wildlife and village culture. The area encompasses 2700 sq km, ranging from lowland tropical rainforests on the Purari River to alpine grasses on the slopes of Crater Mountain. You can hike between the various villages, but it's serious trekking.

## Mt Wilhelm

For many, climbing to the 4509m summit of Mt Wilhelm, PNG's highest peak, is the highlight of a highlands trip. On a clear day you can see both the north and south coasts of New Guinea. If the weather is fine, the climb takes three or four days, but frequently the weather causes delays. Don't try to climb the mountain on your own no matter how fit you are – a guide is essential.

# GETTING YOU THERE

Air Niugini (www.airniugini.com.pg) flies from the PNG capital, Port Moresby, to Tari on Monday, Friday and Sunday. PMV buses leave Tari early each morning (excluding Sunday) for Mt Hagen via Mendi. There are flights into Port Moresby from Australia, Fiji, the Solomon Islands and several Asian hubs.

# EXPLORING THE NEW GUINEA RAINFOREST

A couple of highland lodges are well geared towards birdwatchers.

✿ **Kumul Lodge** (www.kumullodge.com.pg) You can see birds of paradise in the grounds of this lodge, 40 minutes from Mt Hagen. The bungalows are built from bush materials and have large windows and balconies overlooking the surrounding forest. It offers guided walks up the mountain for birders.

✿ **Ambua Lodge** (www.pngtours.com) This lodge offers commanding views across the Tari Basin and Huli homelands. In 2001 it was listed as one of the 10 best ecotourism facilities worldwide by *National Geographic Adventure* magazine. At 2100m, the lodge enjoys a refreshing mountain climate and attracts many birdwatchers and orchid enthusiasts.

## FAST FACTS

Bird of paradise courtship displays can last for hours.

European explorers didn't make it into New Guinea's rugged interior until the 1930s; they expected unbroken forest, but found heavily cultivated valleys and more than 1 million people.

There are more than 700 recorded bird species in Papua New Guinea, around half of which are endemic.

# RAINFOREST HIKING
## The Amazon, South America

Everyone has fantasised about a hiking trip through the Amazon in search of epic wonderment. But in a rainforest this legendary it's actually the little things that make it special. Give it some time, forget your preconceived notions, and the Amazon cannot fail to impress.

## On Screen

*Planet Earth* shows us that the Amazon is both large and small, from the mighty Amazon River and its botos (freshwater dolphins), right down to the tiniest ants and microscopic fungal spores. Its quintessential experiences are more sublime than they are superlative: hiking beneath dense forest canopies that shroud out the tropical sun, keeping step with the signature calls of birds and insects, and contemplating the massive networks of complex interactions that keep the whole system functioning.

## When

The Amazon has two seasons, rainy and dry. The rainy season runs from December to June, with temperatures ranging from 23°C to 30°C, and almost daily rains in April and May. The dry season lasts from July to November, with temperatures from 26°C to 40°C, though sporadic showers are still possible. As with any area as large as the Amazon, regional differences can be stark.

**(top) Squirrel Monkey**
Squirrel monkeys belong to the family Cebidae. There are about 55 Cebidae species, of which 35 or so are found in the Amazon River basin.

**(bottom) Leaf-Cutter Ants**
Leaf-cutter ants harvest pieces of leaves, take them back to the nest and chew them up to feed to the fungus cultures that the ants farm for food.

# EXPERIENCE

After a couple of days on the trails, you've been surprised to discover that the Amazon is not in fact home to jaguars and anacondas at every turn. But that doesn't mean that it's not rich in biodiversity.

Up ahead, your guide draws your attention to an enormous fig tree rising tall and strong. As you draw nearer, a chorus of bestial shouts and hollers echoes thunderously across the canopy. In a measured whisper, your guide informs you that more than 40 different kinds of birds and monkeys can feed from a single fig tree. Assuming your luck holds out, you're about to see a few species up close and personal.

With binoculars in hand, your guide hones in on some small monkeys with massive moustaches – emperor tamarins. You watch as the regal group gorges itself on juicy ripe figs. Their urgency is certainly understood – several crashes and thuds later, the tamarins have all been bullied away by the capuchins. But as your guide is quick to point out, their victory will be short lived. In the distance, the voluminous hoots of the howler monkeys are rapidly closing in.

You purposely left your watch behind in Manaus, but keeping rough track of the hours in the Amazon is facilitated by the harmony of the insects, who time their calls to fall between each others' notes. In the cool air of early morning, sound travels farther and the chorus is especially rich. At midday little stirs and the hot, dense air muffles sound. As evening wears on, new sets of nocturnal players warm up for their upcoming choral performance.

Indeed, there are insects everywhere you look; your guide tells you that a single acre of the Amazon may hold up to three million ants. Mental note: before going to bed tonight, make sure your hammock is properly slung high up off the ground.

Pausing in his tracks, your guide drops to his hands and knees, and points out one of the most bizarre creatures you've ever laid eyes on: somewhat reminiscent of iridescent vomit, a slime mould cruises along the undergrowth, feeding on bacteria and rotten vegetation. Although it's almost time to set up camp and prepare dinner, you've unfortunately just lost your appetite.

**Mundurucú Girls Chasing Butterflies**
There are hundreds of indigenous tribes living in the Amazon. The Mundurucú tribe, traditionally known for their elaborate tattoos (a practice they no longer adhere to), claims the land along the Tapajós and Trombetas Rivers.

# TAKING ACTION

## As You Saw It

While you're out hiking in the Amazon, try to see the proverbial forest through the trees. Cliché as this might sound, most travellers in the rainforest focus solely on the path ahead, thus missing out on the plethora of amazing things happening around them. Make a mental note to always look up, down, left, right and behind – as you never know what you'll find hiding out among the leaf clutter. And do take a guide – the simplest way of maximising your wildlife-watching opportunities is to travel with someone who knows the rainforest. Even if you've already logged a significant amount of outdoors experience back home or elsewhere on the road, the Amazon is best experienced through the eyes of a local.

## Adding to the Experience

The Amazon comprises a number of diverse national parks to explore.

✿ **Parque Nacional das Montanhas do Tumucumaque** The largest national park in the Amazon (and Brazil), spanning nearly 4 million hectares in the state of Amapá.

✿ **Parque Nacional do Jaú** Next in line, this park protects around 2.3 million hectares of the Jaú and Carabinani River systems, both major tributaries of the Rio Negro located northwest of Manaus.

✿ **Parque Nacional do Araguaia** Located on Ilha do Bananal, Tocantins, arguably the world's largest river island.

✿ **Parque Nacional do Pico da Neblina** Located almost 1000km up the Rio Negro in the northwest corner of Amazonas state, this park contains the eponymous 3014m Pico da Neblina (Foggy Peak), the highest point in Brazil.

## Alternative Great-Forest Experiences

The Amazon may be the largest rainforest on the planet, but there is one larger swath of trees: the Taiga, located in the northern latitudes of Eurasia and North America (see p278).

# WHILE YOU'RE THERE

The 50,000-sq-km Ilha de Marajó, slightly larger than Switzerland, lies at the mouths of the Amazon and Tocantins Rivers. It was the ancient home of the Marajoara indigenous culture, notable for their large ceramic burial urns. Today Marajó's friendly residents live in a few towns and villages and on the many *fazendas* (ranches) spread across the island. This is a world apart, where bicycles outnumber cars and water buffalo graze around town. Legend has it the buffalo are descended from animals that swam ashore from a French ship that sank while en route from India to French Guiana. The island

## KILLER CORDYCEPS

Although million member–strong colonies of ants may seem invincible, they're not. Far from it. Spores from the *Cordyceps*, a parasitic fungus, can infect the brain of an ant, which is then directed (by its own addled mind – like something out of a bad science fiction movie) to climb upwards, in a death march. If the workers discover an ant in its death throes, it will be carried far away from the colony, and crisis (for the colony, at least) will be averted. After death, a fungal growth erupts from the ant corpse and releases deadly spores high into the air. Any nearby ants risk infection, and ultimately the same fate. The fungus is so virulent that it can wipe out whole colonies in a matter of weeks.

There are thousands of different species of *Cordyceps,* and each specialises in just one type of insect host. These attacks do have their upside, as the fungi keep any one species of insect from getting the upper hand – the more numerous a species, the more likely an attack.

is well known for its buffalo cheese, buffalo steaks and buffalo-mounted police force.

## GETTING YOU THERE

Manaus is serviced by international flights, including direct connections to Miami and Buenos Aires, in addition to frequent domestic air services. Manaus lies along limited bus routes, though arriving and departing by riverboat is much more atmospheric.

## EXPLORING THE AMAZON

Virtually every foreigner you see in Manaus is planning a trip or returning from one, and they are the best source of honest, up-to-date information. Different tour operators specialise in different things; thinking carefully about what sort of trip you want can help determine which operator is best for you. How much do you want to rough it? Do you want to sleep out in the forest or do day trips from a lodge? Do you want a bed or a hammock? Private bathroom, shared, or pit toilet? There is no shame in choosing more or less comfort – you are there to enjoy yourself after all.

## UNCONTACTED

The notion that there are indigenous tribes who have yet to be contacted by the outside world living deep in the Amazon rainforest is not as illusory as you might think. Brazil has more uncontacted indigenous groups than any other country. A report in 2007 by Funai (National Foundation of the Indian), Brazil's indigenous-affairs agency, estimates there are 67 such groups. Anthropologists have long known that uncontacted groups exist, though estimating how many, and how numerous they are, is obviously difficult. Contacted tribes often tell of uncontacted families living in remote areas of their territories, and occasionally members of an uncontacted group will emerge from the jungle, having left or been expelled from their land.

## FAST FACTS

Over the course of a year, a single Amazonian tree can suck up hundreds of tonnes of water.

Excess water absorbed by trees returns to the air as vapour. In the largest stretch of rainforest on earth, half of all the rainfall comes from clouds produced by the trees themselves.

Humidity creates the perfect conditions for a world where life is built on the ongoing cycle of growth and decay.

In the Amazon, decomposition happens faster than anywhere else on the planet.

# THE FOREST OF INFINITE DIVERSITY

Rainforests of Borneo

THAILAND

PHILIPPINES

MALAYSIA

BRUNEI

MALAYSIA

Kuching

Celebes
Sea

BORNEO

INDONESIA

Java Sea

Banda
Sea

EAST
TIMOR

Arafura
Sea

INDIAN
OCEAN

Timor
Sea

**(left) Canopy Sky Walk, Gunung Mulu National Park, Malaysian Borneo**
World Heritage–listed Gunung Mulu National Park is a 52,864-hectare park dominated by Gunung Mulu, a 2377m-high sandstone pinnacle, and at least 295km of explored caves.

**(right) Nepenthes (Tropical Pitcher Plants)**
The name *Nepenthes* was first coined by Carolus Linnaeus in 1737 in reference to Homer's *Odyssey*, in which *Nepenthes pharmakon* is a magical potion that quells sorrows with forgetfulness, given to Helen of Troy by an Egyptian queen.

**The world's third-largest island is a seething hotpot of biodiversity. Despite well-documented problems with deforestation, you'll still find incredible opportunities for striking out into truly primal and untamed expanses of jungle, some unchanged for millions of years. Here lurk orang-utans, endangered rhinos, elephants, clouded leopards, flying lemurs and carniverous pitcher plants.**

## On Screen
The rainforest is a land of plenty – plenty of resources and plenty of competition. *Planet Earth* reveals just a few of the astonishing ways in which animal and plant species have evolved, with specialised methods of reaching food – or getting the food to come to them.

## When
In a rainforest it rains all year, though rainfall is a little heavier here between October and March. You might want to time your Borneo sojourn to coincide with a local event – perhaps Sarawak's traditional Gawai Dayak harvest festival on 1 and 2 June.

FELIX HUG/LONELY PLANET IMAGES

MARK DAFFEY/LONELY PLANET IMAGES

# EXPERIENCE

In the thick black night of the rainforest, sounds are amplified to deafening levels: insect whirrs, avian trills and squawks, the calls of unidentifiable animals. You stand rigid, waiting for your eyes to grow accustomed to the gloom. A large leaf detaches itself from the canopy above and drifts above your head, edges fluttering gently, before grasping the trunk of a tree nearby.

Grasping? That's not a leaf! A pair of bulbous brown eyes stares at you, unblinking, above furry wings. It's a colugo: a flying lemur. Except it's not a lemur and it doesn't actually fly – though that's splitting hairs. As it arcs backwards you can see the parchmentlike flaps of skin stretched between its long limbs – a living kite wing – but also a baby clamped to its belly. It hops up towards the young, tender leaves that lured it to this tree, munching hurriedly before launching off again to glide towards another likely dining spot 50m or more yonder. This bizarre creature is only one of countless unique biological adaptations you'll spot on your sweaty romp through the jungle.

As dawn brings a mosaic of sunlight to the forest floor, more of the dizzying array of plants – and the creatures that live on, with and in them – become apparent. A cluster of bulbous, mottled plants catches your eye: pendulous, liquid-filled gourds dangling beneath an umbrella leaf. These pitcher plants do what only animals are supposed to: they lie in wait to trap their prey. You crouch, checking first for irate ants, and watch the plant in predatory action.

An unwary passing beetle catches a whiff of sweet nectar in the underside of a flat leaf, and lands for a sip. Reaching for the sugary treat, it slips – the rim of the pitcher is waxy and treacherous – and tumbles with an audible plop into the water-filled depths, joining a suspended graveyard of previous victims.

Anchored to the rim of the pitcher you spy a translucent pink spider, sitting and watching as patiently as you are while an ant also flounders and succumbs to its watery doom. When the death throes have shuddered to a halt, the red crab spider lowers itself on a silk lifeline to fish out the ant. It's a handsome meal for the spider, a postponed one for the pitcher plant, which will enjoy – if a plant can enjoy – the digested remains exuded by the arachnid.

But that's not this spider's only stunt. Spotting a mosquito larva wriggling at the bottom of the pitcher, the spider prepares for a scuba dive, filling an air bubble on its abdomen and plunging into the water to retrieve the juicy morsel before again hauling itself up the safety rope.

You straighten up, every drop of sweat now itching; more than ever you're aware of the incredible audacity of the hungry multitude of organisms surrounding you, striving every which way to get a bite. Even though you know you're within touching distance of your bunk at park headquarters, the sheer density of the jungle – and the dizzying diversity of species being pointed out by your ranger guide – ensures a sense of dislocation from 'civilisation'.

**Orang-utan**
The Malay word orang-utan means 'person of the forest'. Found only in Sumatra and Borneo, orang-utans are highly intelligent and use a variety of sophisticated tools.

# TAKING ACTION

## As You Saw It

Numerous reserves around Borneo offer the chance to get that 'lost in a primal forest' feeling. Bako National Park – a mere hop from Kuching, capital of the Malaysian state of Sarawak in north Borneo – encompasses 27 sq km of lush coastal jungle. As advertised, colugos glide, pitcher plants trap and visitors sweat in regulation fashion.

The park's population of proboscis monkeys is another big draw. A series of marked trails leads you through the various subhabitats – take a night walk to spot colugos on the wing.

## Adding to the Experience

Park rangers at Bako sometimes guide night treks for added insight. Borneo also has a wealth of other national parks and wildlife centres, covering a range of habitats and hosting varied animal species. Some more remote locations, such as Sabah's Danum Valley and Maliau Basin Conservation Areas (the latter is described as a 'Lost World'), are harder to access and offer an even wilder experience. It's also sometimes possible for committed – and, ideally, qualified – visitors to join volunteer programs assisting with conservation and wildlife rehabilitation; if you're keen to get your hands dirty, investigate via organisations such as Wild Asia (www.wildasia.org).

## Alternative Pitcher Plant–Spotting Experiences

Carnivorous pitcher plants can be found in moist forests around the globe.

✿ **Karri forests around Nannup & Pemberton** (Western Australia) The state's far southwest hosts the Albany pitcher plant.

✿ **Masoala National Park** (Madagascar) Exotic Nepenthes pitcher plants can be found on the island's humid east coast.

✿ **Gunung Leuser National Park** (Sumatra, Indonesia) Besides pitcher plants, you're also likely to encounter orang-utans at the rehabilitation centre near Bukit Lawang.

✿ **Sinharaja Forest Reserve** (Sri Lanka) This is the island's most important swath of virgin rainforest.

# THE HEADHUNTERS & THE WHITE RAJAH

For about 500 years the Dayak warriors of Borneo's interior practised a truly gruesome tradition: headhunting. Skirmishes involving warrior groups, as well as individual expeditions by lone men (often to woo a would-be bride), resulted in countless craniums being lopped off, smoked and hung up in traditional longhouses to impress – or instil fear in – visitors.

One man who wasn't so impressed was James Brooke, an Englishman who came to wield astonishing power in Borneo. Born in India in 1803, Brooke became first a soldier and later a trader, though without great success in either endeavour. Buying a ship, *The Royalist,* he sailed to Borneo to trade – arriving in 1839 just in time to help the Sultan of Brunei deal with a siege and suppress an uprising. The grateful (or cowed) sultan subsequently declared Brooke the Rajah of Sarawak. As rajah, Brooke stamped his mark on the fiefdom, cracking down on piracy and headhunting and enforcing a paternalistic but generally benevolent government that essentially regarded the rajah as both king and judiciary. Two subsequent Brookes inherited the position of rajah before Sarawak was handed to the British after WWII.

Headhunting continued sporadically well into the 20th century (the heads of Japanese WWII soldiers were taken), though it's not practised by the Dayaks today. At least, most visitors have returned with cranium intact...

# WHILE YOU'RE THERE

### Kuching
Explore Sarawak's lithe main city – its name means 'cat' – delving into Chinatown and browsing the busy weekend market.

### Semenggok Wildlife Rehabilitation Centre
Visit this excellent centre, just 24km south of Kuching, at feeding time to see orang-utans swinging in from the forest.

### Talang-Satang National Park
Snorkel, dive and – if you're lucky – watch baby sea turtles released into the wild on these four islands off the coast just west of Kuching.

### Longhouses of Batang Ai
Sip rice wine with the villagers in the traditional longhouse, then set out into the Batang Ai National Park in search of orang-utans.

### Wind Cave & Fairy Cave
Head to these bat-chattering limestone grottoes near Bau for a subterranean experience. With more time, you can reach the truly massive caves at Mulu or Niah, in the far northeast of Sarawak.

# GETTING YOU THERE

Bako National Park is accessible only by boat; from Kuching, take a bus to Kampung Bako (about an hour), then charter a boat for the hop to park headquarters.

# EXPLORING BAKO NATIONAL PARK

You can book accommodation in Bako directly with park headquarters (www.sarawakforestry.com). Alternatively, operators in Kuching offer day trips or overnight tours; Borneo Adventure (www.borneoadventure.com) is an award-winning outfit with strong community and conservation credentials.

## FAST FACTS

The colugo is sometimes called a 'flying lemur' – though it glides rather than flies (it's not powered flight) and it's definitely not a lemur, which are endemic to Madagascar only.

Despite its relatively modest size, Bako National Park hosts 184 bird species, and around 275 rare proboscis monkeys.

Nine species of the world's largest flower, the rafflesia, are believed to bloom in Borneo's rainforests. The rafflesia grows to 1m in diameter, but only lasts for a week or two before decomposing. Even while fresh, it emits a smell of rotting meat.

Borneo has a land area of about 745,000 sq km, which is home to some 15,000 plant species, of which over one-third are found nowhere else in the world.

Borneo's orang-utans are under severe threat, mostly from habitat loss due to deforestation; the International Union for Conservation of Nature (IUCN) estimates the current population may be less than 50,000. The Sumatran species is Critically Endangered; fewer than 8000 are believed to survive.

# TRACKING CHIMPANZEES
## Kibale Forest National Park, Uganda

CONGO (ZAÏRE)

Fort Portal

UGANDA

KENYA

Kampala

**KIBALE FOREST NATIONAL PARK**

Lake Victoria

RWANDA

TANZANIA

BURUNDI

Winston Churchill called Uganda the 'Pearl of Africa'. It boasts the tallest mountain range in Africa (the glacier-capped Rwenzoris), as well as the mighty Nile River's origins (Lake Victoria, the continent's largest lake) and one of the highest concentrations of primates in the world. The merging of habitats from eastern, western and northern Africa also produces arguably the world's best birdwatching.

## On Screen

One of the more gruesome moments in the *Planet Earth* series is the depiction of a group of chimpanzees launching a raid against a rival group. The footage reveals both that chimps are capable of committing violent homicide against their own kind, and – startlingly – that cannibalism is also practised. In an environment where every calorie consumed can increase one's chances of survival and procreation, a vital protein source is not readily discarded.

## When

Chimp tracking is not a seasonal activity, but the best times for a visit to the Ugandan jungle are the dryer months of January and February and June to September. Travel during the wet seasons is possible (to most destinations), but slower; and you probably won't enjoy your time in the great outdoors as much.

**Chimpanzee**
Kibale Forest National Park is home to 13 different species of primate, including chimpanzees, colobus monkeys and bush babies.

# EXPERIENCE

Hiking through equatorial rainforest is an intense experience in its own right, but it takes on a new element of suspense – and even hints of danger – when you are tracking chimpanzees. The tension in your group is palpable, as the dense vegetation makes it difficult to catch more than a glimpse of what lies ahead; the extreme humidity and the tropical sun beating down on your head certainly don't help. You drain the contents of your canteen and munch on some fried banana chips in hope of a quick energy boost. Precious fluids appear to be leaving your body in litres at a time, though remarkably your guide hasn't even broken a mild sweat.

You stick close to your guide as he hacks through the obstructive greenery with mighty swipes of his panga blade. Penetrating ever deeper into the forest, you fend off blood-sucking mosquitoes, biting flies and stinging nettles, all the while developing a deep respect for your primate cousins, who apparently thrive in these conditions.

Suddenly your guide freezes in his tracks, and starts bellowing greeting calls to the chimpanzee sentries that you hadn't yet noticed eyeing you from a distance. With their bulky frames and well-defined muscles, these magnificent creatures are much bigger and stronger than you could have possibly imagined. And you're trespassing in their territory – were you a lesser primate, this act would most certainly incur violence, and you wouldn't stand a chance.

Like infantry preparing for battle, the chimpanzees fall into line. A wave of second thoughts race through your head, but your guide reassures you that everything will be alright. And moments later everything is alright. The chimps have moved on, signalling that you are free to pass. From here on out your movements must be cool and calculated – you can still feel watchful eyes glaring at you from behind the brush, though fortunately the worst risk is over.

Further on you spot an enormous alpha male hunkered down on a fallen tree trunk. He is surrounded by a group of subordinates, who are busy sifting through his coat for salt particles and parasites. As you point your telephoto lens at him, the alpha male acknowledges your presence with a mighty yawn. You breathe a sigh of a relief. All is peaceful here in Kibale.

**Rwenzori Mountains National Park, Uganda**
The main attraction of Rwenzori Mountains National Park is the luxuriant vegetation found above 3000m, which includes giant lobelias and groundsels.

# TAKING ACTION

## As You Saw It

Chimps are always on the move throughout their home territory, so you're going to have to employ the services of an expert tracker to catch up with them (fortunately the rangers of Kibale Forest are some of the best trackers on the continent). Although elusive, you stand a high chance of finding them on any particular day – and even if you don't, you'll most likely see other primates, in addition to the incredible number of birds (more than 350 species) that live here.

If you come across a group of chimps on the move, you need to be swift with the camera – they have a tendency to quickly disappear into the underbrush or climb up into the canopy and out of sight. If you are lucky enough to locate a party sitting still awhile, your time will be memorable and highly entertaining – chimpanzees are engaging animals whose amusing (and sometimes frightening) antics are deservedly famous.

## Adding to the Experience

If you can't shake the primate kick, be sure to also check out the Bwindi Impenetrable Forest, one of Africa's most celebrated national parks. The steep mountainous terrain is home to almost half of the world's surviving mountain gorillas, an estimated 340 individuals. One of the world's most ancient habitats, the Bwindi Impenetrable thrived right through the last Ice Age (12,000 to 18,000 years ago) when most of Africa's other forests disappeared. This antiquity has resulted in an incredible diversity of flora and fauna, even by normal rainforest standards. And we do mean rainforest – up to 2.5m of rain falls here annually.

## Alternative Chimp-Spotting Experiences

Despite being an endangered species, chimps continue to reign over a number of exotic locales.

❀ **Queen Elizabeth National Park** (Uganda) At one of Uganda's top safari parks, you'll find chimps hiding out in the safe confines of Kyambura Gorge.

❀ **Gombe Stream National Park** (Tanzania) This chimpanzee-rich habitat was where Dr Jane Goodall performed much of her groundbreaking research.

❀ **Nyungwe Forest National Park** (Rwanda) This patch of old growth equatorial forest is one of the continent's richest biomes.

# WHILE YOU'RE THERE

**Ngamba Island Chimpanzee Sanctuary**, 23km from Entebbe, is home to around 40 orphaned or confiscated chimpanzees that are unable to be returned to the wild. Also known as Chimp Island, humans are confined to about one of the 40 hectares while the chimps wander freely through the rest. Trips must be booked in advance with Kampala tour companies, which can also arrange transport to Entebbe. Feedings can be watched from a raised platform, and the staff gives informative talks on chimp life. There's also an overnight experience available where you can

## KIBALE ECOLOGY

Kibale is a rich slice of rainforest where several vegetation zones overlap. The main attraction is the high density of primates that inhabit the forest, but birdlife is also prolific. In addition, some 250 species of trees have been recorded in the park, all with crooks and boughs festooned with dense mats of moss. Bracket fungi cling to broad tree trunks, and orchids grow high up in the canopy. Permanent streams cut through the forest, and swamps fill low-lying areas; the northern and southern boundaries support stands of grasslands and west of the park is a scenic field of volcanic craters.

spend two days on the island and one night in a self-contained, solar-powered safari tent.

## GETTING YOU THERE

Kamwenge-bound minibuses from Fort Portal pass Kibale Forest's main visitor centre; there are also daily buses connecting Fort Portal to Kampala. While most visitors to Uganda touch down in Kampala, Fort Portal is also a major regional hub.

## EXPLORING KIBALE

The following operators can help you get your bearings and put you on the road to Kibale:

✿ **Afri Tours & Travel** (www.afritourstravel.com) One of the better all-round tour companies in Uganda, offering safaris at prices for every pocket.

✿ **Great Lakes Safaris** (www.safari-uganda.com) One of the newer safari companies in Uganda, the team has been generating rave reviews for friendly service and flexibility.

✿ **Mantana African Safaris** (www.kimbla-mantana.com) Known throughout East Africa for its luxury lodges and tented camps, Mantana offers a limited range of safaris around Uganda.

## CHIMP COMMUNITIES

Chimps are highly sociable creatures that form complex communities ranging upwards of 100 individuals. During the day these communities break down into smaller units to forage for food, a behaviour that has been dubbed by anthropologists as 'fission-fusion'. Since they can cover a great distance over the course of just a few hours, tracking chimpanzees can be a rigorous enterprise that requires patience and stamina.

# SHALLOW SEAS
*Planet Earth, Episode Nine*

Planet Earth is about 70% ocean, yet most marine life congregates in just 8% of that expanse – the shallow waters fringing the continents. It is here that coral reefs flourish, providing sculptural subaquatic pleasure gardens for myriad fish (and besnorkelled onlookers). This is where humpbacks migrate, feeding off the krill-rich briny waters; and where the most fearsome predator of them all, the great white shark, picks off seal snacks in a bone-chilling combination of aerial acrobatics and brute, toothy strength. It's great news for travellers – we landlubbing humans don't need to sail, swim, dive or gaze far offshore to see the ocean at its most alive.

# DUGONG &
# DOLPHIN WATCHING

## Shark Bay, Central West Coast, Australia

Timor Sea

INDIAN OCEAN

**SHARK BAY** ●

Perth ●

AUSTRALIA

---

**A Unesco World Heritage Site, Shark Bay encompasses more than 1500km of coastline, stretching along two jagged peninsulas and around numerous islands. As well as boasting beautiful white-sand beaches, fiery red cliffs and turquoise lagoons, it is one of Western Australia's most biologically rich habitats.**

## On Screen

*Planet Earth* introduces us to two of the most charismatic species of marine mammals known: the dugong and the dolphin. More than 3m long and weighing almost 500kg, dugongs are the largest herbivores in the sea and eat nothing but sea grass; dolphins are highly intelligent hunters that use echolocation, coordinated team strikes and lightening-fast instincts to make short work of their prey.

## When

North of Shark Bay, dry and wet seasons replace winter and summer. The dry lasts from about June to August, and the wet from about December to February, with monsoon rains falling from January. The rain can render roads impassable, and Port Hedland weathers a serious cyclone at least every two years. Southwest of Shark Bay temperate climate patterns result in mild winters and warmer summers with frequent dry spells.

**(top) Dugong**
Dugongs are more closely related to elephants than to other marine mammals, such as whales and dolphins, but their closest living aquatic relatives are the manatees.

**(bottom) Aboriginal Rock Art**
These scenes, created by the Worrorra people on a cave ceiling at Raft Point in Collier Bay, are said to depict a 'great fish chase', showing figures representing rock cod and dugong and their Wandjina captors.

"Most life in tropical waters groups around coral reefs and sea-grass meadows."

Cape Peron
The northern tip of Peron Peninsula is protected
by Francois Peron National Park. Once a sheep
station, the park is home to many rare and
endangered species.

# EXPERIENCE

Western Australia (WA) is big. Seriously big. This
becomes abundantly obvious as you clear Perth's city
limits and immediately find yourself all alone on the
edge of the outback. Perth has the proud distinction of
being the world's second-most-isolated metropolitan
area (Honolulu being the first). It takes 10 hours and
change to drive north up the coast to your destination,
Denham, passing through what is best described as
glorious tracts of nothingness.

Petrol stops are prized moments to stretch
your legs and converse with the frontier-minded
locals that live here on the veritable edge of
Australian civilisation. You appreciate their defiant
WA attitude, with an independence shaped by
extreme distance from the eastern states where
more than 80% of the population lives.

Arriving in Denham you strike up a conversation
with a friendly old-timer, who tells the somewhat

tall-sounding tale that the entire town used to be covered in mother of pearl. But while the pearling fisheries have long since closed up shop, you notice that there are still a few old buildings with shell-brick facades.

After another fueling stop – in the form of fried barramundi fillets and a pint of Emu Bitter – you board a tour boat and set out for the world's largest sea-grass meadows, in Shark Bay. You've travelled a long way to see the dugongs, and the laid-back captain assures you that he knows exactly where they're hiding out – and right he is.

Minutes later, you're snapping photos of bulky sea cows grazing to their hearts' content. The captain tells you that a herd can clear a patch of sea grass the size of a football field in a single day.

Before long you're back in the car, though your next destination, the tourist resort of Monkey Mia, is only 26km northeast. In the 1960s wild bottlenose dolphins started turning up here in shallow waters, looking for handouts from local fisherman. Today marine biologists rigidly control the feeding, while simultaneously conducting behavioural research.

Standing ankle deep in the sun-drenched turquoise waters of the Indian Ocean, you find yourself surrounded by a pod of eager dolphins. They're splashing about like mischievous children, all the while eyeing your bucket, which they know contains their next meal. Not to keep them waiting any longer, you toss a fish into the gaping mouth before you. The bottlenose squeals in delight before firing off a succession of rapid clicks that you imagine might be a pleasant greeting and thank you for the meal, although they are well beyond your linguistic comprehension.

# TAKING ACTION

## As You Saw It

Dugongs and dolphins are in such abundance in this stretch of WA coastal waters that up-close-and-personal encounters are virtually guaranteed. Boat tours from Denham bring you to the various seasonal spots where dugongs tend to congregate; while controlled dolphin feedings at Monkey Mia provide a rare opportunity to intimately interact with the smartest mammals in the sea. You also stand a good chance of spotting wildlife while kayaking, swimming, snorkelling, scuba diving or even while on a scenic drive.

## Adding to the Experience

In a striking contemporary building in downtown Denham, the cutting edge Shark Bay World Heritage Discovery Centre is one of WA's best museums, with compelling exhibitions on Shark Bay's natural environment, its Aboriginal peoples, the many explorers who've ventured here and how understanding these entanglements can help us experience a sense of place. At Monkey Mia, plenty of other diversions beyond dolphin feeding are on offer, including Aboriginal heritage walks, sailing, camel trips, diving and stargazing.

## Alternative Marine Mammal–Watching Experiences

Marine mammals inhabit attractive tourist destinations the world over.

✿ **Belize** (Caribbean Sea) For manatees.

✿ **Amazon River** (South America) For botos (freshwater dolphins). See p66.

✿ **Petersburg** (Alaska) For steller sea lions.

# WHILE YOU'RE THERE

Laid-back, liveable Perth has wonderful weather, beautiful beaches and an easygoing nature. About as close to Southeast Asia as it is to Australia's eastern state capitals, Perth's combination of big-city attractions and relaxed and informal surrounds offers an appealing lifestyle for locals and a variety of attractions for visitors. WA's mining boom has seen Perth blossom like the state's wildflowers in spring.

It's a sophisticated, cosmopolitan city with myriad bars, restaurants and cultural activities all vying for attention. But the best bit is that when you want to chill out, that's also easy to do. Perth's pristine parkland, nearby bush, and river and ocean beaches – along with a good public transport system – allow its inhabitants and visitors to spread out and enjoy what's on offer.

## BLOOMING WILDFLOWERS

Western Australia (WA) is famed for its 8000 species of wildflower, which bloom between August and November. The southwest has over 3000 species, many of which are unique to this region. All over WA you will find flowers commonly known as everlastings because the petals stay attached after the flowers have died. Common flowering plants include mountain bell, Sturt's desert pea and various species of banksia, wattle, kangaroo paw and orchid.

Even some of the driest regions put on a colourful display after a little rainfall at any time of the year. You can find flowers almost everywhere in the state, but the jarrah forests in the southwest are particularly rich. Coastal national parks such as Fitzgerald River and Kalbarri also have brilliant displays, as do the Stirling Ranges. Near Perth, the Badgingarra, Alexander Morrison, Yanchep and John Forrest national parks are excellent choices. There's also a wildflower display in Kings Park, Perth. As you go further north, flowers tend to bloom earlier in the season.

## GETTING YOU THERE

Private transport is something of a requisite in WA, especially if you want to escape the cities and towns and surround yourself with nature; but bear in mind that driving distances in WA are mind-boggling, so make appropriate safety preparations – make sure you carry adequate water, spare tyres and extra fuel. The rewards are obvious – hit the road and enjoy the sensation of limitless space around you. Since there are many enticing areas of the state that don't have sealed roads, a 4WD is recommended, even in the dry season.

## EXPLORING SHARK BAY

The website www.sharkbay.org offers a comprehensive listing of everything going on in the Shark Bay World Heritage Area.

# DIVING SHALLOW SEAS
Indonesia

The diversity on land and in the sea runs like a traveller's fantasy playlist, but it's also the mash-up of people and cultures that makes Indonesia so appealing. Bali justifiably leads off, but there are also the tribes deep in Papua, funeral-mad Toraja of Sulawesi, artisans of Java, mall rats of Jakarta, and the list goes on...

## On Screen

The warm tropical waters surrounding the Indonesian islands contain 10 times as many species of marine life as there are in the whole of the Caribbean. Indonesian reefs contain such an amazing variety of life because they lie at a giant crossroads – where the Indian Ocean meets the Pacific. Legendary dive sights also happen to be exotic destinations in their own right: Bali, Nusa Tenggara, the Gili Islands, Sulawesi, the Togean Islands, and the incredible Raja Ampat Islands in Papua.

## When

Indonesia is hot and humid year-round, with wet and dry seasons. Generally, the wet season starts later the further southeast you go. In North Sumatra the rain begins to fall in September, but in Timor it doesn't fall until November. In January and February it rains most days. The dry season is from around May to September.

**Pygmy Seahorse, Komodo Island**
Growing to only 2cm in length, pygmy seahorses are found only on gorgonian corals of the genus *Muricella,* and have evolved to resemble their host.

# EXPERIENCE

In between sips of syrupy sweet Balinese coffee, you unfurl your country map and pause to appreciate some of the most impressive geography on the planet. With the equator as its spine, Indonesia arcs between Malaysia and Australia in one hell of a sweep. You proceed to run a few simple calculations in your head, but somehow the maths doesn't seem to work out; with 17,000 islands to explore and 30 days total on your tourist visa, you'd best not waste any more time planning.

Your first destination is in the neighbourhood. Emerging from your bungalow, you suit up on the beach, take your first deep breath of compressed air and wade right into the shallow seas. Thirty metres out and 30m down, you soon find yourself hovering above the coral-encrusted remains of the *Liberty,* a sunken freighter that was torpedoed by the Japanese in WWII. In between bursts of bubbles from the regulator, you stabilise your buoyancy and pause to reflect on the uniformed men who lost their lives in these same waters decades ago.

Bali is littered with surf spots and dive sites – not to mention amazing cuisine and a remarkably rich heritage – but you're not going to fall into the same trap as your fellow travellers, you're going to press on with a purpose. It's time to board a bus, and then a plane, and then a taxi, and then a ferry before arriving in the Raja Ampat Islands off the coast of Sorong. This particular group is home to over 600 uninhabited islands.

Fortunately every dive here counts for two elsewhere. Quite simply, Raja Ampat offers some of the best – if not the best – diving in the whole of Indonesia. The reefs have hundreds of different brilliantly coloured soft and hard corals, and the marine topography varies from vertical walls and pinnacles to reef flats and rock gardens. Surrounded by marine life from head to toe, you suddenly realise what it must be like to swim in a fishbowl.

You soon lose all track of time, but judging by the lack of empty pages in your logbook, you know it's almost time to go home. It's going to take several more trips to Indonesia if you want to check off another dozen or so islands, but diving is truly addictive and pretty soon you're going to need another fix anyway.

(top) Traditional Bajau Fishing Huts, Togean Islands
The Togean Islands were officially designated a national park in 2004, extending protection to their rich coral reefs and fauna.

(bottom) White-Eyed Moray Eels, Lembeh Strait
Lembeh Strait boasts a whole raft of weird-looking creatures, including ambush-predator frogfish, camouflaged pipefish and a variety of moray eels.

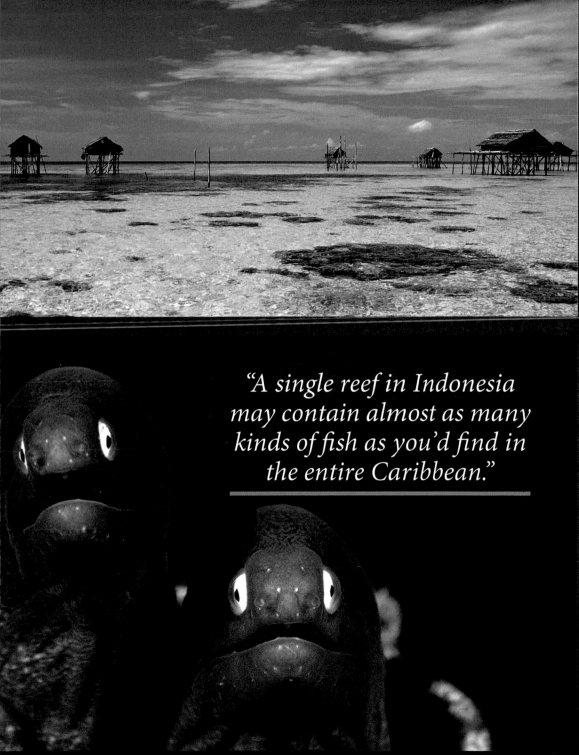

"A single reef in Indonesia may contain almost as many kinds of fish as you'd find in the entire Caribbean."

# TAKING ACTION

## As You Saw It

With so many islands and adjacent reef systems to choose from, Indonesia offers countless opportunities to re-create the spectacular underwater scenes witnessed in *Planet Earth*. In fact, you're really limited only by the length of your tourist visa, the padding in your wallet and the levels of postdive nitrogen rapidly accumulating in your bloodstream!

## Adding to the Experience

Diving Komodo National Park is one of the big draws to Labuanbajo in Nusa Tenggara. Currents are strong and unpredictable, with cold upswellings and dangerous down currents thanks to the convergence of the warm Flores Sea and the cooler Sumba Strait. These conditions nourish a rich plankton soup that attracts whales, mantas, dolphins, turtles and sharks. Factor in pristine coral and clouds of colourful fish, and the diving is nothing short of exhilarating. But it isn't easy, so it's best to tune into local conditions on shallower dives before you venture into the depths.

## Alternative Diving Experiences

Choosing the so-called 'best dive spots in the world' is always a heated subject among divers, though here are three of our nominations.

✿ **Yongala** (Great Barrier Reef, Queensland, Australia) One of the world's top dive sites, this wreck went down in 1911, and was discovered half a century later.

✿ **Blue Corner Wall** (Palau, Micronesia) Sheer rock formations and some of the world's largest schools of fish.

✿ **Thistlegorm** (Red Sea, Egypt) Another world-class wreck, this one went down in 1941, and was discovered a decade later by the legendary Jacques-Yves Cousteau.

# WHILE YOU'RE THERE

## Sulawesi

If you think Sulawesi looks crazy on the map, just wait until you see it for real. The massive island's many-limbed coastline is lined with sandy beaches, fringing coral reefs and a mind-boggling variety of fish. Meanwhile the interior is shaded in with impenetrable mountains and jungles thick with wildlife, such as rare nocturnal tarsiers and flamboyantly colourful maleo birds.

## Togean Islands

Yes, it does take some determination to get to the Togean Islands, but believe us, it takes much more determination to leave. Island hop from one forested, golden-beach beauty to the next; hammocks are plentiful, the food is fresh and the welcome homey. There are lost lagoons and forgotten coves where you can plunge into crystal-clear seas to explore all three major types of reef system – atoll, barrier and fringing. Colours absolutely pop. Fish are everywhere.

## LIFE IN INDO

The most populous Muslim nation is no hardline Islamic state. Indonesians have traditionally practised a very loose-fitting, relaxed form of Islam. Although there's little desire to imitate the West, catching a Hollywood movie in an American-style shopping mall after prayers at the mosque is a common occurrence for many. Internet usage in Indonesia is soaring and millions of Indonesians work overseas – mainly in the Gulf, Hong Kong and Malaysia – bringing extraneous influences back to their villages upon their return. A boom in low-cost air travel has also enabled the newer generations to travel internally and overseas conveniently and cheaply, while personal mobility is much easier today thanks to cheap imports of motorcycles and cars.

## Nusa Tenggara

Nusa Tenggara is lush and jungle green in the north, more arid savannah in the south, and in between has almost limitless surf breaks and technicolour volcanic lakes. It's a land of pink-sand beaches, schooling rays, pods of whales, troops of monkeys and the world's largest lizard: the swaggering, spellbinding komodo dragon.

# GETTING YOU THERE

Jakarta and Bali are the two main transport hubs of Indonesia, but other useful international connections include Balikpapan (Kalimantan), Mataram (Lombok), Manado (Sulawesi), Medan (Sumatra), Palembang and Padang (Sumatra), and Solo and Surabaya (Java). Garuda Indonesia (www.garuda-indonesia.com), Indonesia's national airline, serves Australia and points across Asia.

# EXPLORING INDONESIA'S SHALLOW SEAS

Throughout Indonesia, PADI-linked dive operators number in the hundreds, so you'll have no problem getting sorted, assuming of course you've brought along your scuba certification card. If not, and you have the time to get qualified (typically less than a week), the Gili Islands, Pulau Bunaken and Labuanbajo in Nusa Tenggara all offer good selections of PADI-linked dive schools.

## AN UNLIKELY ALLIANCE

Banded sea kraits are a highly venomous species of sea snake found in tropical Indo-Pacific oceanic waters. Since they're too slow to catch fish in a straight chase, they seek prey hiding out in the nooks and crannies of the coral. As one band of hunters cruises for prey, another joins it, eventually forming large caravans that are dozens strong. Sea kraits also form a rather unlikely alliance with schools of predatory yellow goatfish and trevally. The big fish scare the prey into cracks – where the snakes can catch them – and anything fleeing the kraits will swim straight into the gaping mouths of the eagerly waiting schools. There's simply nowhere to hide. This remarkable cooperation between snakes and fish has only recently been observed, for it happens only on the most remote reefs in Indonesia. Perhaps such phenomena were once a common sight in the shallow seas, but today no more than 6% of Indonesia's reefs are in their pristine state.

# HUMPBACK MIGRATIONS
## Central Pacific, off the Coast of Maui, Hawaii

Kaua'i

Ni'ihau

O'ahu

Honolulu

Moloka'i

Lana'i

Maui

**HUMPBACK MIGRATIONS**

Kaho'olawe

PACIFIC OCEAN

**HAWAII**

Hawai'i

*"His tropical nursery is warm and safe – but his days here are numbered. His mother is starving."*

**(left) Mother & Calf**
It is thought that humpback whalesongs are used for communication and attracting mates. This may become challenging as humans conduct undersea activities, such as testing high-powered sonar systems and military technologies, and explosions for mining and oil exploration.

**(right) Haleakalā Crater, Maui**
Haleakalā National Park was first established to preserve Haleakalā Crater, but was later extended to also protect Kipahulu Valley, the scenic pools along 'Ohe'o Gulch, and the coast.

The seasonal migration of the humpback whale is one of nature's grandest spectacles. With luck, a single humpback will make this journey around 70 times during the course of its life, cruising back and forth between the shallow polar seas and tropical, equatorial waters, such as those around Hawaii. Beyond the cavorting whales, Hawaii is all about fiery volcanoes, Pacific Rim cuisine, coral-reef cities, and drinking mai tais with hibiscus flowers in your hair.

## On Screen
Two of the biggest stars of *Planet Earth* are a humpback whale mother and her newborn calf. Together they undergo an epic journey from winter birthing grounds near the equator to the polar seas, the whales' krill-laden summer feeding grounds.

## When
From November through May some 10,000 humpback whales crowd the shallow waters along the western coast of Maui for breeding, calving and nursing. During this time these majestic creatures are easy to spot from shore, particularly when they perform their awe-inspiring acrobatic breaches.

MIKE PARRY/MINDEN PICTURES

SCOTT DARSNEY/LONELY PLANET IMAGES

# EXPERIENCE

The polar seas in the summer months support the greatest concentrations of marine life on our planet. Humpback whales must migrate from their tropical birthing grounds near the equator to feed in these richer, shallower waters. And so begins what will most likely be the greatest maritime expedition that you and your sailing crew will ever undertake.

Away from all land, the ocean is virtually empty: a watery desert that receives plenty of sunlight, but lacks the necessary nutrients for life. All creatures here are locked in a constant search to find food, and a struggle to preserve precious energy. But these equatorial seas make for excellent nurseries, as their crystal-clear waters are warm, and there are no predators about.

Peering over the stern of your yacht, you watch in awe as a whale calf breastfeeds; it will consume up to 500L of mother's milk per day. But you don't have to be a marine biologist to realise that the mother is starving; thin and emaciated, she has lived off nothing but her fat for months now. Empathy takes hold, but there is nothing nutritious for a whale onboard the ship.

CENTRAL PACIFIC, OFF THE COAST OF MAUI, HAWAII

Now that the calf has doubled in size, the mother must set a course towards either the South or North Pole while she still has the energy to migrate. Raising your sails, you leave the tropics and pursue the whales through colder, rougher and much more dangerous waters. Mother and calf stay close, signalling each other by slapping the surface of the water with their fins. You and your crew take heed; you don't want to lose anyone to the foamy seas either.

Winter storms are violent, threatening to drive the whales and your sailing vessel off course. But the turbulence the storms create stirs the water and draws nutrients up from the depths. As the spring sun strengthens, algae fields the size of the Amazon rainforest turn the seas green and are fed upon by krill, the most abundant animal (by weight) on the planet.

At long last the mother humpback can gorge herself around the clock, laying on the fat reserves to survive another year. By midsummer all of the surface nutrients will have been absorbed, and as the algae die off the food chain will collapse. The whales will return to warmer waters, and you and your crew will set a course for home, thus completing the migratory cycle.

# TAKING ACTION

## As You Saw It

Short of chartering a yacht and following migrating humpbacks to the literal ends of the earth (which of course is always an option if you've got the cash to burn), your best opportunity for whale-watching is to pay a visit to the Hawaiian Islands. As an added bonus, while winter weather in the US mainland can bring all manner of snow, sleet and hail, Hawaii enjoys tropical warmth year-round, with coastal temperatures averaging a high of 28°C and a low of 20°C. Think the whales aren't happy to be in Maui? Listen to them singing at www.whalesong.net.

## Adding to the Experience

In the summer months consider migrating yourself to the extreme northern city of Juneau. Alaska's cruise-ship capital, and the gateway to numerous scenic attractions – including Glacier Bay National Park & Preserve and Admiralty Island National Monument – Juneau also happens to lie along the humpback's polar migration route. If you can't be there alongside the humpbacks as they travel the Pacific, watching them in two destinations as far-flung as Hawaii and Alaska helps to put their incredible journey into perspective.

## Alternative Aquatic Mammal–Spotting Experiences

Our planet's waterways are full of charismatic mammals that are worth seeking out.

✿ **Shark Bay** (Australia) A Unesco World Heritage Site, the world's largest sea-grass meadow is home to dugongs (see p240).

✿ **Amazon River** This river is so massive that it has the resources to support botos (freshwater dolphins; see p66).

✿ **California** (USA) Along the Californian coast, rich waterways support large fish populations, which in turn are a valuable food source for sea lions.

# WHILE YOU'RE THERE

## Maui

According to some, you can't have it all – perhaps those folks haven't been to Maui. Consistently landing atop travel-magazine reader polls as one of the world's most romantic islands, Maui

# HAWAIIAN CULTURE

Compared to 'the mainland' – the blanket term for the rest of the USA – Hawaii may as well be another country. In fact, some Native Hawaiians would like to restore Hawaii's status as an independent nation. Geologically, historically and culturally, Hawaii developed in isolation and, like its flora and fauna, its society is unique. Locals treasure their customs and sensibilities, and guard them against the diluting influence of *haole* (white or mainland) ways.

In Hawaii, no ethnicity claims a majority, but this diversity is also distinct from typical American multiculturalism. Hawaii has large Asian populations and very small African-American and Mexican-Hispanic communities, with about 20% of residents identifying themselves as full or part Native Hawaiian.

As befits a tropical paradise, Hawaii has a decidedly casual personality. Except in cosmopolitan Honolulu, aloha shirts and sandals are acceptable attire for any occasion, socialising revolves around food and family, and fun means sports and the outdoors. In local and Hawaiian sensibilities, caring for the land and caring for the community are integral and intertwined. Then there is aloha – or alooooooooHA, as they say at the luau. It is of course a greeting but, more than that, it describes a gentle, everyday practice of openness, hospitality and loving welcome – one that's extended to everyone, local and visitor alike.

has a wealth of glorious beaches, luxe resorts, friendly B&Bs, gourmet cuisine, fantastic luaus and world-class windsurfing, whale watching, snorkelling, diving and hiking. What's missing? More adventure? Drive the jungly road to Hana or traverse the moonlike volcanic crater of Haleakala. More privacy? Maui is the gateway to secluded Moloka'i and Lana'i.

## O'ahu

O'ahu – the centre of Hawaii's government, commerce and culture – is pre-eminent among Hawaii's islands; so much so that the others are referred to as 'Neighbour Islands'. It's home to three-quarters of the state's residents and is the destination of two-thirds of all visitors to the state. Honolulu is one of the USA's major cities, and its nearby Waikiki beaches gave birth to the whole tiki-craze Hawaii fantasia.

If you want to take the measure of diverse Hawaii, O'ahu offers the full buffet in one tidy package: in the blink of an eye you can go from crowded metropolis to remote turquoise bays teeming with sea life. Meaning 'the gathering place', O'ahu is arguably the nation's best combination of urban living, natural beauty and rural community.

# GETTING YOU THERE

Honolulu International Airport (HNL; www.honoluluairport.com) on the island of O'ahu is a major Pacific air hub and an intermediate stop on many flights between the US mainland and Asia, Australia and the South Pacific.

# WATCHING THE WHALES

The nonprofit Pacific Whale Foundation (www.pacificwhale.org) runs whale-watching cruises out of both Lahaina and Ma'alaea harbours; or you can get acquainted at the Hawaiian Islands Humpback Whale National Marine Sanctuary Headquarters in Kihei.

## HUMPBACK WHALES

Humpbacks *(Megaptera novaeangliae)* are a species of baleen whale, characterised by their distinctive body shape, long pectoral fins and knobby head. Adults range in length from 12m to 16m, and can weigh in at 35 tonnes. Found across the world, humpbacks are seasonal migrants that can travel over 25,000km each year.

# GREAT WHITE IN FLIGHT
## South Africa

NAMIBIA

BOTSWANA

MOZAMBIQUE

SWAZILAND

ATLANTIC
OCEAN

SOUTH
AFRICA

LESOTHO

Cape Town

GREAT
WHITES

INDIAN
OCEAN

Gansbaai

**(left) Cage Divers Watching a Great White**
Australian Rodney Fox, expedition leader and producer of shark documentaries, is credited with designing and building the first underwater observation cage to dive with and observe great whites after surviving a shark attack in 1963.

**(right) African Penguins at Boulders Beach**
African penguins, as found at Boulders Beach in Table Mountain National Park, are also known as jackass penguins because of their donkeylike braying call.

*Carcharodon carcharias* – the great white shark – is the planet's largest predatory fish: 2000kg of ravenous, streamlined muscle, with a shocking mouthful of around 300 teeth. To get close to one is a humbling and terrifying experience; boat trips can take you to watch them breach and hunt, while the brave can cage dive – a descent into their lair with just a few flimsy-seeming bars for protection.

## On Screen
More chilling than any Hollywood horror, *Planet Earth* captures – in super-slow motion – the instant a great white shark erupts from the ocean and consumes a fur seal in one great gulp. Replayed at nearly one-fiftieth the actual speed (in reality it lasted just a second), we see every twist of movement, every tooth bared, every water drop displaced in this awesome display of raw hunting power.

## When
The best time to see sharks off South Africa is at dawn during the cooler months, from mid-April to mid-September. As the water temperature dips, migratory fish depart, leaving only the year-round marine life and so concentrating shark-feeding activity on fewer areas; this makes them easier to spot. Winter is also the best season for hiking and for spotting game in South Africa's parks and reserves as wildlife congregates around waterholes.

NORBERT PROBST/PHOTOLIBRARY

WALTER G ALLGÖWER/PHOTOLIBRARY

# EXPERIENCE

It's a beautiful day: the sun is glinting off the water, salt spray kisses your cheeks, the sea air blasts away the cobwebs as you roar away from the mainland in a little motorcraft, into a wildlife wonderland. The fur seals seem so carefree, porpoising in the waves as one big happy family; it looks, you think, like they're playing catch 'n' kiss or test driving new flippers. But this appearance of gay abandon is misleading: far from fun and games, their watery dawn dash from rocky home to open water is done at speed for one very large reason...

When it happens, it takes your breath away, chills your blood, makes you run and hide behind the sofa – or it would, but there's no such thing on this suddenly insubstantial-feeling vessel. There's nowhere to escape, nothing to do but watch.

What you've just seen is the most heart-stopping ambush in the animal kingdom. A seal, so contentedly bobbing on the ocean surface, has just been engulfed in an enormous, raw-gummed, razor-toothed mouth, the only remaining evidence of its existence a sorry flipper protruding from the shark's maw like a dangle of spaghetti. (And who dares tell a great white it's a messy eater?)

Without warning, like a geyser erupting in a nondescript landscape, the scene flicked from flat ocean to great-white white-water explosion in an instant. And the force of the thing – so fast did the shark burst from the deep that its whole body left the ocean: first pointy snout, then teeth, fins, blinding-white belly, tail. The whole beast was airborne, a colossal tonnage of flying fish twisting balletically as it reared up, grabbed dinner, cleared the water and dived in again nose first, tail re-entering last, smooth as a knife through butter.

And all is calm again. Well, for a bit. For with such a profusion of food in these cold temperate waters, it's not long before there's another shark strike. However, this time the great white is not so successful. You watch as the open mouth misses its fur seal target, and hold your breath as a thrashing chase ensues. Played out underwater, with just the odd flipper and fin breaking the surface maelstrom, you have no idea who is winning. The shark may be bigger, and faster in a straight line, but the seal is agile, and can twist and turn more sharply. Will the minnow make a getaway?

Suddenly the seal leaps for freedom – but it is an ill-timed escape attempt. Its sleek black body curves just above the great white's lurking mouth; the shark soars up and grabs the seal deftly, like a fielder making a catch.

And then the water is still once more.

### Great White

There is a lack of reliable data on the world's great-white population size, but scientists agree that their numbers have declined sharply over the past 50 years. The decline is attributed to overfishing and accidental catching in gill nets, among other factors, and great whites are now listed as an endangered species.

"The great white shark – the largest predatory fish on the planet."

# TAKING ACTION

## As You Saw It

Some extremely clever camera equipment and a bit of patience are required to re-create the *Planet Earth* experience. If you are lucky enough to be in the right spot at the right time to see a great white nobble a fur seal, you need to suck it up quickly. Without the benefit of slow mo' it's over in a second – a hellish roar of water, a mass of fish flesh, a flash of white belly, the crash of the plunge back in; somewhere in there a seal became lunch. Head out with an experienced local operator that knows the areas sharks frequent and you'll hopefully get your sighting; taking it all in is down to you.

## Adding to the Experience

A boat trip to witness great white sharks in action will bring other treats, too. You'll likely spot the seals that the sharks are after – a cheerful sight as they porpoise off your bow (until getting eaten…). Plus there are dolphins, whales and many birds, including albatrosses, petrels and shearwaters.

There are cage-diving options for the biggest thrill seekers: this involves floating just off the boat in a specifically constructed steel cage, in the shark's domain but safely contained. You breathe through a snorkel or simply hold your breath for repeated dips, so scuba diving experience isn't necessary – just strong nerves. If you're going to cage dive be certain that your chosen operator is licensed.

## Alternative Great White Shark–Spotting Experiences

Great white sharks are found in coastal waters around the globe.

✿ **Isla Guadalupe** (Mexico) For really remote – and possibly the world's best – shark viewing.

✿ **Neptune Islands** (off South Australia) For submersible cage diving: special cages are lowered 18m down onto the seabed (qualified divers only).

✿ **Gulf of the Farallones** (California, USA) For some of the planet's biggest great whites, just 30km off the coast near San Francisco.

# WHILE YOU'RE THERE

## Boulders Beach, Cape Town

Around 3000 African penguins live on this beach near Simon's Town; watch them waddle across the sand, or get in the water to waddle with them (www.sanparks.org).

## Hermanus

Watch whales without leaving the shore; from June to December large numbers of southern right whales cruise just off the coast near Hermanus – bring binoculars.

# LOOK, BUT DON'T BUY

Due to their size, man-eating reputation and the infamy resulting from the 1975 film *Jaws,* great white goodies – teeth, jaw bones, fins – are especially prized and can fetch high prices. In South Africa there have been reports of individuals willing to pay up to US$50,000 for great white shark jaws, and up to US$800 for a single tooth. These lucrative returns encourage poaching and underground trade.

In 2000 a proposal to ban international trade in great white products failed, though the fish are protected in many waters. The International Union for Conservation of Nature lists great white sharks as 'Vulnerable', though it is recognised that one of the key challenges faced by this fine fish is improving its woeful PR.

In an act of atonement Peter Benchley, author of *Jaws,* subsequently became a shark activist, and spent the last years of his life advocating their conservation.

### Bloukrans River Bridge, Eastern Cape

If diving with great whites isn't hair-raising enough, how about the world's highest bungy jump? Cape Town–based Bungy Bus (www .bungybus.co.za) runs overnight trips from the city to this 216m leap.

### Stellenbosch

Steady your shark-shot nerves with a glass of South Africa's finest wine, grown in the scenic vineyards just inland from the coast. Cape Town–based Bikes 'n' Wines (www.bikesnwines.com) leads tasty cycling tours on which you can slurp from the saddle.

## GETTING YOU THERE

The best places to view great whites in South Africa are Seal Island, just off Cape Town, and Dyer Island, a rocky outcrop just offshore from Gansbaai, a little further east along the coast. Both are easily accessible; it's about a 2½-hour drive between the two.

## EXPLORING THE SEAS OFF CAPE TOWN

Book a trip with a licensed operator to see the sharks; and pack seasickness pills – it could be a rough ride. Apex Shark Expeditions (www.apexpredators.com), based in Cape Town, escorted the *Planet Earth* team on its dramatic shark shoot. Apex also runs specialist trips to see pelagic birds.

## NOT SO CHUMMY

There is much controversy about the practice of baiting the water to attract sharks to tourist boats. It is thought that, if fed from boats, great whites make the connection between man and food, leading to more attacks on humans.

It is illegal to feed the sharks, but most operators will throw chum into the water – a pungent mix of fish blood, oil and guts that will attract the creatures but not provide a meal. Some people think this is much the same thing – even if you're not feeding it, the great white's hunting mode is switched on. Before booking a trip, ask your company for their stance on chumming and make sure you are happy with their answers.

## FAST FACTS

Of the 100-plus annual shark attacks worldwide, up to half are attributable to great whites; however, most are not fatal – the shark will often take a 'sample bite' then release the victim.

More than 100 million sharks are killed annually by humans; fewer than 25 humans are killed each year by sharks.

Great whites can travel at speeds of up to 24km/h.

The maximum size of a great white is believed to be around 6m long; females grow bigger than males.

Great white sharks are able to detect the electromagnetic fields emitted by the movement of other living creatures – even fields as faint as half a billionth of a volt.

# PENGUINS ON LIFE-OR-DEATH PARADE
## Marion Island, South Indian Ocean

SOUTH AFRICA

INDIAN OCEAN

MARION ISLAND ●

SOUTHERN OCEAN

ANTARCTICA

**Around 215,000 breeding adult penguins live on Marion Island, one of the most important – and impressive – king colonies in the world. There are also cantankerous elephant seals, feisty fur seals, wandering albatrosses (with 3.5m wingspans) and armadas of passing whales.**

## On Screen

On this tiny speck adrift midway between South Africa and Antarctica, in the gale-blasted latitudes of the Roaring Forties, the *Planet Earth* team documents the island's king penguins, who battle crashing surf and hungry fur seals to somehow survive here.

## When

The weather is pretty consistent, if not pleasant, year-round: cold, rainy, very windy and perpetually cloudy – summer (December to February) highs average just 9°C. King penguins lay from November to March, incubating a single egg – on their feet – for nearly two months. The adults then rear the chicks for about a year.

**King Penguins at Ship's Cove, Marion Island**
Marion Island is the larger of the Prince Edward Islands group, and a South African–designated Special Nature Reserve.

*"Being flightless, the penguins must cross the beach on foot. An unexpected predator is waiting…"*

# EXPERIENCE

Boof! Surf crashes, thick clouds scud, the wind whips – marooned Marion Island is as wild and elemental as planet earth comes. But amid the explosion of sea foam, there are tens, hundreds – no – thousands of king penguins, their sleek bodies pummelled by the ocean but emerging unscathed.

If you were allowed on the beaches of this ridiculously remote isle (once described by a passing sailor as 'a cluster of rugged nipples') you would be overwhelmed – both by the chill blasts, and by the noise and scale of the wildlife spectacle. Sociable kings like to gather in numbers – this is a penguin party (tuxedos mandatory) of 200,000-odd birds, who all like to chat. The blubberous elephant seals who share this beach look on huffily, declaring with fartlike snorts their displeasure at the ruckus.

As they waddle across the shore, returning home from their three-day fishing trip, the penguins are unflustered by their grumpy neighbours. Unflustered, that is, until a ravenous fur seal bursts out of the surf on the hunt for lunch.

Fur seals usually live on krill, but the beasts here have developed a penchant for penguin. It's hard to watch as an open-jawed seal grabs one of the birds by its pretty, slender neck and shakes it around with the zeal of a patriot waving a flag. Other penguins scatter as this monster lollops across the sand; neither bird nor beast is really designed

for land agility – it's an ungainly chase. But the fur seal has considerable size on its side and quickly catches up with its prey as both try to negotiate seaweed-slippery rocks and incoming tides.

However, it's not quite as bleak as it looks for the diminutive kings. Despite being at a physical disadvantage, they know their strengths – their razor-sharp beaks are more than capable of taking out a fur seal's eye; the predator must attack from behind to avoid a blinding, a fact the canny penguins are well aware of.

Now you can see a David and Goliath battle in progress: a ruffled fur seal and a king, neck stretched to make itself appear as big as possible, circle each other, each making proprietary jabs and lunges, probing for signs of vulnerability. The penguins are bold little birds, punching above their weight in order to safeguard their fluff-ball chicks, who bleat for food in the colony just metres away. If parent doesn't make it home, junior will starve – this is a gauntlet the kings must run.

David looks doomed as he tries to escape from the fur seal but stumbles on the wet pebbles; but luck is on his side – he makes it, somehow. Indeed, two out of three of these plucky penguins *do* make it, ensuring the colony lives to squawk, fish, breed and battle another day.

**Fast Food**
When a fur seal charges across a crowded beach, king penguins must get their little legs moving at top speed to get out of the way.

# TAKING ACTION

## As You Saw It

Unfortunately Joe Public is not allowed anywhere near Marion; even researchers are restricted. The South African National Antarctic Programme (Sanap; www.sanap.org.za) does run expeditions, but they comprise only specially skilled, selected scientists and doctors. Sanap's pretrip advice for these elite few includes making sure teeth are in good order before departure ('limited dental care is available from a medic who has done a one-week crash course') and the suggestion to order 'more than your normal quota of beer and liquor'.

## A More-Accessible Experience

So you can't visit Marion (unless you're a very fortunate expert with excellent dental hygiene), but you can re-create a similar experience on the 'nearby' islands of the Southern Ocean. While there are rules about visiting penguin rookeries (for example, not getting too close to the birds – though the inquisitive creatures often flout this themselves), certain sites do allow controlled numbers of visitors. Generally you will need to join an expedition cruise to access king-penguin colonies; check the itineraries of the various boats to see if a king-colony visit is likely.

## Alternative King Penguin–Experiences

There are a few places in the planet's far south where you can get close to massive huddles of king penguins:

✿ **St Andrews Bay** (South Georgia) Three-hundred thousand pungent king penguins cluster at this island's largest rookery.

✿ **Volunteer Beach** (Falkland Islands) A stoic bunch of kings – the penguins here were virtually wiped out in the 19th century, but have rallied and now number 500 breeding pairs.

✿ **Tierra del Fuego** (Argentina, Chile) Mainland king colonies.

✿ **Macquarie Island** (Antarctica) A seriously remote king rookery – permits are required.

# WHILE YOU'RE THERE

## Grytviken, South Georgia

Stop off at this former whaling station to nose around the fascinating South Georgia Museum and raise a dram to the main man – polar explorer Ernest Shackleton's grave is in the cemetery here.

## Sea Lion Island, Falkland Islands

See not just kings but four other species of

## NOT SO COOL FOR CATS

Five domestic cats were introduced to Marion in 1949 to help eradicate a mouse problem at the island's South African base. Oh, the irony: by 1975 the feline population was out of control, swelling to more than 2000.

The problem was that these kitties began feeding on unsuspecting burrowing petrels – a much easier prey than the wily mice they were sent to hunt. In 1975 alone the cats ate nearly half a million birds, driving the grey petrel to extinction on the island.

By 1977, with the mass of moggies numbering around 3400, it was clear something needed to be done, so the Marion Island Cat Eradication Program was initiated. A few felines were infected with a highly specific disease and nocturnal hunting with 12-bore shotguns was undertaken; finally, traps were used. In 1991–1992 only eight cats were trapped and no sightings were recorded. It is now believed that feral cats have been completely eradicated from Marion's shores.

penguin on this tiny offshore outcrop, as well as stonking-great elephant seals. You can stay on the island; it's home, according to the brochure, to 'the most southerly British hotel in the world'.

### Paulet Island, Antarctic Peninsula
Beneath the distinctive cone of this 2km-wide isle, nest 200,000 noisy Adélie penguins; also look out for blue-eyed shags and giant petrels.

### Snow Hill Island, Antarctica
Snow Hill's 4000 pair–strong colony of majestic emperor penguins was first visited as recently as 2004. The island is only accessible by icebreaker; visit late October to November to witness the emperors' winter breeding.

## GETTING YOU THERE

Expedition cruises to the Antarctic most commonly depart from Ushuaia, at the extreme southern tip of Argentina. A range of itineraries is available; a classic voyage would cross the notoriously choppy Drake Passage for the South Shetland Islands and the Antarctic Peninsula, taking two weeks there and back. These trips are not cheap: basic cruises range from around £2,000 (in a shared cabin, on a big boat, in the shoulder season) to £14,000 and up.

## EXPLORING THE ANTARCTIC REGION

For more information on expedition cruises to the region, visit www.iaato.org (the International Association of Antarctica Tour Operators) and see p162.

## FAST FACTS

King penguins are the second-largest penguin species (behind emperors) measuring about 80cm tall.

......................................

King penguins are serially monogamous, staying with one mate for the duration of a breeding cycle, but not necessarily selecting the same mate the following season.

......................................

Marion Island is 19km long by 12km wide, with a high point of 1230m – the permanently snow-capped State President Peak.

......................................

Marion Island was first discovered in 1663 by the Dutch ship *Maerseveen*, but no landing was made; the first recorded landing was in 1803 by a gang of sealers, though they found signs of earlier occupation.

......................................

Marion Island was claimed for South Africa by the South African Navy on 29 December 1947; the South African government made it, and neighbouring Prince Edward Island, a Special Nature Reserve in 1995.

......................................

# EXPERIENCE

Seasickness strikes. Even though you've had a couple of days to get accustomed to the boat's pitching and yawing, the swells rolling in from the Pacific are too much even for your Stugeron-soothed stomach.

'Keep your eyes on the horizon!' advises your neighbour at the deck rail. But you can't see the horizon. There's something black and dense swirling in the way. As you get closer, you realise it's alive: a wheeling mass of birds, churning the surface into a seething maelstrom as they plunge into the glacial blue waters. Shearwaters, in their hundreds, thousands – tens or even hundreds of thousands; before you know it, the ferry is surrounded by seemingly all the world's birds. You've watched Hitchcock movies and you're nervous, but fortunately your krill suit is at the dry cleaners – because that's what they're after.

It's amazing what hunger can make you do, the ship's naturalist explains. These shearwaters – all five million of them – have made the 16,000km journey from Australia, as they do each year, to feast on the krill swarms. And they're only a small part of the crowd: there are 80 million seabirds hereabouts right now, all with a taste for krill.

It's the sun, he says, and the currents stirring up the nutrients; it all creates a warm krill soup. Tasty, you say, but you don't mean it. The ship lurches, and your stomach does the same.

Another dark shape appears among the frenzied birds, breaking the surface smoothly before slipping beneath again. Then a barnacled fin slaps the water, and a vast fluke; 20m away there's another fin, and another. There must be half a dozen humpback whales here, blowing and dipping again to gorge themselves.

Those shearwaters dive to depths of 130m to reach the krill, you're told. A valuable skill, diving, if you're a shearwater. But there are other strategies: if you're a humpback, and you need to gulp down three tonnes of invertebrates each day, having a mouth the size of a garage is pretty much essential.

Whale-mountains erupt and subside all around, a marine ballet with impeccable choreography. You gaze across at a nearby pair, one half the length of the other. It won't be long before that calf says goodbye to its mother, the biologist explains. Big enough to make its own way, it's feeding here before migrating back south alone.

You know they're singing down there. You can't hear it, but that haunting, wordless hymn echoes in your head anyway, and it helps. You've almost forgotten the seasickness, but you'll always remember this sea.

**Humpbacks in Frederick Sound, Alaska**
In addition to humpbacks, Frederick Sound hosts an abundance of sea lions, seals and porpoises.

# TAKING ACTION

## As You Saw It

The massed gatherings of shearwaters and humpbacks showcased on *Planet Earth* take place among the Aleutian Islands, which stretch in an arc from the Alaska Peninsula towards Russia. Whale-watching tours depart from Kodiak, but a fascinating alternative is to board the ferry *MV Tustumena* to sail along the chain; there's a federal naturalist on board to highlight the wonders you'll spot en route.

## Adding to the Experience

There are opportunities for whale-watching in several other parts of Alaska, including the waterways around Glacier Bay, Juneau, Sitka and Petersburg, and further west around the Kenai Peninsula. Sightings – mostly of humpbacks, but also orca, bowhead, minke and gray whales – are also relatively common from the decks of state ferries.

## Alternative Whale-Watching Experiences

Whale-watching opportunities dot the planet.
✿ **Kaikoura** (South Island, New Zealand) Also good for diving with fur seals.

✿ **Sea of Cortez** (Baja California, Mexico) For various whale species, plus the world's biggest fish: the whale shark.

✿ **The Azores** (Portugal) Remote islands floating in the Atlantic off the West African coast.

✿ **Tonga** For the chance of snorkelling with humpbacks during winter and spring.

# WHILE YOU'RE THERE

## Kodiak Island

Go on a bear hunt (with camera, not rifle, naturally) on this vast, wild, rugged island to spot the planet's biggest Bruins.

## Dutch Harbor & Unalaska

At the furthest stop on the *MV Tustumena's* voyage, discover the relics of the Aleutian Islands' all-too-active involvement in WWII – bunkers, batteries and a poignant cemetery.

## McNeil River State Game Sanctuary

To see 20 brown bears flipping salmon straight from the McNeil River Falls, you need to win the lottery – literally: permits to watch this mind-blowing natural event are limited to 10 per day over just four days, available only through a random draw (www.wildlife.alaska.gov).

## Lake Clark National Park & Preserve

Get paddling on the rapids of three rivers – with both frantic white-water sections and more placid parts, there are plenty of options for kayaks and rafts.

# SONG OF THE SEA

The song of the male humpback is one of the longest, most complex and haunting calls in the animal kingdom – but we still don't really know how it's made or even what it's for.

Humpback 'songs' consist of an array of noises – whistles, grunts, squeaks and longer, deeper notes – arranged into repetitive sequences that can last for up to 30 minutes. Each song is unique to males in a particular area, though the songs change gradually over time. It's been suggested that males sing to attract females, to challenge other males, or for some echolocation purpose, but research is yet to prove conclusive.

Whales don't make these noises by vibrating the larynx, but somehow use air circulated within the body underwater, perhaps using sinuses within the nasal system – again, we don't know exactly how. But however – or why ever – they sing, humpbacks produce the most beautiful sound in the ocean.

## GETTING YOU THERE

The departure point for the *MV Tustumena* is Homer, a 40-minute flight from Anchorage.

## EXPLORING THE ALEUTIANS

The *MV Tustumena* sails from Homer monthly from April to October, calling at Kodiak Island, Chignik, Sand Point, King Cove, Cold Bay, False Pass and Akutan on the four-day voyage to Dutch Harbor. Timetables can be downloaded from www.ferryalaska.com.

## THE BEAR FACTS

The Kodiak bear *(Ursus arctos middendorffi)* – which can weigh over 650kg – is found only in the Kodiak archipelago, where around 3500 survive. It's a subspecies of the brown bear and comparable in size to the polar bear, making it the world's largest land carnivore – perhaps partly because of the abundance of spawning salmon during the summer, when the bears effortlessly flip the fish from the rivers.

# SEASONAL FORESTS
## *Planet Earth, Episode Ten*

Life affirming and quietly magnificent, the planet's coniferous and deciduous trees are Mother Nature's sentinels: protective and essential. Take the sub-Arctic taiga forest – a globe-encircling belt of green – which is so vast that, during summer, its oxygen output actually changes the make-up of our atmosphere. Fascinating animal species (wolverine, lemur, a rare type of leopard) call these forests home. But they're also special in themselves: you don't need to spot wildlife to appreciate the grandeur of California's redwoods (topping 100m, the planet's tallest trees) or the silent wisdom of a bristlecone pine – aged 4000-plus, the oldest living organism in the world.

# NORTHERN LATITUDES
## The Taiga, North America & Eurasia

THE TAIGA
NORTH AMERICA

THE TAIGA

ARCTIC OCEAN

PACIFIC
OCEAN

ATLANTIC
OCEAN

INDIAN
OCEAN

**(left) Taiga**
Much of the Taiga was once covered with glaciers. As the glaciers receded they left gouges and depressions in the topography that are now frequently filled with water, creating bogs and lakes.

**(right) Wolverine**
The wolverine (Gulo gulo) is also known as the American glutton, skunk bear, Indian devil and carcajou.

**Heading south from the treeless Arctic tundra, the Taiga is a sub-Arctic zone of lush muskeg, willow thickets and spruce. The cold-adapted creatures inhabiting this great landscape may live and die without ever seeing a single human. Long may it be so.**

## On Screen
*Planet Earth* takes us on a sweeping journey across the Taiga, a nearly continuous belt of coniferous forest that circles the northern latitudes of North America and Eurasia. The Taiga holds as many trees as all the world's rainforests combined, and produces so much oxygen that it refreshes the atmosphere of the entire planet.

## When
From Siberia and Scandinavia to Alaska and the Yukon, the Taiga is impossibly cold in the winter, and in some years it can dip to -50°C in the middle of February. The region is at its warmest and brightest from June to August, when temperatures frequently top 30°C, and white nights are illuminated by a sun that refuses to set.

PETE CAIRNS/NATURE PICTURE LIBRARY

# EXPERIENCE

Harsh and unforgiving in the dead of winter, the Taiga is understandably not everyone's first choice of travel destination. Even when summer finally comes to the northern latitudes, the growing season may last just one month; it can take 50 years for a tree to get bigger than a seedling. But as you pause to take in the majesty of the forest surrounding you – stunted though it may be – suddenly time seems like a luxury that we humans will never have.

In this silent world little stirs, aside from the snow softly crunching beneath your boots. But there are signs of life – stories written in the snow – such as the prints of an arctic fox and the hare it was stalking. And then there are the occasional moose and caribou calls, which comfort you with the knowledge that you're not completely alone out here.

Still, most animals in the Taiga are so hard to glimpse that they're almost like spirits. You could spend your whole life in these woods and never see a lynx. The cat must roam hundreds of kilometres in search of prey, and may never visit the same patch of forest twice. Quite simply, the Taiga is the very essence of wilderness.

Every once in a while, your traverse across the great north leads you to thriving human outposts, physical manifestations of our species' collective will to survive. In Siberia, you travel Soviet-era railways across a vast swath of the planet, stopping regularly to buy fresh-picked wild mushrooms and various cylinders of smoked and cured meats.

By the time you reach Scandinavia, your spirits have been beaten down by the frosty cold, yet there are signs that winter is finally passing. In towns and cities of picturesque wooden buildings, outdoor cafes fill with overeager denizens. Baristas build all manner of espresso-based drinks, which are served to customers with typical Scandinavian sophistication.

One trans-Atlantic flight later, and suddenly you find yourself behind the wheel of a somewhat intimidating 4WD truck. You've still got your snow boots on, and your right foot is pressing the proverbial 'pedal to the metal'.

Your circumnavigation of the globe has finally brought you to the Yukon, a name that is evocative as well as descriptive. There is a long and bitter highway ahead, but Alaska – big, beautiful and wildly bountiful – awaits your imminent arrival.

**Woodland Caribou**

The woodland caribou relies on mature and old-growth forests for its main food sources, ground and tree lichens.

# TAKING ACTION

## As You Saw It

It will take several trips, many months and a decent chunk of change if you want to experience all that the Taiga has to offer. But if you're limited by either time or money, then consider focusing in on just one region. A journey on the Trans-Siberian Railway is comparatively light on the wallet, but Russian infrastructure is not to be relied upon if you have a schedule to keep. In contrast, Scandinavia is one of the most efficiently organised travel destinations in the world, though shoestringers will find themselves pinching every last kroner. Alaska and the Yukon probably offer the greatest diversity of travel experiences, welcoming both free-spending jetsetters and more measured overland travellers.

## Adding to the Experience

A journey on the legendary Trans-Siberian Railway is arguably the best way to traverse the Taiga. This Soviet-built ribbon of steel joins together far-flung dots on the map. Step off the train in Krasnoyarsk, Irkutsk, Ulan-Ude and Chita to admire faded 19th-century grandeur alongside quirky socialist realism. Irkutsk is the gateway to magnificent Lake Baikal, the most touristed spot in Siberia.

## Alternative North American–Highway Experiences

If you have reliable wheels, a decent map and a healthy respect for road distances, check out these classic North American highways.

❀ **Alaska Hwy** (Alaska–Canada) Also known as the Alcan, this vast highway runs from Dawson Creek, British Columbia to Delta Junction, Alaska, via Whitehorse, Yukon.

❀ **Klondike Hwy** (Alaska–Canada) The Klondike runs from Skagway, Alaska to Dawson City, Yukon, and parallels the route used by early prospectors in the Klondike Gold Rush.

❀ **Robert Campbell Hwy** (Canada) Runs from Watson Lake, Yukon to Carmacks, Yukon; nearly 600km of mostly gravel surface.

# WHILE YOU'RE THERE

## Chilkoot

The Chilkoot, the most famous hiking trail in Alaska, was the route used by the Klondike gold miners in the 1898 gold rush. Walking it is both a wilderness adventure and a history lesson. The almost-60km trek takes three to four days and includes the Chilkoot Pass – a steep climb up to 1000m that has most hikers scrambling on all fours. The highlight of the hike for many is riding the historic White Pass & Yukon Route (WP&YR) Railroad from Lake Bennett back to Skagway. Experiencing the Chilkoot and returning on the WP&YR is probably the ultimate Alaska trek, combining great scenery, a historic site and an incredible sense of adventure.

## Whitehorse

The leading city and capital of the Yukon, Whitehorse is also likely to have a prominent role in your trip. The territory's two great highways,

## WOLVERINE

In northern folklore, the wolverine is viewed as a cross between a bear and a wolf. In reality, it's a huge weasel. The wolverine's bulk helps to conserve body heat and broaden its menu – it's so strong that it can bring down an adult caribou. For its size, it's said that wolverines can eat more in one sitting than any other animal. But in the Taiga gluttony is no sin, and it's wise to eat all you can, when you can. And when you can't, you can always store leftovers in the frozen ground.

the Alaska and the Klondike, cross here. As a major transport hub, Whitehorse is home to all manner of outfitters and services for explorations across the territory. Utility aside, Whitehorse can delight: it has a well-funded arts community, good restaurants and a decent range of hotels. Exploring the sights within earshot of the rushing Yukon River can easily take a day or more. Additionally, look past the bland commercial buildings and you'll see a fair number of heritage ones awaiting your discovery.

## Bergen & the Western Fjords

This spectacular region of Norway will dazzle your eyeballs with truly indescribable scenery. Hardangerfjord, Sognefjord and Geirangerfjord are all variants on the same theme: steep crystalline rock walls dropping with sublime force straight into the sea, often decorated with waterfalls, and small farms harmoniously blending into the natural landscape. Summer hiking opportunities exist along the fjord walls and on the enormous Jostedalsbreen glacier. Bergen, a lively city with a 15th-century waterfront, is exceedingly pleasing to behold, and contains some of the country's finest nightlife and restaurants.

## Lake Baikal

Crystal-clear Lake Baikal is a vast body of the bluest water, surrounded by rocky or tree-covered foreshores, behind which mountains float like phantoms at indeterminable distances. Baikal's meteorological mood swings are transfixing spectacles, whole weather systems dancing for your delectation over Siberia's climatic kitchen. Shaped like a banana, Baikal is 636km from north to south and up to 1637m deep, making it the world's deepest lake. Incredibly, it contains nearly one-fifth of the planet's unfrozen fresh water, more than North America's five Great Lakes combined. See p60 for more on Lake Baikal.

# GETTING YOU THERE

Transportation hubs throughout the northern latitudes are served by most of the world's major airlines.

# EXPLORING THE TAIGA

The world-famous Man in Seat Sixty-One (www.seat61.com/Trans-Siberian.htm) can help you make sense of the world's most famous train jaunt.

# TALLEST FORESTS ON EARTH
## Sequoia National Park, California, USA

Growing only along North America's western edge, coast redwoods and sequoias (another redwood species) combine to pack a small area of California with the largest and tallest organisms on earth – natural skyscrapers that seem to scratch at the sky. To walk beneath them is to be humbled by the size and potential of nature.

## On Screen

*Planet Earth* takes you to the tops of the tallest forest on earth, an ancient place where humans trying to scale the trees look like insects, and where life thrives far above any visitors' eyes. Great grey owls take their comical maiden flights, falling from branch to branch, while pine martens stalk distracted squirrels in a game of life and death.

## When

Hiking through the giants of the redwood forests is best through the summer and autumn dry seasons, from around May to November.

### A Bristlecone Pine

Bristlecone pines are thought to be one of the world's oldest living organisms, and their timber persists for a long period after a tree's death. As tree growth rings can provide insights into past climates and climatic events, studies of bristlecone pine wood have revealed environmental conditions stretching back to almost 9000 years ago.

"*Animals may be sparse in America's conifer forests – but the trees themselves make up for it.*"

# EXPERIENCE

A sheet of mist slices across the top of the conifer forest, the tall trees drinking from the air's moisture even as you stuff your own water bottle into your pack. From here, across the open Crescent Meadow, it looks like many other woodlands: thick, straight and tall, its foliage like a quiver of arrows pointed at the sky, but not massive. But you know that's only a veneer; somewhere deep inside this forest are the biggest living things on earth.

You begin walking, threading between Crescent Meadow and Log Meadow. As the Trail of the Sequoias heads into the appropriately named Giant Forest, massive trunks spear out of the ground – you begin to suspect that you will have neck ache tomorrow from constantly looking up in search of their tops.

After crossing Crescent Creek and climbing to crest a small ridge, you wind back down into a hollow that might be the true 'valley of the giants'. It is here that some of the most impressive trees on earth are rooted, and soon you are among them. By the track junction with the Congress Trail you stand dwarfed by the President, said to be the third largest tree in the world, its widening trunk like a giant hoof stamped into the earth. The nearby Chief Sequoyah tree is a mess of injuries, as scarred and worn as you'd expect of any living thing so many hundreds of years old.

You begin to imagine shapes and faces in the burls and bark around you – forest spirits watching you pass – as you continue to your ultimate destination: the mighty General Sherman tree. Although not really that much bigger than the other forest giants around it, General Sherman feels as vast as its fame, because you know that, by volume, it is the largest organism on the planet. It is tall enough – 83.8m – but it's the sheer bulk of the thing that really sets it apart, with its trunk more than 11m across at the ground. Still, it is difficult to imagine that this one bit of wood weighs as much as 10 blue whales.

You look up and it seems unclear where the tree ends and the sky begins, one merging with the other. Perhaps the canopy is actually just a dense green cloud?

Famous sequoias in this grove include the House and Senate Groups, and the President, General Lee and McKinley trees.

# TAKING ACTION

## As You Saw It

If you want to rope up and ascend into the redwood canopy, as per the images in the *Planet Earth* series, grab yourself – at a minimum – a biology degree. These heights are the exclusive domain of forest-canopy scientists.

For a shorter route, recreational tree climbing, which uses similar roping and safety features as rock climbing, is a growing pastime – in 2008 it was estimated that there were around 13,000 recreational tree climbers in the USA. Tree Climbers International (www.treeclimbing.com) was formed in the early 1980s and offers courses from beginner to instructor training, as well as public climbing days in Atlanta. (Note that US national parks are designated 'no climb' zones.)

## Adding to the Experience

General Sherman may be considered the largest tree on earth, but it is not the tallest. In the summer of 2006, researchers found three new record-breaking trees in Redwood National Park along the northern California coast. The tallest, Hyperion, measures a whopping 115.5m – that's nearly 40 storeys high! Coming in a close second and third are Helios at 114.5m and Icarus at 113.1m. These trees displaced the old record-holder, the 113.1m-high Stratosphere Giant in Rockefeller Forest. But you won't be able to find them, the trees bear no signs – too many boot-clad visitors would compact the delicate root systems, so the parks service is not telling where they are.

## Alternative Tall-Tree Experiences

In the southwest corner of Western Australia, around the town of Pemberton, the endemic karri tree is also among the tallest in the world, growing to around 90m. Eight of the tallest karris once served as fire lookout trees, with platforms built in their canopies and metal spikes hammered into their trunks as ladders. Today three of the trees have been designated as 'climbing trees', allowing visitors to ascend to their tops: Diamond Tree (51m high), Gloucester Tree (60m) and Dave Evans Bicentennial Tree (75m).

# A TALL STORY

Though they covered much of the northern hemisphere millions of years ago, redwood trees now grow only in China and two areas of California (and a small grove in Oregon). Coast redwoods (*Sequoia sempervirens*) are found in a narrow, 725km strip along California's Pacific coast between Big Sur and southern Oregon. Giant sequoias (*Sequoiadendron giganteum*) grow only on the Sierra Nevada's western slopes and are most abundant in Sequoia and Kings Canyon and Yosemite National Parks.

The tallest trees reach their maximum height some time between 300 and 700 years of age. Because they're narrow at their bases at this age, they generally aren't the ones you notice as you walk through the forest. The dramatic, fat-trunked giants, which make such a visually stunning impact from the ground, are ancient – as much as 2000 years old. But they're not as tall as the younger ones because their tops will have been blown off in intense storms over the centuries.

What gives these majestic giants their namesake colour is the redwoods' high tannin content. It also makes their wood and bark resistant to insects and disease. The thick, spongy bark also has a high moisture content, enabling the ancient trees to survive many naturally occurring forest fires.

Coast redwoods are the only conifers in the world that can reproduce not only by seed cones (which grow to about the size of an olive at the ends of branches), but also by sprouting from their parents' roots and stumps, using the established root systems. Often you'll see a circle of redwoods standing in a forest, sometimes around a wide crater; this 'fairy ring' is made up of offspring that sprouted from one parent tree, which may have deteriorated into humus long ago.

# WHILE YOU'RE THERE

### Giant Forest Museum

For a primer on the intriguing ecology, fire cycle and history of the big sequoias, drop in at the excellent Giant Forest Museum (right by the Giant Forest). Follow up your visit with a wander around the paved (and wheelchair-accessible) 2km interpretive Big Trees Trail, which starts from the museum parking lot.

### Ancient Bristlecone Pine Forest

From the tallest to the oldest, it's little more than 100km as the crow flies from the Giant Forest to the parched and stark slopes of the otherworldly Ancient Bristlecone Pine Forest in California's White Mountains. This forest contains the most ancient trees in the world: Methuselah, the oldest, is estimated at 4700 years of age, making it older than the Great Sphinx of Giza.

### High Sierra Trail

One of the USA's ultimate mountain hikes, this trail is all about highs – 116km in length, it traverses the heart of the High Sierra. Leaving from beside the Giant Forest in Sequoia National Park, it ranges east to the summit of Mt Whitney, the highest peak in the contiguous US. Expect to take around eight days to complete the trail.

# GETTING YOU THERE

From the town of Visalia, visitors to Sequoia National Park can catch the handy Sequoia Shuttle (www.sequoiashuttle.com), which has five daily departures to the Giant Forest Museum from late May to early September. If driving, leave Hwys 65 or 99 and go east on Hwy 198 to the national park entrance.

# EXPLORING SEQUOIA NATIONAL PARK

Throughout the year, Sequoia National Park rangers offer a variety of walks around, and talks about, the park and the giant trees that underpin it, including walks to the General Sherman tree. For information see www.nps.gov/seki.

## FAST FACTS

Coast redwoods can live for 2200 years, grow to 115m tall and achieve a diameter of 7m at the base, with bark up to 30cm thick.

Deciduous and coniferous woodlands are the most extensive forests on earth.

The General Sherman tree is estimated to weigh almost 6000 tonnes.

# TINY PREY, TINY PREDATORS

## Valdivian Forests of Southern Chile

PACIFIC
OCEAN

BOLIVIA

BRAZIL

PARAGUAY

URUGUAY

**VALDIVIAN FORESTS**

Puerto Varas
Puerto Montt

ARGENTINA

ATLANTIC
OCEAN

**CHILE**

**(left) Southern Pudú**

Pudús often establish complex networks of paths and tunnels through the thick vegetation of their habitat, allowing them to move about virtually unseen.

**(right) Gunnera Tinctoria**

Native to southern Chile and also known as Chilean rhubarb, gunnera has been introduced to other places throughout the world as an ornamental and edible plant – its leaves can grow up to 2.5m across.

**Chile's forests, volcanoes and lakes are ripe for exploration. Strike out on a hiking trail, kit up to climb one of the rumbling peaks dominating the skyline, raft or kayak the waterways, or just ponder the impenetrable mysteries of nature: for example, why do creatures so tiny feed on rhubarb so gargantuan?**

## On Screen

In a land of giants, sometimes making yourself small is a strategy for survival. Within the lush rainforests lining the lower slopes of smoking volcanoes in Chile's Lake District, huge gunnera plants – giant rhubarb – conceal a menagerie of miniature creatures. *Planet Earth* stoops to introduce a rarely seen family of minute deer – and the equally small-scale predator that hunts them.

## When

Chile's southern half is best visited in the austral summer, from December to March; some areas are almost cut off in the winter months, and just chilly and damp the rest of the time. Conversely, there's a range of decent ski resorts in this region – some June to October to get on the piste.

"*This is a bizarre world of miniature creatures.*"

# EXPERIENCE

The night air is chilly after the warmth of the summer day. Zipping your fleece, you decide to head away from the camp for a clearer view of the volcano; the red glow from its peak has become angry and raw in the gathering darkness. As you delve deeper into the forest your friends' chattering fades, replaced by the chirrup of crickets and the faint whisper of the breeze through the trees.

The moon is full, and bright enough – as your eyes adjust to the gloom – to light your way as you step off the trail. Pushing through the ferns in the undergrowth you spot a movement among the gunnera – rhubarb on steroids, its cabbagey leaves the size of tea trays. At first it's hard to make out what's making that staccato crunching; then, coyly, a furred form emerges from the shade – no bigger than a cat, it looks something like a horned marmot. It's a pudú – at less than 45cm tall, the world's smallest deer; this male is standing guard as his mate gets stuck into the gunnera leaves, tearing off mouthfuls as her tiny offspring nuzzle underneath to suckle.

You're still crouching, mesmerised but conscious of the pins and needles tickling your legs, when you become aware of something else studying the scene just as intently as you are. The cat looks harmless enough – it's kitten-sized, at best – but the leopardesque markings betray its predatory intentions. The kodkod – a cousin of the ocelot – sniffs the night air and glares hungrily at the infant pudús, each of which would make a hearty feast for such a compact cat. You'd lay heavy odds on the Lilliputian leopard, but he clearly thinks differently; it seems the size and weight the defensive-minded dad has over him means an attack is just not worth the risk.

Eyes narrowed and head bowed he slinks away into a neighbouring clearing, and you follow – partly to stretch your legs, but also curious to watch the hungry cat's next move. As you arrive, you see what's drawn him here: a flickering and whirring from the forest floor announces the arrival of newly hatched moths, vulnerable and, to the kodkod, enticing – in-flight snacks, if you will. Scampering over, he bats one out of the air, crunching greedily, then another. Ready for one more, he leaps – and misses; this one's got the hang of flying, looping around the bemused cat to bat him on the rump before fluttering up out of reach. That's enough humiliation for one evening, clearly, and the cat evaporates into the undergrowth.

You stroll back to camp to warm yourself. En route you gaze up – while you tower over the pocket-sized species adapted to life in this quirky Gulliver's world, you're still dwarfed by the volcanoes and soaring trees.

Hiking to Puyehue–Cordón Caulle

The Puyehue–Cordón Caulle volcanic complex encompasses the Puyehue volcano and Cordón Caulle fissure complex. Cordón Caulle, a geothermal area occupying a 78-sq-km depression, is the largest active geothermal area in the southern Andes.

# TAKING ACTION

## As You Saw It

Many of Chile's parks are well set up for curious explorers. Parque Nacional Puyehue and Parque Nacional Vicente Pérez Rosales – Chile's oldest national park – form a contiguous band of protected land along Chile's Argentine border. Both encompass a range of habitats, including Valdivian rainforest as well as volcanoes, lakes and waterfalls. Both parks also have campsites, lodges and refuges from which to strike out into the forests. You don't need to be a naturalist to spot wildlife – just lucky; the pudú and kodkod aren't just pretty, they're pretty rare and secretive, too.

## Adding to the Experience

Hiking trails lace most areas of the parks. To get a sense of scale, ascend one of the peaks: in Vicente Pérez Rosales, Volcán Osorno (2660m) is a challenge not to be underestimated (ice-climbing gear is likely to be needed); a jaunt up to the crater lookout on Volcán Casablanca (1990m) in Puyehue shouldn't be beyond most hikers, and the views are spectacular. Horse trekking offers another way to strike out and explore more distant sections of the parks.

## Alternative Rainforest Experiences

Temperate rainforests dot the planet – and usually offer absorbing hikes.

✿ **Olympic Peninsula** (Washington State, USA) Large herds of Roosevelt elk roam the state's western slopes.

✿ **Haast region** (South Island, New Zealand) Head off on the trails through kahikatea and rimu forests.

✿ **Devon and Cornwall** (southwest England) The damp valleys on the UK's south coast host verdant wet woodlands; visit Fowey and some of the more lush gardens in southern Cornwall.

✿ **Shikoku** (Japan) Best known for its temple pilgrimage circuit, Shikoku also has lush forests.

✿ **Tasmania** (Australia) Ten percent of the state is covered with rainforest – take a hike around Cradle Mountain to explore some of it.

# WHILE YOU'RE THERE

## Termas de Puyehue

Chile's premier hot-springs resort (www.puyehue.cl) is the place to head to ease those aching bones posthike with a soak and some luxurious treatments.

## THE DAY THE EARTH MOVED

The array of cones and peaks that punctuate many of Chile's most memorable landscapes are also reminders of its position in the Ring of Fire – the volcanically active coastal countries bordering the Pacific Ocean. Essentially, to pervert a popular proverb, this is what happens when an unstoppable force meets another unstoppable force: the westward-drifting South American tectonic plate – at the edge of which Chile is perched – is in constant collision with the adjacent, eastward-moving Nazca plate, which is being forced to slide underneath. In geological terms, the Nazca plate is being subducted; this does not make for a happy tectonic plate, and (as well as having created the Andes) causes periodic earthquakes and volcanic eruptions.

On 22 May 1960 the plates shifted in epic fashion: the resulting tremor, known afterwards as the Valdivia Earthquake, was the most powerful ever recorded, measuring up to 9.5 on the Richter scale. Several thousand people died, not just from the damage on land but also from a number of tsunamis that devastated the Chilean coast and Hilo on Hawai'i, with waves reaching as far as Japan and the Philippines. It also triggered the eruption of a vent on Volcán Puyehue, which blasted lava and ash across the area, changing the landscape forever.

### Parque Nacional Nahuel Huapi, Argentina

Slip over the border for more natural wonders in this diverse park; the photogenic focal point is the bluer-than-you'd-believe Lago Nahuel Huapi.

### Puerto Varas

The fast-rising adrenalin centre of the Lake District is the go-to place for climbing, canyoning, rafting, kayaking and horse trekking – not to mention rich German-style cakes.

### Sail to Patagonia

The busy port city of Puerto Montt is the launching point for boats south into Patagonia; join the locals aboard a Navimag ferry (www.navimag.com) sailing through the glacier-lined channels to Puerto Natales, gateway to Torres del Paine. See p22 for more on Torres del Paine.

## GETTING YOU THERE

Both parks are accessible from gateway towns on the main Ruta 5 running north from Puerto Montt. Buses from the town of Osorno make the 75km journey east into and across Parque Nacional Puyehue, while frequent minibuses from Puerto Varas serve Petrohué in Parque Nacional Vicente Pérez Rosales.

## EXPLORING CHILE'S PARKS

It's straightforward to traverse the area independently – paved roads access both parks – but many visitors organise trips with operators in Puerto Varas, which can organise transport and activities.

# THE RAREST CAT IN THE REMOTEST FOREST
## Broadleaf Forests of the Russian Far East

Very few travellers make it to Russia's Far East. Even those who ride the Trans-Siberian Railway tend to branch off for Mongolia rather than ride it to its terminus on the Sea of Japan. So this is virgin territory for the intrepid, whose spirit of adventure will be richly rewarded. The land here is surprisingly bountiful; unlike the wastes of Siberia, the forests at this more southerly latitude provide better sustenance and are home to Asiatic black bears, roe and sika deer, wild boars, raccoon dogs and, of course, Amur leopards.

## On Screen

*Panthera pardus orientalis* – the Amur leopard – is the planet's rarest big cat. So it's all the more impressive that, out in the vastness of eastern Russia, the *Planet Earth* team manages to capture (on film) a mother and cub padding across the snow and dining on a frozen deer carcass – though the cameraman had a long, chilly wait first.

## When

The Russian broadleaf forests are harsh in winter – temperatures lurk below freezing all season long. The naked trees provide less cover for the cats then, but you'd still be incredibly lucky to bag a sighting. Summers are much warmer, and the forests are lush and full of life, though this is when the monsoon dumps most of the region's rainfall.

**(top) Amur Leopard**
With a population of less than 40 individuals in the wild, the Amur leopard is listed as Critically Endangered on the International Union for Conservation of Nature (IUCN) Red List.

**(bottom) Manchurian Fir**
Kedrovaya Pad's forests are dominated by Manchurian firs; the tallest trees in the Russian Far East, they can grow to 55m tall and 2m in diameter.

"Only 40 Amur leopards survive in the wild – and their numbers are falling."

# EXPERIENCE

You can't feel your toes. Or your fingers. Or your ears, nose or any other extremities for that matter – it's perishingly cold, and you've been sitting still as a statue in the unheated hide for hours. But, when – finally – something stirs, you know the wait has been worth it. It's an incredible privilege. More people probably live on your street than will ever see an Amur leopard in the wild. And there are two of them, right there in front of you, padding silently through the snow: a mother and her year-old cub.

They've already frightened off the vultures – minutes earlier you were watching an ugly, unkempt bunch of the birds clawing at an unfortunate sika deer carcass. The vultures were a sorry-looking sight: big, powerful birds, sure, but the tramps of the forest, nonetheless – scabby faced, balding, feathers askew. Quarrelsome, too – fighting among themselves to win the best scraps of meat.

But then one of them heard something (you didn't catch it, your senses not nearly so finely tuned to the twig cracks and bird caws of this vast woodland). The vulture pulled up from its meal, a droplet of blood still hanging from its hooked beak, and surveyed the area. Something was amiss. In a moment the carrion-eating birds were gone, abandoning their buffet.

You soon spot why. Without vegetation to hide them, the leopards' brown-orange rosetted bodies are clearly visible against the snow. A curse for them: there's no way to sneak up on their prey without cover. But a blessing for you, because you don't want to take your eyes off these beautiful creatures. They're not nearly as big as the Amur tiger, the other rare feline that stalks the region, but they're still large – mum is maybe 30kg. And they're gorgeous, with thick coats – more luxuriant than the pelt of an African leopard – to help them cope with the freezing winter temperatures. The youngster is particularly fluffy, not having fully grown into his fur. Nor has he yet attained any of mum's grace; while she moves about the rocks with elegance, he gingerly inches down a tree trunk, unsure of his paw-steps.

He is utterly reliant on her for food. As the female leopard sets about the deer, trying to soften the hide of this priceless discovery, which has frozen in the subzero temperatures, junior looks on hungrily. It will be another year before he can fend for himself; they just need to hold on, make it through this most unforgiving season.

You pull your hat down against the chill, and wish you had a leopard's coat to keep you warm. But while you may shudder, you can leave this frosty forest at will; these big cats must endure a few more weeks before spring arrives, with its kinder climate and more-abundant food. These are two of 40 remaining wild Amur leopards; their survival is critical to the whole species' existence. As you leave, bound for a warm bed and a hot meal, you wish them luck.

Its body growing to only about 15cm long, the Siberian chipmunk is the only chipmunk genus found outside North America.

# TAKING ACTION

## As You Saw It

Kedrovaya Pad Zapovednik, a nature reserve nestled into the slopes of the Black Mountains and conveniently close to Vladivostok (20km), is perhaps the best place to head for a chance of an Amur leopard sighting, albeit a very slim chance. The leopards are no respecters of borders and, in this sliver of the Far East, the Russian, Chinese and North Korean boundaries collide – leopards may cross, but without the requisite paperwork (near impossible for North Korea) you cannot follow. Plus there are so few of the leopards to see; you will need lottery-win-level luck, as well as the desire, equipment and endurance to sit in a hide, in the cold, for a very long time, on the off chance a leopard strolls by. That said, all of the cats that live in Kedrovaya Pad have been fitted with radio collars so that scientists can track their movements.

## Adding to the Experience

You might not see an Amur leopard in Kedrovaya Pad or the surrounding area, but this is a fascinating – and very little-visited – region to explore. Nestled in the spurs of the eastern Manchurian mountains, Kedrovaya is full of dense forests, sandstone canyons, rivers, pools and waterfalls. Amid all this you might spot wild boars, roe deer, Asiatic black bears, Siberian weasels and many types of birds, including the rare grey goshawk. In springtime warblers are profuse and the rivers and waterfalls torrential with snow melt; in autumn the trees turn vibrant rust and gold.

## Alternative Leopard-Spotting Experiences

There are generally considered to be eight subspecies of leopard worldwide; most are endangered to some degree.

✿ **South Luangwa National Park** (Zambia) Possibly the continent's best odds of seeing *Panthera pardus pardus* (African leopard); for an extra thrill, head out on a walking safari.

✿ **Yala National Park** (Sri Lanka) Has concentrated, though still elusive, populations of *Panthera pardus kotiya* (Sri Lankan leopard).

✿ **Kanha National Park** (India) Offers the chance of spotting both tiger and *Panthera pardus fusca* (Indian leopard) – if you're lucky.

✿ **Alborz Mountains** (Iran) Great trekking with a possibility of sighting *Panthera pardus saxicolor* (Persian leopard).

# WHILE YOU'RE THERE

## Vladivostok

The Russian Far East's most cosmopolitan town has a dramatic setting – all peaks, peninsulas and bays. Ride the funicular railway for the best view of it all, then take a boat to one of its outlying islands.

## BACK FROM THE BRINK

Things don't look good for the Amur leopard: the number of wild individuals remaining is critically low. But hope is not lost; conservationists believe the Amur can be saved. Although the current population is just 40, this number has been stable for the past 30 years, despite increasing development in their traditional territories. Breeding has been successful too: indications are that the species reproduces well in the wild, and zoos worldwide are involved in captive breeding programs. It is hoped that some of these animals may be reintroduced to the wild, in the areas south of Sikhote-Alinsky where prey populations are healthy and, thanks to increased conservation awareness, suitable land has been protected.

See the Amur Leopard and Tiger Alliance website (www.amur-leopard.org) for extensive information on conservation efforts.

### Gaivoron

The Russian Academy of Sciences' biological research centre (235km north of Vladivostok) is home to two Amur tigers – your only chance of a guaranteed sighting of the leopard's larger cousin.

### Khankaisky Zapovednik

Board a boat through the wetlands to view the rich birdlife of this reserve, stopping to picnic on the shores of Lake Khanka.

### Sikhote-Alinsky Biosphere Zapovednik

Home to the Russian–American Siberian Tiger Project (www.wcsrussia.org), this mountainous and densely forested reserve conserves the habitat of the world's biggest cat, which tracks prey along the rivers, wends up the hillsides and seeks shelter on the rocky outcrops.

## GETTING YOU THERE

The best, and most atmospheric, way to access Far East Russia is to catch the Trans-Siberian Railway from Moscow to Vladivostok. The journey completed nonstop takes 6½ days; consider making stop-offs en route (for example, Yekaterinburg and Lake Baikal). Life on board is a fascinating mix of endless Siberian tundra views, cups of tea from the carriage *samovar* (hot-water urn) and vodka shared with Russian businessmen and Mongolian traders. Kedrovaya Pad reserve is 20km from Vladivostok.

## EXPLORING THE RUSSIAN FAR EAST

Russia Experience (www.trans-siberian.co.uk) is an expert in arranging trips to Russia, including journeys along the Trans-Siberian Railway to Vladivostok. It can give all sorts of advice on exploring the area.

## FAST FACTS

Male Amur leopards generally weigh 32kg to 48kg, but can weigh up to 75kg; females are smaller, weighing 25kg to 43kg.

There are around 300 Amur leopards in captivity, mostly in zoos in Europe, North America and countries of the former Soviet Union; most of these zoos are involved in conservation breeding programs.

Amur leopards survive the cold thanks to their chunky coats, which increase in thickness from 2.5cm in summer to 7.5cm in winter.

There are eight subspecies of leopard in the world, found across Africa and Asia; the Amur leopard is only found in the Russian Far East and northeast China.

Russia's nature reserves are known as *zapovedniks,* meaning 'sacred' or 'prohibited from disturbance'; they are generally areas of scientific research.

# EMERGENCY RATIONS IN THE BARREN FOREST

## Teak Stands of Central India

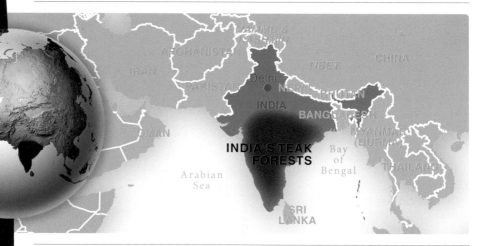

**Indian wildlife isn't all big cats and bigger pachyderms; watching the behaviours of smaller, more easily spotted beasts and birds among the changing habitats connects you to the country more surely than a ride in a safari jeep. But there's no denying the power of witnessing a successful hunt.**

## On Screen

This is the real *Jungle Book:* the cast of animals – tigers, monkeys, birds and deer – playing out the dramas of life (and death) in the forests that Kipling loved and described so vividly. *Planet Earth* captures the mundane and the miraculous: the moments of inaction in dry clearings, as well as the triumph of the forest's most feared hunter – the tiger.

## When

India's seasons are as dramatically varied as its wildlife; the comfortable time in most parts of the country for visitors is winter – the cool, dry season between November and February. Come March and April temperatures soar, but undergrowth thins and teak leaves crackle and drop, improving wildlife spotting. The monsoon arrives to drench the land in June.

# EXPERIENCE

Shuffling through the broad, dry leaves carpeting the forest floor in a crackling blanket, you could be in any deciduous woodland in autumn – but for the searing heat. As each dead leaf drifts down, a fraction less shade remains, and the tropical sun sears ever more harshly through the skeletal canopy of denuded branches. You're breathless as you lope languidly towards a clearing in the teak forest; it's a heat so palpable you can hear it: the chirping hum of cicadas and the buzzing cloud of flies being ineffectually swatted by the whisk-tails of gaur – huge forest buffalo – as they chew the desiccated bark off trees.

In the glade you spot a gathering of chitals – elegant spotted deer – and langur monkeys. For most, even the slightest movement is too much effort; they lounge around, chattering intermittently, waiting for the evening to bring respite from the oppressively parched air. One monkey leaps into action, though, spying something worth scampering for. Your eyes follow his path up to the small, tender blossoms of a mahua tree, protruding from slender fingers in the uppermost branches. As his black hands grasp at the pale, liquid-filled globes and pack them into his maw, the rest of the family wakes and scuttles up to join him; soon the boughs are loaded with munching monkeys. A parakeet, all pastel lilac, yellow and turquoise livery, darts in to share the feast.

The chitals also wander over, foraging among the leaf detritus at the tree's base for blossoms knocked loose by the gluttonous primates above, and barking in anticipation as they await the next delivery of treats from on high. They alternate their attention, one moment bowing to snuffle for the juicy mahua blooms, the next lifting their heads and sweeping their gaze around the clearing edge, scouring the brush for danger. It's a neighbourhood-watch arrangement from time immemorial: deer and monkey share security details, each ready to alert the other to any sign of predators.

One langur, reassured by the serene calm of the deer, drops from the lowest branch and heads away for a moment alone. It's the wrong moment. In the tall, arid grass lining the clearing's edge you spot a glinting patch of orange, the swish of a black-striped tail; but the monkey is oblivious to its peril. A golden flash erupts from the undergrowth. The tiger leaps the few paces from its hiding place to the unfortunate monkey – dinner – in the blink of a slitted feline eye. With a brief snarl and a shake of the tiger's great head the monkey hangs limp and lifeless, neck firmly clamped between the predator's jaws. Bird and animal screech and chatter in alarm – but too late. Shere Khan will feast tonight.

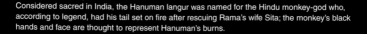

Considered sacred in India, the Hanuman langur was named for the Hindu monkey-god who, according to legend, had his tail set on fire after rescuing Rama's wife Sita; the monkey's black hands and face are thought to represent Hanuman's burns.

# TAKING ACTION

## As You Saw It

Teak forests dot central and southern India, but tiger numbers in them are sparse, despite the establishment of tiger reserves and the Project Tiger program; witnessing a kill would be an almost lottery-level stroke of luck. Pench Tiger Reserve in eastern Madhya Pradesh offers the hope of a sighting among the teak; nearby Kanha National Park's sal forests are reputedly the country's top location for tiger sightings, though visitor numbers are correspondingly high. Madhya Pradesh's other tiger reserves, Bandhavgarh and Panna National Parks, are also hot spots for spying stripes.

Get up early between February and June, book a gypsy (jeep) and go on a morning drive for the best chance of a sighting – but be prepared to share the moment.

## Adding to the Experience

Opportunities for tracking pugmarks through prime tiger territory in the big parks are few, though walking safaris are available in some reserves – try Wayanad, Parambikulam or Chinnar Wildlife Sanctuaries in Kerala, southern India. An elephant-back safari can bring you trunk to snarling muzzle with a tiger – an electric encounter; you can take an elephant ride in Kanha, Pench and several other tiger reserves.

## Alternative Tiger-Spotting Experiences

Though it has the lion's share of the global population, India doesn't have the monopoly on tiger sightings.

✿ **Chitwan & Bardia National Parks** (Nepal) For tiger encounters on foot, elephant or from a canoe.

✿ **Sundarbans** (Bangladesh) Home to infamous man-eating tigers among the mangroves. See p78 for more on the Sundarbans.

✿ **Royal Manas National Park** (Bhutan) Where tigers roam one of the most pristine areas of the eastern Himalayas.

✿ **Gunung Leuser National Park** (Indonesia) For the faint prospect of spotting a rare Sumatran tiger (but a good chance of meeting an orang-utan).

# WHILE YOU'RE THERE

Bear in mind the vast scale of India; these attractions, though near Pench and Kanha in relative terms, are several (worthwhile) hours' journey hence.

# TIGER, TIGER, BURNING OUT...?

The planet's largest cat – species *Panthera tigris* – terrorises prey across southern and eastern parts of Asia. At least it used to; today small populations of the surviving six subspecies cling on in pockets of the Indian subcontinent, southern China, far eastern Russia and Southeast Asia.

The Bengal tiger, most numerous of the extant subspecies, is championed by India's Project Tiger program, launched in 1973 to research and conserve these mesmerising beasts. Some 40-odd tiger reserves were created, a success story that led to a resurgence in numbers from around 1200 in the early 1970s to an estimated 3500 in the 1990s.

Accuracy in counting tigers is, though, notoriously difficult – it's not a case of spotting cats and ticking a tally sheet; previous censuses used pugmark identification. Whether due to previously inaccurate estimates, alleged manipulation of results by officials or increased poaching, the 2008 census suggested a fall in numbers to 1411 adults across India (excluding the Sundarbans), with one reserve – Sariska – losing its entire population of tigers. Trials of a census technique involving DNA samples from droppings began in the Indian Sundarbans in 2009.

## Khajuraho

Built 10 centuries ago, this extensive complex of Hindu temples is alive with ornate and extremely erotic figures – the karma-sutra carvings are beautifully executed and seriously adults-only in theme.

## Maheshwar

Climb the ramparts of the fort for views of the sacred Narmada River, lined with ancient ghats and temples.

## Pachmarhi

This Raj-era hill station is a blessed relief from the sweltering summer heat of the plains below; come for highland hikes past caves and waterfalls.

## Orchha

Palaces and temples dating back to the 16th and 17th centuries peer out from the jungle – meaning 'Hidden Place', Orchha is aptly named.

## Mandu

A village that hides a city; this mountainside settlement is the remains of a mighty Afghan citadel dating back 1000 years. Wander among ancient palaces, mosques, temples and tombs.

# GETTING YOU THERE

The nearest major railhead to Pench is Nagpur, a 2½-hour bus ride away; Kanha's closest train station is Jabalpur, a four-hour coach journey. Bandhavgarh is an hour from the station at Umaria by bus or shared jeep, while the bus to Panna from Khajuraho also takes an hour.

# EXPLORING INDIA'S PARKS

Upmarket lodges tend to organise jeep and elephant-back safaris as well as birdwatching tours; many have their own expert naturalist guides. If you're staying in more modest accommodation, you can still join safaris, but investigate the quality of their guides before booking.

## JUNGLE BOOK

The inspiration for Rudyard Kipling's *Jungle Book* hero Mowgli was probably the case of a 'wolf-boy' reported near Pench in 1831. Several locations described in the book can be found in the districts near Pench, including the Waingunga River Gorge, where Mowgli's nemesis, the vicious tiger Shere Khan, was defeated.

# CALL OF THE LEMUR
## Madagascar

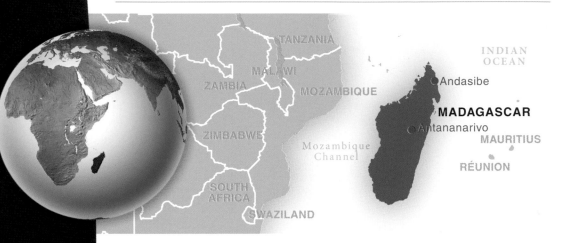

**Madagascar barely qualifies as part of Africa: the two are separated by hundreds of kilometres of sea and 165 million years of evolution – long enough for Madagascar's plants and animals to have evolved into some of the weirdest forms on the planet. Nowhere else can you see more than 70 varieties of lemur, including one that sounds like a police siren; the world's biggest and smallest chameleons; and the last stomping ground of the elephant bird, the largest bird ever recorded.**

## On Screen

*Planet Earth's* cameras capture the arrival of Madagascar's wet season across the baobab forests, bringing with it the rarely seen spectacle of baobab flowers peeling back like bananas in their night-time bloom. This creates a mini–food chain as mouse lemurs and giant hawk moths sip on the baobab's nectar, and the lemurs in turn dine on the moths.

## When

Madagascar has two distinct seasons: the wet (November to March) and the dry (April to October). The seasonal conditions shown on *Planet Earth* were in the wet, but travel possibilities are more extensive in the dry. The best times to visit Parc National d'Andasibe-Mantadia are from September to January and in May.

**Lemur Calling**

*Verreaux's sifakas* are tree-dwelling lemurs of the Madagascan forests. The name *sifaka* comes from the noisy barking call they make during territorial confrontations.

"The baobab nectar is starting to flow...
The sugary nectar is packed with energy –
an ideal way for lemurs to start their day".

# EXPERIENCE

Away in the distance, deep in the forest as the sun rises, an eerie siren cries – sounding as though a pod of whales has found its way onto the land. This is the call of the indri – the largest and most entrancing of Madagascar's 70-plus lemur species, and the reason you are here in Réserve Spéciale d'Analamazaotra, part of the larger Parc National d'Andasibe-Mantadia.

You begin walking towards the sound, though you know it may be some time before you reach it, and by then the indri will probably be gone. This haunting territorial call can travel up to 3km and may only sound for a couple of minutes. But there will be more, because with around 60 family groups of lemur in this park, there is no better place to see this unique animal.

Across the island's red soils you wander deeper into the forest, the land beginning to steam as the heat of the day arrives. The forest stirs very little, but you know that it's filled with the sort of strange creatures – the remarkable evolutionary twists and turns – that only island isolation seems to create. Such as a moth with a tongue up to 30cm in length. And a cockroach that hisses. And the golden bamboo lemur, which eats cyanide in quantities that would kill most other animals.

But the indri calls again and you are drawn forward once more, out of your forest thoughts – it is truly a siren call. Shortly your guide stops and points into the branches of a tree, where unblinking eyes stare down at you from inside a haphazard bundle of grey and black fur. It is the indri, looking something like a koala with Inspector Gadget arms and legs. The round eyes and soft fur make you think of teddy bear you once owned, and it's easy to see why this animal has been described as looking like a four-year-old child in a panda suit.

Looking closer, you see that the indri is not as misshapen as it first appears – those extra bits and bulges are two babies clinging to their mother. Despite the youthful weights, the mother swings easily between the branches – indri can leap up to 10m between trees. The babies untangle themselves in a stretch of arms and legs to leap about briefly by themselves before returning to their mother's warmth and comfort. Another siren rings out. Another lemur making itself heard on this island known to the outside world for little else.

The trees lining Avenue du Baobab are of the species *Adansonia grandidieri* (Grandidier's Baobab). Named after the French botanist and explorer Alfred Grandidier (1836–1921), this is the largest and most impressive of the baobab species.

# TAKING ACTION

## As You Saw It

To observe nocturnal mouse lemurs – the world's smallest primate – you will need to take a night walk through the forests. Night walks can be organised in parks such as Réserve Spéciale d'Analamazaotra, Parc Mitsinjo, Réserve de Nosy Mangabe and Parc National d'Ankarafantsika.

## Adding to the Experience

To really immerse yourself in the wild world of lemurs, consider joining a 'voluntourism' project working in the Madagascan forests.

✿ **Azafady** (www.madagascar.co.uk) Runs lemur research programs in the Anosy region several times a year.

✿ **Earthwatch** (www.earthwatch.org) Conducts volunteer projects in Madagascar.

## Alternative Baobab Experiences

Baobabs may be the distinctive image of Madagascar, but there are a couple of unique baobab sights and experiences elsewhere in the world, too.

✿ **Baobab Tree Bar** (Modjadjiskloof, Limpopo Province, South Africa) Said to be the largest baobab on earth, with a 47m circumference, this tree's hollowed centre has been turned into a pub with space for more than 50 people.

✿ **Prison Tree** (Derby, Western Australia) This boab (an Australian species of baobab) tree in the Kimberley is said to be over 1000 years old. With a girth of 14m and a hollow trunk, prisoners were once locked up inside the tree en route to Old Derby Gaol.

# WHILE YOU'RE THERE

## Avenue du Baobab

One of the most photographed spots in Madagascar is the avenue of baobabs on either side of the road about 15km north of Morondava, on the way to Belo sur Tsiribihina. The best times to visit are at sunset and sunrise, when the colours of the trees change and the long shadows are most pronounced. Some of the trees here are 1000 years old.

## Tsaranoro Massif

Just outside the western boundary of Parc National d'Andringitra in central Madagascar is the Tsaranoro Massif. It has an approximately 800m-high sheer rock face considered by rock climbers to be one of the most challenging climbs

# BOTTLED BEAUTIES

There are eight species of baobab in the world, and six of them are found only in Madagascar (the seventh grows in both Madagascar and eastern Africa, and the eighth is found only in northwest Australia). In many areas they are known as upside-down trees because when they have no leaves their branches resemble tree roots. But the most striking feature of baobabs is their swollen, bulbous trunks, which fill each wet season with up to 120,000L of water to get the trees through the next dry season.

Illegal felling of baobab trees in protected areas such as Montagne des Français remains a problem in Madagascar, as poor locals raze the trees to grow rice. In 2002 long-time Diego Suarez area resident York Pareik created the Parc Botanique des Mille Baobabs, in part to help stop baobab poaching. He planted 5000 baobabs on the property and hopes to counter the poaching by teaching locals about the importance of sustainable living and why it's so destructive to cut down the baobab trees, which are an important part of the local ecosystem. The park features flora and fauna native only to northern Madagascar, including five of the country's seven species of baobab.

in the world (there are also routes for beginners). Camp Catta (www.campcatta.com), on the western edge of the park, specialises in rock climbing.

### Belo sur Mer

This seaside village's star attraction is the string of seven gorgeous, little known and seldom visited coral-fringed islands off its coast. Diving here is excellent, thanks to the proximity of a deep passage through the Canal de Mozambique – you get to see some really big fish, deepwater critters (such as the octopus) and even sea turtles.

# GETTING YOU THERE

By air, Madagascar is well connected with the Indian Ocean islands of Mauritius and Réunion, and reasonably accessible from mainland Africa. Air Madagascar also flies from the capital city, Antananarivo, to Marseille, Paris and Bangkok. Most visitors to Réserve Spéciale d'Analamazaotra stay in the village of Andasibe. To reach it from Antananarivo, take a *taxi-brousse* (bush taxi) to Moramanga, where you'll find direct *taxis-brousses* to Andasibe, which can drop you at your hotel of choice.

# EXPLORING RÉSERVE SPÉCIALE D'ANALAMAZAOTRA

Guides gather at the main entrance to Réserve Spéciale d'Analamazaotra from about 6.30am waiting for clients; it's worth being a bit selective, as some of the less qualified guides show very little effort or enthusiasm. A list of official National Association for the Management of Protected Areas in Madagascar (Angap) approved guides is displayed at the main park entrance near Andasibe, with details of their skills and qualifications; as well as a list of fixed guide fees.

## FAST FACTS

Madagascar is the world's fourth-largest island, behind Greenland, New Guinea and Borneo.

............................................

In 2005 two new species of lemur – Goodman's mouse lemur and the northern giant mouse lemur – were discovered in Madagascar.

............................................

Lemurs are endemic to Madagascar.

............................................

The baobab's fruit is known as 'monkey bread' and is rich in vitamin C.

............................................

# OCEAN DEEP

*Planet Earth, Episode Eleven*

Covering most of the planet but less understood than the surface of the moon, the oceans are planet earth's final frontier. Unsurprising perhaps: a human body would be crushed just a few hundred metres below the surface but, at its deepest, the ocean plunges to a forbidding 11km. Somehow, though, a profusion of creatures has adapted to life in this chill, dark, unwelcoming place. From the whitetip sharks and speeding dolphins that patrol the uppermost realms, to the quirky creatures – winged deep-sea octopus, bioluminescent vampire squid – that survive at the bottom of the abyss, the ocean is an example of nature at its most tenacious.

# DRAGON CHIMNEYS

## Okinawa Trough, Western Pacific, Off the Coast of Japan

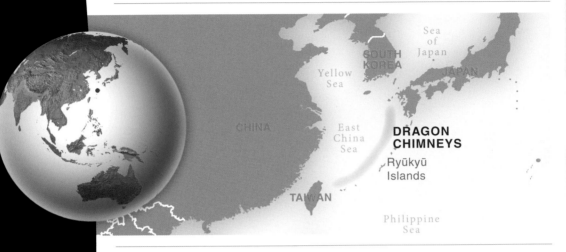

Here be dragons... Navigating the thick plumes of these ocean dragons' smoking nostrils is a rather extraordinary experience. Surprising though it may be, there is life that thrives in this deep, dark, watery world – one of the least explored environments on the planet.

## On Screen

Deep, deep down in the western Pacific, the *Planet Earth* crew's submarine navigates the smoky plumes of the aptly named Dragon Chimneys. Along the Okinawa Trough off the coast of Japan, in places where the ocean floor has wrenched itself apart, underwater vents erupt in the darkness, emitting clouds of superheated water laden with dissolved minerals.

## When

The success of any deep-sea expedition is dependent on a slew of factors, including weather patterns, ocean currents and seasonal variants. Indeed, there is no perfect time to take the plunge, and even if the conditions are favourable, there is still a hefty amount of risk to contend with as extreme pressures can quickly turn sophisticated technology to compressed scrap metal.

**Chinese Trumpetfish**
The trumpetfish swims only slowly, so it relies on camouflage and stealth to ambush its prey, and also to hide from predators.

# EXPERIENCE

Your epic journey begins in the Ryūkyū Islands, a chain of scattered land masses that runs southwest from the Japanese island of Kyūshū to Taiwan. Deep-sea diving is a monumental effort requiring months of comprehensive planning by a large and highly skilled support team, so the predive atmosphere is a heady mix of eager anticipation, overwhelming excitement and a few frayed nerves.

Now that the skies and seas are cooperating, the first major challenge is finding the exact location of the Dragon Chimneys. They lie between 1000m and 2000m below – fairly shallow when it comes to oceanic trenches (some of which can swallow Mt Everest whole), but still a long, long way down. When you're measuring depth by thousands of metres at a time, success relies on exact calculations. Fortunately, your colleagues are some of the finest oceanographers in the world – operating the sophisticated imaging tools and software required to map the ocean floor is routine to them.

To penetrate such extreme depths, you take a manned submersible – a so-called midget submarine that is not fully autonomous, and must rely on either a support facility or mother ship to replenish power and breathing gases. Down here the pressure can be several hundred times greater than at the surface; the sub's thick sheets of titanium plating are all that's protecting you from a gruesome death – when the hatch is sealed and you're lowered down into the abyss, you must place full and complete trust in its craftsmanship. Every time the submersible flexes and strains and croaks in protest, you shoot your fellow crewmembers nervous looks.

Finally the external spotlights from the submersible illuminate a thick black plume reminiscent of a dragon's smoking nostrils. Although no sunlight can penetrate this far down, there are remarkable signs of life all around. Alongside the vent furry-armoured squat lobsters graze for bacteria. As you all stare through the reinforced glass in complete wonderment, the tension seems to simply drift away.

The density of crustaceans is astounding, and with each revolution around the Dragon Chimneys, the submersible captures detailed images of this remote oasis of marine life. But your time is severely limited. The instrument panel is illuminated, signaling you are near the end of your supply of vital fuel and oxygen. It's a wrench to return to the mother ship, but there are data feeds and video footage for your team to sort. You, on the other hard, are free to wind the day down with a bottle of Sapporo lager in hand.

**Hypselodoris Apolegma**
*Hypselodoris Apolegma* is a nudibranch that feeds on sponges and is found in the western Pacific.

# TAKING ACTION

## As You Saw It

Unfortunately, without some seriously impressive skills to fill a resume, you're unlikely to make it to the Dragon Chimneys. Of course, education is the key to locked doors, so if the great ocean depths are your dream, hit the books hard. Marine biology, oceanography and nautical engineering are all great focuses to have in this business.

## A More-Accessible Experience

As oxygen-loving human beings, we prefer to spend the vast majority of our time above the water. Even though the Dragon Chimneys may be off your travel list, don't overlook the incredible destination that is the Ryūkyū Islands. While the island of Okinawa tends to garner most of the attention, the Ryūkyū chain is home to an astounding diversity of terrestrial ecosystems, including subtropical beaches, mangrove forests and bamboo jungles. The islands are also rich in history and culture, not to mention their incredible culinary style, which blends Chinese and Japanese influences.

## Alternative Diving Experiences

The ocean depths aren't within easy reach for everyone, though fortunately the shallows seas are.

✿ **Indian & Pacific Oceans** (Indonesia) The coral reefs at this great ocean crossroads are the most biodiverse marine environments on the planet. See p246 for more information.

✿ **Great Barrier Reef** (Australia) Arguably the most famous marine tourist destination, the world's largest reef extends for over 2600km.

# WHILE YOU'RE THERE

The warm waters surrounding the Ryūkyū Islands are home to an outstanding variety of tropical fish and pelagics, including dolphins, whale sharks, hammerheads and manta rays. There are also a variety of hard- and soft-coral reefs, as well as a smattering of underwater wrecks, cavern systems and even the odd archaeological ruin.

## Manta Way

One of the most famous sights in the island chain, Manta Way is located in the straits between Iriomote-jima and Kohama-jima, and is absolutely teeming with manta rays in the late spring and early summer.

## Manta Scramble

Located off the coast of Ishigaki-jima, this popular dive spot virtually guarantees a manta-ray sighting, particularly in the spring and summer.

# THE RYŪKYŪ KINGDOM

Prior to the Middle Ages the Ryūkyū Islands were ruled by *aji* (local chieftains), who battled for control of small fiefs and struggled among themselves for power and fame. In 1429 the islands were united by Sho Hashi of the Chūzan kingdom, which led to the establishment of the Ryūkyū Kingdom. During this era Sho Hashi increased contact with China, which contributed to Ryūkyū's music, dance, literature and ceramics flourishing. In this 'Golden Era' weapons were prohibited, and the islands were rewarded with peace and tranquillity.

With little means of defence, however, the Ryūkyū Kingdom was not prepared for war when the Shimazu clan of Satsuma (modern-day Kagoshima) invaded in 1609. The Shimazu easily conquered the Ryūkyūs, and then established severe controls over their trade. While the rest of Japan closed its doors to the world prior to Commodore Matthew Perry's arrival in 1853, the Shimazu continued to trade with China under the guise of the now vanquished Ryūkyū Kingdom.

### Irizaki Point

If swimming alongside sharks doesn't absolutely terrify you, this famous spot off the coast of Yonaguni-jima is frequented by enormous schools of hammerheads in the winter.

### Underwater Ruins

One of the most unusual dive spots in the region is also located off the coast of Yonaguni-jima, and is home to a mysterious underwater archaeological ruin of unknown origin.

### Mini Grotto

This popular dive spot off the coast of Miyako-jima is home to an elaborate series of underwater caves, which beckon to be explored – assuming you have sufficient experience.

## GETTING YOU THERE

All Nippon Airways (ANA; www.ana.com) and Japan Airlines (JAL; www.jal.com) connect the Japanese archipelago to most major cities around the world.

## EXPLORING THE RYŪKYŪ ISLANDS

While they're off the radar for most international travellers, the Ryūkyū Islands benefit from excellent tourist infrastructure that caters primarily to the domestic Japanese market. You're most likely going to have a few lost-in-translation moments as you island-hop but, fortunately, the locals are very friendly and always willing to help. Frequent flights, diverse accommodation options, several established dive operators and excellent Okinawan cuisine are added bonuses.

## FAST FACTS

The Okinawa Trough, which runs along the ocean floor between Japan and Taiwan, marks the edge of the continental shelf of the East China Sea.

Oceanographers classify the Okinawa Trough as a back-arc basin behind the much deeper Ryūkyū Trench.

Despite its comparative small size, the Okinawa Trough reaches a maximum depth of more than 2700m.

The Ryūkyū Trench reaches a mind-boggling maximum depth of more than 5000m.

# 9° NORTH

Guatemala Basin, Between Mexico & the
Galápagos in the Eastern Pacific

MEXICO
● Acapulco
GUATEMALA
NICARAGUA
● 9° NORTH
COSTA RICA
PANAMA
VENEZUELA
COLOMBIA
PACIFIC
OCEAN
ECUADOR
GALÁPAGOS
ISLANDS
(ECUADOR)
BRAZIL

**(left) Cerro Azul, Galápagos Islands**
Isla Isabela, the largest of the Galápagos Islands, was formed by the merger of six volcanoes (including Cerro Azul), of which all but one are still active.

**(right) Johnson Sea Link Working on a Bush of Tubeworms**
The tubeworms shown are over 1.5m long and extend far into the sediment below.

**Too far down for any sunlight to penetrate, the underwater volcanoes in this deep-sea world blast scalding, toxic, mineral cocktails into the surrounding waters. But this apparently inhospitable environment is home to some incredible marine life...as long as the volcanoes are erupting.**

## On Screen

In a camera-equipped submersible in the shadowy depths of the eastern Pacific, the *Planet Earth* team comes across a site known to oceanographers and marine biologists as 9° North. Here, superheated water (at temperatures of more than 400°C) spews from the earth's crust, enabling the world's fastest-growing marine invertebrates to reach astounding lengths.

## When

There's no preferred season for exploring the ocean depths, but vents do not erupt indefinitely, and they may suddenly become inactive. If eddies deep in the earth's crust divert their volcanic energy elsewhere, an entire microworld can be extinguished in an instant; chimneys that once teemed with life can unpredictably turn into cold, sterile mineral monuments.

TUI DE ROY/MINDEN PICTURES/NATIONAL GEOGRAPHIC

IMAGE COURTESY OF GULF OF MEXICO 2002, NOAA/OER

# EXPERIENCE

From Acapulco in Mexico, your fully equipped maritime vessel – complete with an expert team of oceanographers, marine biologists, nautical engineers, boat captains and support crew – embarks on a journey into the open ocean. Northwest of the Galápagos Islands, at N9° W104°, you will leave the relative comfort of the mother ship in favour of a manned submersible, or midget, submarine.

Your destination lies more than 2000m below the sea – well beyond the reach of even the sun's strongest rays, and well below a tolerable depth for your more familiar marine life. But not all life is dependent on energy from the sun; peculiar kinds of creatures are found in great abundance here at 9° North.

After descending into the murky abyss you finally reach the ocean floor, which is home to an immense chain of volcanic mountains. In some places fissures rive the crust like great scars and blast superheated water loaded with dissolved minerals into the icy depths. The view is epic, as clouds of sulphides solidify into towering chimneys as tall as a three-storey house.

A quick glance at your instruments reminds you that, at more than 400°C, this scalding cocktail of chemicals would be lethally toxic to most forms of life. But then you see it – a fissure venting superheated water supporting a spectacular display of giant tubeworms.

The worms are a visual showstopper, but in order to truly understand the significance of 9° North you have to shift your focus to a micro scale: the greatest discovery yet made at this site is the bacteria living in the razor-thin interface between the extremely hot and the very cold water. According to your scientific papers, evidence suggests that this organism is able to photosynthesise in the absence of sunlight, using nothing more than the dim light coming from the hydrothermal vents. Thus far, over 50 different species have been found living here, though each new expedition brings with it new discoveries.

And 9° North's revelation that photosynthesis is not limited to dry land has another significance: given the ongoing search for extraterrestrials, this discovery extends the possible range in which astronomers can look for life on other planets.

**Galápagos Sea Lions**
Galápagos Sea Lions are unique to the Galápagos Islands and (occasionally and in smaller numbers) coastal Ecuador and Colombia.

# TAKING ACTION

## As You Saw It

Only a few privileged individuals get to lay their own eyes on 9° North; for a chance you would need to have begun studying and training at a young age. For starters, an advanced degree in either marine biology or oceanography is probably a good idea, along with specialist training in deep-sea exploration and the engineering of manned submersibles. Brushing up on your Spanish language skills wouldn't hurt either, as you'll probably be spending a good chunk of time in Latin America between expeditions.

## A Less-Intense Experience

If you're looking to dive underwater – at a modest 10m to 40m – then consider a holiday at the Mexican resort destination of Acapulco. Although the Caribbean Sea tends to garner much of the diving spotlight, Acapulco is rife with dive sites, especially if you're a fan of towering underwater pinnacles, rocky caverns, shipwrecks and seamounts. Average year-round temperatures are a comfortable 24°C, while visibility tends to be somewhere between 5m and 20m. If this still doesn't sound convincing to you, consider the appeal of diving the ocean depths without having to rely on titanium plating to save your life from skull-crushing pressures.

## Alternative Deep-Ocean Experiences

On the other side of the ocean, off the coast of Japan, Dragon Chimneys (western Pacific, Okinawa Trough) is a series of exploding underwater vents that fosters its own unique marine life. Again, they are only accessible to experts. See p316 for more information on this site.

# WHILE YOU'RE THERE

Much like the revolutionary scientific idea with which they've become synonymous, the Galápagos Islands may inspire you to think differently about the world. You can't help thinking you've stumbled upon an alternate universe, some strange utopian colony organised by sea lions and arranged on principles of mutual cooperation. The creatures that call the islands home truly act as if humans are nothing more than slightly annoying paparazzi.

# GETTING YOU THERE

Aeromexico (www.aeromexico.com) is Mexico's largest air carrier, while LAN Airlines (www.lan.com) services destinations in Ecuador. Visitors to the Galápagos arrive by boat, usually from Ecuador – tours can last from three days to three weeks, though four- to eight-day trips are the most common.

## ALIEN ORGANISMS?

Europa, a planet-sized satellite of Jupiter, has long been thought to have some of the necessary attributes to harbour life. However, it is far too distant from the sun for traditional forms of photosynthesis as we know it to take place. With that said, it is believed that under the ice-covered surface of Europa there are vast liquid oceans, which might contain thermal vents similar to the ones found at 9° North. If these were to exist, some scientists postulate, Europa could support photosynthetic organisms analogous to the ones residing on our own deep ocean floor.

# EXPLORING THE PACIFIC

If you're looking for the proper education and training to dive the ocean depths, here are a few of the world's leading institutions.

✿ **Woods Hole Oceanographic Institute** (www.whoi.edu) Located in Woods Hole, Massachusetts, this is the largest private nonprofit oceanographic institution in the world.

✿ **Center for Ocean Engineering** (http://oe.mit.edu) At the Massachusetts Institute of Technology (MIT), this is one of the academic and industrial leaders in hydrodynamics, ship structural mechanics and propeller design.

✿ **Scripps Institution of Oceanography** (http://scripps.ucsd.edu) At the University of California, San Diego (UCSD), this is one of most important centres for ocean and earth science research, education, and public service in the world.

## GALÁPAGOS GEOLOGY

The oldest of the Galápagos islands visible today were formed roughly four to five million years ago by underwater volcanoes erupting and rising above the ocean's surface (the islands were never connected to the mainland). The formation of the islands is an ongoing process as the archipelago is relatively young compared with the age of the earth (which is about 1000 times older).

The Galápagos region is volcanically very active – more than 50 eruptions have been recorded since its discovery in 1535. The most recent eruptions occurred in April 2009 on the islands of Fernandina and Llaima.

## FAST FACTS

Ocean vents are typically located near areas of tectonic plate movement known as ocean ridges.

Below ocean depths of about 2200m, water reaches critical pressure and can no longer boil.

Underwater eruptions account for more than three-quarters of the planet's total magma output.

Bacteria at deep ocean vents thrives on hydrogen sulphide, a highly toxic chemical to most known organisms.

Tubeworms are capable of absorbing life-sustaining nutrients directly into their skin.

# PACIFIC VOLCANOES

## Pacific Ocean, Off the Coast of French Polynesia

VANUATU

SAMOA

FIJI

TONGA

COOK
ISLANDS

TAHITI
(FR)

**PACIFIC
VOLCANOES**

FRENCH
POLYNESIA
(FR)

PACIFIC
OCEAN

NEW
ZEALAND

---

**Volcanoes are impressive terrestrial features, but *Planet Earth* showed us that they can also lie below the surface of the ocean. Here, often at extreme depths, volcanoes form the base of unique and complex marine ecosystems.**

### On Screen

From the deep ocean floor of the Pacific, sheer cliffs soar upwards, culminating in drowned volcanic peaks. Powerful currents sweep up these sunken seamounts, transporting nutrients from deeper water to their summits. The hard rock provides firm anchorage for communities as varied as they are colourful. Life is abundant on this extinct volcano, even though it is several kilometres below the reach of the sun.

### When

Since deep-sea conditions are fairly constant – very cold and very dark – it's probably best to plan your visit in accordance with the surface's seasonal climate variations, to best enjoy your time above water. In French Polynesia, the dry season runs from May to October.

**(top) Bora Bora, French Polynesia**
Because the islands of French Polynesia are volcanic, and so literally sprang up in the middle of nowhere, they have very little natural wildlife other than birds and marine life. All mammals on the islands were introduced by settlers.

**(bottom) Nautilus Pompilius**
Although often used for any species of Nautilidae, the name Chambered Nautilus more specifically refers to the species Nautilus pompilius, the largest in the genus.

# EXPERIENCE

Most people spend their lives trying to get to Tahiti, yet you're itching to escape the island and get back out to sea. But with storm clouds threatening in the distance, it's going to be at least another day before you can set sail from Pape'ete and safely clear the outer reef. Resigned to wait it out in proper style, you mix yourself another mai tai.

The next morning you awaken to a picture-perfect South Pacific sunrise. Climbing out from your cabin and up onto the main deck, you notice puddles of fresh water evaporating in the strengthening sun. The storm must have hit, yet you slept through the night without so much as a minor stir. Mental note: check the proportions in your mai tai recipe – you might be going a bit too heavy on the rum.

The research vessel spurs to life as the crew heads to their stations. Before long Pape'ete is a distant memory, and all that you see before you is bright blue skies and deep blue seas. A perfect Polynesian day by all accounts; but where you're heading there is only one season – the cold stillness of an interminable winter night.

As you descend into the depths in a submersible, the pressure builds and temperature falls. Five-hundred metres below the ocean's surface, mysterious animals appear in the abyss. While some resemble creatures familiar from shallower waters, others defy classification.

It takes several months for organic detritus of dead and dying animals and plants – so-called marine snow – to drift this far down; you, on the other hand, have made the journey in under an hour. So far it has been uneventful, but when you trust your life to a bucket of bolts, boredom is generally preferable to drama. And then, a flash of life – a sea spider, a small relative of shrimps and crabs, feasts on the gently sinking marine snow. You admire its feathered, leglike appendages, which it uses to maintain buoyancy and enmesh the nutritious particles.

More than 1km down, where the water is 20° colder than the surface, an enormous mola mola (ocean sunfish) glides in front of the submersible and scoops up a delicious morsel of gelatinous jellyfish. A true oceanic wanderer, the mola mola is the heaviest bony fish in the world, topping the scales at 1000kg. Here in the shadowy depths it can blissfully cruise about, evading predation.

As you watch the mola mola feast on its prey, a low grumble emerges from your belly and echoes through the cabin. You radio up to the chef onboard the mother ship, innocently inquiring about the catch of day.

**Mola Mola (Ocean Sunfish)**
The name 'mola' comes from Latin for millstone, in reference to the fish's roundish shape. The common name 'ocean sunfish' comes from the mola mola's habit of lying at the surface of the ocean appearing to sun itself.

"The huge mola mola lives on jellyfish more than half a mile down, where the water is 20 degrees colder."

# TAKING ACTION

## As You Saw It

Your mother was right – hard work will get you everywhere in life, including to the very bottom of the deep sea. Only if you've got a science PhD, a naval career or engineering knowledge of submersibles, might a voyage into the abyss be within reach.

## A More-Accessible Experience

Short of devoting most of your life to academic and professional training, your best bet for exploring the Pacific volcanoes is to strap on some scuba or snorkelling gear and dive down to the summits of the more shallowly submerged. These summits are found in abundance in the ocean waters surrounding French Polynesia, and are home to large communities of marine life – and thus the target of scuba divers and snorkellers (depending on the depth). Fortunately pretty much every hotel and resort in French Polynesia has an on-site dive centre to help get you sorted.

Alternatively, there are even some summits that break the ocean surface; you can stay dry while exploring these ones. The island of Bora Bora is a spectacularly mountainous example, rising to Mt Hue (619m), Mt Pahia (661m) and Mt Otemanu (727m). The whole island is only 9km from north to south, and 4km at its widest point.

## Alternative Volcanic-Island Experiences

Our planet is home to several other volcanic island chains.

✿ **Hawaiian Islands** This volcanic-derived archipelago consists of eight major island in addition to several islets, atolls and seamounts.

✿ **Cook Islands** Comprising 15 major islands spread over 2.2 million sq km of ocean, the Cook Islands are sunken volcanoes topped by coral growth.

✿ **Aleutian Islands** The westward sweeping arm of the US state of Alaska, this archipelago contains more than 300 volcanic islands sitting at the north of the Pacific Ring of Fire. See p270 for more on the Aleutian Islands.

# WHILE YOU'RE THERE

## Pape'ete

The capital of French Polynesia, Pape'ete is a medium-sized town of weather-beaten architecture with a lively port, lots of traffic and plenty of smiling faces to pull you through it all. You'll either love its compact chaos and colourful clutter or you'll run quickly from its grimy edges and lack of gorgeous views.

Sip a cappuccino at a Parisian-style sidewalk cafe, shop the vibrant market for anything and

## GEOLOGY OF TAHITI

Tahiti is neatly divided into two circles – the larger and more populated Tahiti Nui (Big Tahiti) to the northwest and the smaller Tahiti Iti (Little Tahiti) to the southeast – connected by an isthmus. Tahiti Iti has its highest point at Mt Ronui (1332m).

The narrow coastal fringe of Tahiti Nui, where the vast majority of the population is concentrated, sweeps rapidly inwards and upwards to a jumble of soaring, green-clad mountain peaks. The mountainous centre of Tahiti Nui is effectively one huge crater, with the highest peak being Mt Orohena (2241m). A fringing reef encloses a narrow lagoon around much of the island, but parts of the coast, particularly along the north coast from Mahina through Papenoo to Tiarei, are unprotected. There are 33 passes through the reef, the most important of which is the Pape'ete Pass into Pape'ete's harbour. Less than 10km east is Baie de Matavai (Matavai Bay), the favourite anchorage point of many early explorers.

everything from pearls to sarongs, dine at a *roulotte* (mobile food van) on a balmy evening or dance the night away. All roads in French Polynesia eventually lead to Pape'ete, so you might as well scope it out between beach-combing sessions.

### Bora Bora

From above, the promise of wonderland is instantly made good, with glinting turquoise sea and dazzling white sandy stretches of picture-postcard beachfront. Add sumptuous resorts in a sensational lagoon setting and indulgent gourmet food in fancy restaurants and it's no wonder Bora Bora makes such a convincing claim as a piece of paradise. This diva of an island is not only for unbridled pampering, though; when you've finished sipping your mai tai, check out diving, snorkelling, parasailing, walking under the sea and even hiking in the interior.

## GETTING YOU THERE

French Polynesia's main carrier, Air Tahiti Nui (www.airtahitinui.com), services many international destinations.

## EXPLORING THE PACIFIC

Your initial base in French Polynesia will be Pape'ete on the island of Tahiti, which welcomes most international arrivals. Less packaged than some of the outlying islands, Tahiti is a great place for independent exploration, both on land and in the sea. Of course, if you're looking for all-inclusive hedonistic luxury, look no further than Bora Bora, which is floating just around the corner.

## FAST FACTS

Tahiti was not the first of the Polynesian islands to be populated. Oral accounts have the first settlers arriving in Tahiti from nearby Ra'iatea, which was once the most politically important island despite being much smaller than Tahiti.

••••••••••••••••••••••••••••

Over time Tahiti's importance increased as more and more European visitors made the island their preferred base, and it soon became a minor pawn in the European colonial game.

••••••••••••••••••••••••••••

Tahiti's population is about 170,000, constituting more than 60% of French Polynesia's entire population.

••••••••••••••••••••••••••••

## LIFE OF THE NAUTILUS

A nautilus spends its days hiding hundreds of metres down, but as night falls at the surface it ascends to the shallow reefs in search of small fish, shrimp and other crustaceans to prey on. Its graceful shell contains gas-filled flotation chambers that control its depth, and a jet of water squirted from a siphon powers its locomotion. Because it devotes so little energy to swimming, a nautilus can get by on only one meal a month. The nearest relatives of the nautilus are squids and octopuses, though over evolutionary time both of these latter groups have lost their shells. In a surprising twist of fate, however, the octopus is now one of the nautilus's major predators. Fortunately for the nautilus, its small tentacles carry highly developed chemical sensors that can detect traces of both prey and predator.

# destination index

000 Photo pages

# general index

# the traveller's guide to planet earth

**PUBLISHER** Chris Rennie

**ASSOCIATE PUBLISHER** Ben Handicott

**PROJECT MANAGER** Jane Atkin

**DESIGNER** Mik Ruff

**ART DIRECTOR** Nic Lehman

**MANAGING LAYOUT DESIGNERS** Indra Kilfoyle, Celia Wood

**LAYOUT DESIGNERS** Jim Hsu, Paul Iacono

**MANAGING EDITOR** Sasha Baskett

**COORDINATING EDITOR** Angela Tinson

**EDITOR** Anna Metcalfe

**CARTOGRAPHER** Corey Hutchison

**IMAGE RESEARCHERS** Rebecca Dandens, Jane Hart

**PRE-PRESS PRODUCTION** Ryan Evans

**PRINT PRODUCTION** Yvonne Kirk

**WRITTEN BY** Andrew Bain, Sarah Baxter, Paul Bloomfield, Matthew D Firestone

**THANKS TO** Mark Adams, Ellen Burrows, David Connolly, Anthony Dorment, Jo Foy, James Hardy, Martin Heng, Charity Mackinnon, Suyin Ng, Tony Wheeler, Juan Winata

**THANKS TO BBC** Mark Brownlow, Jacob DeBoer, Harriet Frost, Jake Lingwood

Thanks to Alastair Fothergill, series producer for *Planet Earth*, the production teams and film crews involved in the series and the local organisations and communities who helped make *Planet Earth* possible.

**PHOTOGRAPHS**

Front-cover photographs: Earth's curvature view from space (Adastra/Getty Images); (from left to right) West MacDonnell Ranges, Australia (Bethune Carmichael/Lonely Planet Images); Sea lion (Getty Images); Dunes of Erg Chebbi, Morocco (Sune Wendelboe/Lonely Planet Images); Waterways meandering through the taiga, North America (BBC).

Back-cover photographs: Lechuguilla Cave, New Mexico, USA (Gavin Newman/BBC); (from left to right) Gazelles (BBC); Gentoo penguin (Getty Images); Hippopotamus (Getty Images).

pp2-3: Aerial view of Halong Bay, Vietnam (Huw Cordey/BBC).

Section-opener images: Mountains pp8-9: Mt Taranaki, Egmont National Park, New Zealand (David Wall/Lonely Planet Images); Fresh Water pp28-9: Spectacled cayman in the waters of the Pantanal wetland, Brazil (Peter Scoones/BBC); Caves pp84-5: Ludi Yan (Reed Flute Cave), Guilin, China (Keren Su/Lonely Planet Images); Deserts pp110-11: Dunes of Erg Chebbi, Morocco (Sune Wendelboe/Lonely Planet Images); Ice Worlds pp154-5: Polar bear swimming in the Arctic Ocean near Alaska (Steven Kazlowski/Photolibrary); Great Plains pp174-5: Ostriches in Chobe National Park, Botswana (Adrian Bailey/Lonely Planet Images); Jungles pp212-3: Boy in a carved canoe, Parembei Village, Papua New Guinea (Jerry Galea/Lonely Planet Images); Shallow Seas pp238-9: Coral reef in Komodo National Park, Indonesia (Mark Webster/Lonely Planet Images); Seasonal Forests pp276-7: Forest in autumn, New England, USA (Christian Guy/Photolibrary); Ocean Deep pp314-5: Spiral wire coral and diver, Mauritius (Reinhard Dirscherl/Photolibrary)

Many of the images in this guide are available for licensing from Lonely Planet Images: lonelyplanetimages.com.

Printed by Toppan Security Printing Pte. Ltd.

Printed in Singapore

**LONELY PLANET OFFICES**

**Australia**
Head Office
Locked Bag 1, Footscray, Victoria 3011
☎03 8379 8000, fax 03 8379 8111

**USA**
150 Linden St, Oakland, CA 94607
☎510 250 6400, toll free 800 275 8555
fax 510 893 8572

**UK**
2nd fl, 186 City Rd,
London EC1V 2NT
☎020 7106 2100, fax 020 7106 2101

**Contact**
talk2us@lonelyplanet.com
lonelyplanet.com/contact

**The Traveller's Guide to Planet Earth**
1ST EDITION
Published November 2010

**Published by**
Lonely Planet Publications Pty Ltd
ABN 36 005 607 983
90 Maribyrnong St, Footscray, Victoria 3011, Australia

ISBN 9781741798852

text & maps © Lonely Planet Publications Pty Ltd 2010

photos © as indicated 2010

*Planet Earth* is a BBC/Discovery Channel/NHK co-production in association with the CBC.

Quotes shown on images are from *Planet Earth* narration.

BBC Earth represents a heritage of more than 50 years of BBC natural-history programming, which includes the fantastic *Planet Earth* and *Life* series. Our mission is to entertain and inspire audiences worldwide with the wonders of the natural world.

Wherever you see BBC Earth you know you'll find gripping stories, astounding images and some surprising characters!

We can be found online, in your local book store, on TV and DVD, or come and join us at our exhibitions and live events. However you choose to explore, we want to help you dive in and meet your planet.

Visit us at bbcearth.com/lifeis or follow us on twitter at BBCEarthLifeIs and join the conversation.

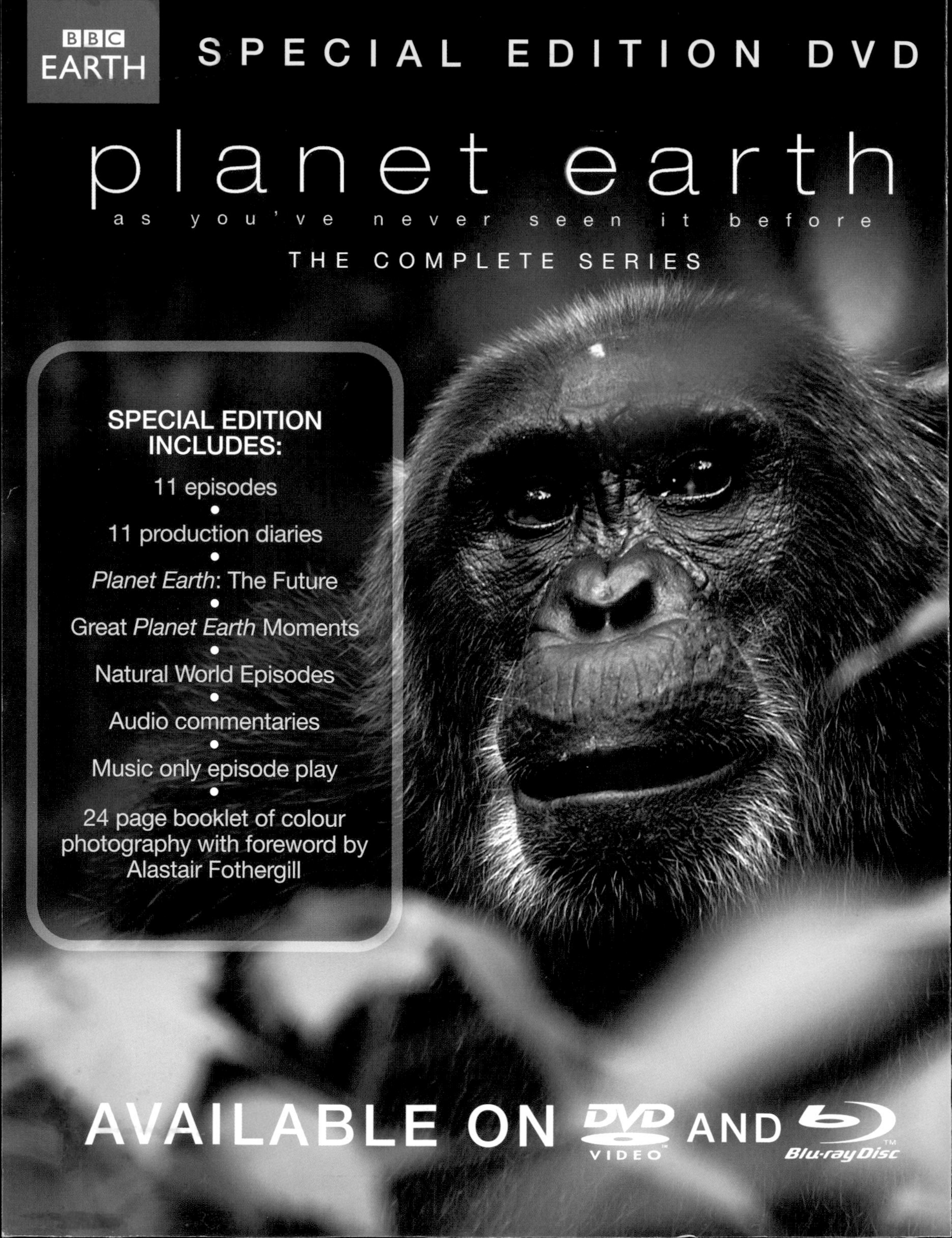
BBC EARTH
SPECIAL EDITION DVD
planet earth
as you've never seen it before
THE COMPLETE SERIES
SPECIAL EDITION INCLUDES:
11 episodes
11 production diaries
Planet Earth: The Future
Great Planet Earth Moments
Natural World Episodes
Audio commentaries
Music only episode play
24 page booklet of colour photography with foreword by Alastair Fothergill
AVAILABLE ON DVD VIDEO AND Blu-ray Disc